FIREARMS

FIREARMS

by

Iain Bradley, M.A., LL.B.
Solicitor with the Procurator Fiscal Service

W. GREEN/Sweet & Maxwell
EDINBURGH
1995

First Published 1995

© 1995
W. GREEN & SON LTD

ISBN 0 414 01089 2

A CIP catalogue record for this book is available from the British Library

Typeset by LBJ Enterprises Ltd, Aldermaston and Chilcompton.
Printed by Headway Press, Reading.

ACKNOWLEDGMENTS

The debt which I owe to the staff at W. Green and Son and to the typesetters involved in the production of this volume is self-evident. The assistance of others will not be apparent to the reader but is gratefully acknowledged.

Frank Gallagher, Advocate, generously gave me an extended loan of a laptop computer which proved invaluable in the preparation of this book. Robert Shiels, the author of the companion volume, *Offensive Weapons*, gave much helpful guidance and assistance as did the staff in the Crown Office library. My colleagues in the Procurator Fiscal's Office in Glasgow, particularly those in Team D, contributed their views on the format of the text and index while Graham Kerr, Gordon Macleod and Colin Simmons in IT and Derek Murray in Reprographics sought to enlighten a computer–illiterate. Needless to say however the views expressed are mine alone.

My greatest debt is owed to my wife Seonaid who gave me constant and patient support. This book is dedicated to her.

PREFACE

Since it came into force on August 1, 1968, the Firearms Act 1968 has been the principal statute regulating the possession of firearms and ammunition in Great Britain. As Schedule 7 to the Act indicates, the Act was intended to be a consolidating measure; a variety of statutory provisions, most notably the Firearms Acts 1937 and 1965 and the Air Guns and Shot Guns etc. Act 1962 were repealed and superseded by the new Act. Yet the Act's longevity has not been easily won, for it has been extensively augmented and amended by a series of statutes whose effects, in an already complex area of law, have not always been readily discernible.

The Firearms Act 1982 closed a loophole created by some imitation firearms which had proved to be capable of conversion into working weapons. While the 1968 Act had enacted that any imitation firearm which had been converted into a working weapon could only be possessed by the holder of a firearm certificate, this provision had not extended to readily-convertible (but unconverted) replica firearms, a deficiency the 1982 Act remedied. The later Act had to be read in conjunction with the 1968 Act since its provisions supplemented, rather than amended, the principal Act.

More far-reaching, however, was the Firearms (Amendment) Act 1988 which gave effect to recommendations contained in the White Paper "Firearms Act 1968: Proposals for Reform". The tragic events at Hungerford may not have been directly responsible for the subsequent statute, but certainly produced a climate of public and parliamentary opinion receptive to reform of the existing legislation. The 1988 Act enacted reforms whose tone was much less permissive than the earlier legislation and, unlike the 1982 Act, the majority of the 1988 Act's provisions were fully incorporated in the body of the principal Act.

The reforms heralded more rigorous control, and more frequent reviews, of firearms licences (particularly shot gun certificates) and introduced peremptory police powers to call in firearms from individuals. Penalties for the use of firearms in pursuance of criminal offences were increased and the classification of prohibited weapons was considerably expanded. (Yet further increases in maximum terms of imprisonment have recently been included in the Criminal Justice and Public Order Act 1994; these amend the Table of Punishments in Schedule 6 to the 1968 Act. Similar adjustments were made to the equivalent Northern Irish legislation, the Firearms (Northern Ireland) Order 1981 (S.I. 1981 No. 155). Additions, applying only to England and Wales, have also been made to Schedule 1 to the principal Act.)

Broadly, the 1988 Act sought to proscribe the possession of multiple-shot, self-loading and pump-action rifles, automatic and semi-automatic weapons such as machine guns and burst-fire weapons as well as most varieties of military armaments. Thenceforth, lawful possession of firearms of these types required the authority of the Home Secretary, or the Secretary of State for Scotland, and it can be assumed that such consent was expected to be given only exceptionally.

A compensation scheme was created to enable the possessors of any such weapons held until then under firearm or shot gun certificates to be recompensed on surrender of the weapons to the authorities. The scheme took effect from September 23, 1987, the day after a speech delivered by the Home Secretary to the Police Superintendents' Conference in which these proposals were announced.

Prior to the 1988 Act the courts had experienced difficulties in dealing with weapons, particularly prohibited weapons, modified to varying degrees. Modifications were intended to qualify firearms for certification under the Acts, effectively circumventing restrictions on possession. In the court context much centred upon the nature, and permanence (or otherwise), of the modifications undertaken and it is fair to say that the status of an individual weapon (and, accordingly, the liability of its possessor to prosecution for contravening the Acts) could rarely be predicted with confidence.

Section 7 enacted that conversion of a prohibited weapon or a section 1 firearm, usually achieved by limiting the repeated firing capabilities or by boring out rifling in a weapon barrel, would not alter the classification of the weapon concerned.

Yet, having broadened the classification of prohibited weapons, enacted a more rigorous licensing regime for holders of firearms and shot guns as well as firearms dealers, and having closed the potential loophole created previously by converted weapons, the Act contrarily introduced a new category of de-regulated weapons in section 8. In part this measure can be regarded as making amends to collectors and other members of the shooting lobby for extending the prohibited weapon classification to firearms (and consequently, in effect banning a wide range of firearms). Whether the benefits of this reform outweigh its potential risks is debatable.

Section 8 provides that de-activated firearms can be freely possessed, without any form of certificate, provided they can be established to be incapable of firing. Accordingly, they can be likened in law to the bulk of imitation firearms which are incapable of firing any sort of missile and which can be bought and sold without reference to the Firearms Acts. While the section stipulates that de-activated firearms are not firearms for the purposes of the Acts, it is silent as to what they are; they may not be imitation firearms either, a matter of some importance having regard to the way in which the Act is framed.

A further anomaly concerns a class of large magazine smooth-bore shot guns which have enjoyed some popularity amongst clay pigeon shooters; these multiple-shot weapons ceased to be treated as shot guns for the purpose of certification under the Act after 1988 and now require possession of a section 1 firearm certificate. Given the Act's general disdain for multiple-shot weapons this approach makes sense, but the result is that some shot guns cannot be possessed in Great Britain on the strength of a shot gun certificate.

Two distinct problems then arise. First, this classification can also apply to several powerful close-assault shot guns, designed for military use, which can discharge a fearsome array of munitions and are as far removed from the traditional sporting guns envisaged in the legislation as can be imagined.

On a more general level, this classification is at variance with the approach taken by other Member States in the European Community which have continued to treat these weapons as shot guns and issue permits accordingly. The position now is that an E.C. citizen coming to Great Britain with a shot gun permit and a European Firearms Pass (E.F.P.) could be in breach of the Firearms Acts if he either imported his multiple-shot shot gun or if he sought to use such a weapon in Great Britain. Section 17 of the 1988 Act introduced visitors' permits as a means of imposing some control over both the temporary importation of firearms into Great Britain and their acquisition there by foreign nationals.

Section 17 was rapidly overhauled by the Firearms Acts (Amendment) Regulations 1992, which gave effect to the E.C. Directive on the Control of the Acquisition and Possession of Weapons, Directive 91/477.

The object of the Directive is to develop partial harmonisation of firearms controls between Member States, to facilitate the freer movement of firearms between these countries by abolishing checks at internal borders, and to develop stronger controls on the movement of firearms at external borders. E.C. nationals who are licensed to possess firearms in their own country are entitled to be issued with a European Firearms Pass which operates much like a passport, identifying the weapons lawfully possessed or acquired by the E.F.P. holder. Harmonisation so far has focused upon achieving a common nomenclature for firearms and ordnance but even here the difficulties are substantial; for example, both Parliament and the courts in Britain have long since given up trying to provide a definitive meaning for the phrase "antique firearm", and no doubt similar pitfalls await the Member States in agreeing a common standard for de-activation of firearms.

Yet these questions of harmonisation really do not address the fundamental issue, which must surely be to achieve a consensus as to the tests of suitability of individuals who seek to be licensed to possess firearms.

Social attitudes towards firearms differ widely internationally: the restrictive British approach which (interest groups apart) views firearms with a mixture of disdain and trepidation reflects a society with very different social mores from, for example, much of the United States of America where the right to bear arms has all too literally confused liberty with licence. While the contrasts between Britain and her European partners may be less marked, they are real enough to make one sceptical about the desirability of harmonisation in the firearms field, particularly as the Community expands into a wider Union.

The Firearms Acts 1968 to 1992, as amended by the 1994 Act, now provide a comprehensive body of legislation, but if it is suggested (to repeat the old saw) that a camel is simply a horse designed by a committee, then the creature which Parliament and the European Community have sired is decidedly more cameline than equine in form. Study of the Firearms Acts makes it clear that every device known to the parliamentary draftsman (except the most obvious one, consolidation) has been deployed over the years. The results have been more workmanlike than elegant, providing completeness at the expense of accessibility.

In an endeavour to make the statutes more coherent, this volume presents the Acts in a consolidated form which reflects the alterations to the principal Act, the 1968 Act. The law is stated as at March 1, 1995.

All opinions expressed, unless the context admits otherwise, are mine alone and cannot be held to reflect the views or policy of any Government department or enforcement agency.

IAN BRADLEY,
Glasgow, May 1995

CONTENTS

TABLE OF CASES

TABLE OF STATUTES

TABLE OF STATUTORY INSTRUMENTS

TABLE OF E.C. LEGISLATION

TABLE OF ABBREVIATIONS

The 1968 Act	Firearms Act 1968
The 1982 Act	Firearms Act 1982
The 1988 Act	Firearms (Amendment) Act 1988
The 1992 Act	Firearms (Amendment) Act 1992
The 1994 Act	Firearms (Amendment) Act 1994
The principal Act	the 1968 Act cited above
The 1992 Regulations	Firearms Acts (Amendment) Regulations 1992 (S.I. 1992 No. 2823)

ARRANGEMENT OF SECTIONS OF ACTS
THE FIREARMS ACT 1968

PART I
GENERAL RESTRICTIONS ON POSSESSION AND HANDLING OF FIREARMS AND AMMUNITION

PROHIBITION OF CERTAIN WEAPONS AND CONTROL OF ARMS TRAFFIC

SPECIAL EXEMPTIONS FROM SECTIONS 1 TO 5

PART III
LAW ENFORCEMENT AND PUNISHMENT OF OFFENCES

PART IV
MISCELLANEOUS AND GENERAL

THE FIREARMS ACT 1982

THE FIREARMS (AMENDMENT) ACT 1992

THE FIREARMS ACTS (AMENDMENT) REGULATIONS 1992

(S.I. 1992 No. 2823)

THE FIREARMS (AMENDMENT) ACT 1994

THE FIREARMS ACT 1968

An Act to consolidate the Firearms Acts 1937 and 1965, the Air Guns and Shot Guns, etc., Act 1962, Part V of the Criminal Justice Act 1967 and certain enactments amending the Firearms Act 1937. [30th May 1968]

PART 1

PROVISIONS AS TO POSSESSION, HANDLING AND DISTRIBUTION OF WEAPONS AND AMMUNITION; PREVENTION OF CRIME AND MEASURES TO PROTECT PUBLIC SAFETY

General Restrictions on Possession and Handling of Firearms and Ammunition

Requirement of firearm certificate

1.—(1) Subject to any exemption under this Act, it is an **1–01–01** offence for a person—

(*a*) to have in his possession, or to purchase or acquire, a firearm to which this section applies without holding a firearm certificate in force at the time, or otherwise than as authorised by such a certificate;

(*b*) to have in his possession, or to purchase or acquire, any ammunition to which this section applies without holding a firearm certificate in force at the time, or otherwise than as authorised by such a certificate, or in quantities in excess of those so authorised.

(2) It is an offence for a person to fail to comply with a **1–01–02** condition subject to which a firearm certificate is held by him.

(3) This section applies to every firearm except— **1–01–03**

[¹(*a*) a shot gun within the meaning of this Act, that is to say a smooth-bore gun (not being an air gun) which—

(i) has a barrel not less than 24 inches in length and does not have any barrel with a bore ·exceeding 2 inches in diameter;

(ii) either has no magazine or has a non-detachable magazine incapable of holding more than two cartridges; and

       (iii) is not a revolver gun; and]
    (*b*) an air weapon (that is to say, an air rifle, air gun or air pistol not of a type declared by rules made by the Secretary of State under section 53 of this Act to be specially dangerous).

1–01–04 [²(3A) A gun which has been adapted to have such a magazine as is mentioned in subsection (3)(*a*)(ii) above shall not be regarded as falling within that provision unless the magazine bears a mark approved by the Secretary of State for denoting that fact and that mark has been made, and the adaptation has been certified in writing as having been carried out in a manner approved by him, either by one of the two companies mentioned in section 58(1) of this Act or by such other person as may be approved by him for that purpose.]

1–01–05 (4) This section applies to any ammunition for a firearm, except the following articles, namely:—
    (*a*) cartridges containing five or more shot, none of which exceeds .36 inch in diameter;
    (*b*) ammunition for an air gun, air rifle or air pistol; and
    (*c*) blank cartridges not more than one inch in diameter measured immediately in front of the rim or cannelure of the base of the cartridge.

NOTES

1–01–06 (1) Substituted by the Firearms Act (Amendment) Act 1988 s.2(2).
(2) Inserted by the 1988 Act, s.2(3).

OBSERVATIONS

1–01–07 (a) The exemptions from the general licensing provisions while in possession of a section 1 firearm are specified in sections 7 to 13 of the Act and, for practical purposes, relate to firearms dealers, auctioneers, warehousemen, operators of slaughterhouses or the employees thereof (in the course of their employers' business), theatrical and film performers, and authorised crew members of ships and aircraft as well as aerodrome staff.

    Exemptions related to recreational shooting and sports events are found in section 11, *infra*.

1–01–08 Although it is not specifically exempted by section 1's provisions, it should be noted that s.58(3) exempts antique firearms held solely as a curiosity or ornament from the licensing provisions of the Act; such weapons possessed with the intention of being used or maintained for use must be licensed appropriately. A fuller discussion follows at 4–06–03, *infra*.

(b) Possession of a section 1 firearm, or ammunition for such, **1–01–09** without holding a firearm certificate or being exempted from the requirements of the section's provisions (as described above), is an absolute offence.

In *R. v. Hussain* [1981] 1 W.L.R. 416 police visited H's house and found, in a box of motorcycle parts, a metal tube some eight inches long with a spring-activated striker pin. When shown the article H stated "It is a small gun. Kids use them in my country"; expert testimony was divided on the lethality, or otherwise, of the weapon, a matter of importance given the terms of section 57(1) of the Act, which provides the statutory definition of a firearm.

Delivering his judgment, Eveleigh L.J. stated (at 417H):

> "In summing up to the jury the judge told them the meaning of the expression 'firearm' and in effect directed them that if the article was a firearm the accused would be guilty of the offence if they found he was in possession of that article, even though he might not know that it was a firearm. On behalf of the defendant it is submitted that this direction was wrong and that, as counsel put it, it is necessary for the prosecution to prove that the accused had the knowledge of the nature of the article in order to establish the mens rea required for the offence."

[His Lordship repeated the terms of section 1(1) above and continued:]

> "The subsection makes no reference to the state of knowledge of the accused. It is drafted in absolute terms and can be contrasted with other sections of the Act where the accused's state of mind is specifically referred to."

His Lordship narrated the provisions of section 24(1) and (5) **1–01–10** and section 25 as examples of offences where *mens rea* was a determining factor.

The judgment moved on to consider, as support for this line of reasoning, the case of *Warner v. Metropolitan Police Commissioner* [1969] 2 A.C. 256, a case decided shortly before the ·

Firearms Act 1968 came into force, and which was a decision dealing with the absolute nature (or otherwise) of section 1 of the Drugs (Prevention of Misuse) Act 1964, the statutory precursor of the Misuse of Drugs Act 1971.

Much time and energy has been expended in efforts to equate "possession" as applied in the Misuse of Drugs Act with its application in the Firearms Act, initially to some effect. No such efforts will be made here: put shortly, the Misuse of Drugs Act 1971, section 28(2), provides that it shall be a defence for a person charged with contravening section 4(2) and (3), section 5(2) and (3), section 6(2) or section 9 if he can prove that "he neither knew of nor suspected nor had reason to suspect the existence of some fact alleged by the prosecution which it is necessary for the prosecution to prove if he is to be convicted". Grudging as this concession may seem, it finds no echo in the Firearms Act, with the exception of a statutory defence contained in section 1(5) of the 1982 Act in relation to a limited class of imitation firearms; see 4–05–17 and 6–05–01 below.

1–01–11   The prosecution has to prove that an accused was in possession of a firearm and that he knew he had something. It is not necessary to prove knowledge on his part to the extent that he knew that the thing he possessed was a firearm. The absolute nature of liability, for those who do not possess the requisite certificate or other authority, is potentially harsh. A yet more extreme example of the application of absolute liability is found in *R. v. Waller* [1991] Crim.L.R. 381. Here W was given a holdall to look after for a few days by a friend. W thereafter removed a black plastic bag from the holdall and did not examine its contents. He stated later that he thought the bag (which the police examined and found to contain a sawn-off shot gun and cartridges) might contain a crowbar.

1–01–12   Convicting him of contravening section 1(1), the judge followed the *ratio* in *Hussain*, cited above. Before the Court of Appeal it was argued on W's behalf that this was a "parcel or container" case of the sort considered in *Warner*; knowledge of possession of a bag would not necessarily imply knowledge on the part of an accused of its contents and, if ignorance or error thereof could be shown, then a defence might be made out. The appeal was dismissed, the court following *Hussain* and citing *R. v. Bradish* [1990] 1 Q.B. 981, which is discussed at 1–05–12. It was noted that there were important public policy reasons for construing offences in the Firearms Act as importing strict liability unless the contrary was stated. The Act's provisions in which the accused's state of mind was of moment were limited and expressly defined. Greater weight had to be placed upon the problems of enforcing the legislation, if a defence of the *Warner* sort could be made out, than upon the possibility that an innocent possessor might be unfairly convicted.

(c) The aim of section 1(3)*(a)*(i) is to distinguish between shot **1–01–13** guns which are ordinarily lawfully possessed by virtue of a shot gun certificate granted under section 2 of the 1968 Act, and a much less common category of large capacity smooth-bore weapons which require a firearm certificate. These section 1 weapons are capable of firing more than two rounds at a time and have enjoyed a following amongst clay pigeon shooters partly because of this factor; such guns are characterised by a lack of recoil which can make them easier to handle.

As was mentioned in the Preface, the parameters of section 1(3)*(a)*(i) are equally met by some non-recoiling military close-assault weapons which, if licensed, would only require a firearm certificate for lawful possession.

It is of note that the Wildlife and Countryside Act 1981, **1–01–14** section 5(1)*(c)*(iv) prohibits the use for killing or taking any wild bird of a shot gun whose internal diameter at the muzzle exceeds 1.75 inches; a similar use of automatic or semi-automatic weapons was precluded by section 5(1)*(c)*(iii), but possession of these is now illegal since they were declared prohibited weapons by section 1 of the Firearms (Amendment) Act 1988. See section 5 of the principal Act, *infra*.

(d) De-activated weapons, *i.e.* weapons which have been ren- **1–01–15** dered incapable of firing in accordance with the standards set in section 8 of the Firearms (Amendment) Act 1988 and consequently (as that Act provides) have ceased to be firearms which are no longer the subject of certificate control, are discussed at 7–08–01/05.

(e) All air weapons are firearms in view of the ubiquity of **1–01–16** section 1(3)*(b)* of the 1968 Act, but only those which are declared to be "specially dangerous" require to be held under a firearm certificate. The Firearms (Dangerous Air Weapons) Rules 1969 and the Firearms (Dangerous Air Weapons) (Scotland) Rules 1969 (S.I.s 1969 No. 47 and 1969 No. 270) respectively, stipulate that air weapons with a muzzle energy exceeding 6ft 1bs. and other air weapons whose muzzle energy exceeds 12ft 1bs. are specially dangerous and are subject to certification in terms of section 1 of that Act. It should be noted, however, that restrictions apply to the possession and use of any air weapon by young people under the age of 17. (See section 22 *infra*).

1–01–17   It is often forgotten that section 1 of the 1968 Act differentiates between low power air weapons and other firearms only as a means of determining which weapons will, or will not, be subject to the Act's certification requirements. The offences specified in sections 16 to 25 are committed when any firearm is involved.

1–01–18   Weapons powered by compressed gases other than air (notably CO_2) are subject to certification requirements without regard to their muzzle energy figures; it is obviously anomalous that low power weapons using other compressed gases have to be certificated when similar power air weapons do not. See *R. v. Thorpe* [1987] 1 W.L.R. 383; [1987] 2 All E.R. 108 and *Peat v. Lees,* 1994 S.L.T. 245; 1993 S.C.C.R. 256 which are discussed at 4–05–16, *infra*.

Air weapons disguised as other objects were declared specially dangerous by the Firearms (Dangerous Air Weapons) (Amendment) Rules 1993 (S.I. 1993 No. 1490) and the Firearms (Dangerous Air Weapons) (Scotland) (Amendment) Rules 1993 (S.I. 1993 No. 1541); they require a firearm certificate to be lawfully possessed.

(f) Statutory definitions are mostly to be found in section 57, *infra*.

1–01–19   (g) What meaning does "possession" have in the Act? One can only agree with Lord Parker's observation, approved in *Hall v. Cotton, infra*: "The term 'possession' is always giving rise to trouble." The tenor of the Act indicates that the term demands a broad interpretation: the legislation would be rendered meaningless if the concept could only apply to situations where an individual had immediate access to the ammunition or firearms in question. Possession in this narrow form can be found in the Prevention of Crime Act 1953 and would be an appropriate construction in some circumstances in the Firearms Act. However, a broader meaning, in the sense of knowledge and control, in addition to ordinary physical custody, of items has to be employed much as is done in the Misuse of Drugs Act 1971.

Perhaps it was that similarity in approach, in both the Firearms and Misuse of Drugs Acts, to the concept of possession that led to so much wasted effort being expended in applying the *Warner* judgment to firearms cases where it was wholly inappropriate.

Complex considerations can arise when weapons are temporarily left in the hands of other persons, whether they are licensed to possess firearms or not, or when a certificate holder keeps his firearm at an address different from that specified in his certificate.

In *Hall v. Cotton* [1987] Q.B. 504; [1986] 3 W.L.R. 681; [1986] **1–01–20** 3 All E.R. 332 an appeal followed the dismissal of informations against C, charged with contravening section 3(2) of the Act by transferring two shot guns to T, and against T, the recipient of the guns, who was charged with possessing them without holding a shot gun certificate. It was established that before their families went off on holiday together, C brought his two certificated shot guns to T's house for safekeeping. Only a lodger remained in T's house while the families were away but he had no involvement with the weapons. On the families' return from holiday the guns still remained with T for some weeks for the purpose of being cleaned by him.

The Justices opined that C had not transferred possession of the guns to T before or after the holiday and founded upon the case of *Sullivan v. Earl of Caithness* [1976] Q.B. 966.

Stocker L.J. [1986] 3 All E.R. 332 at 334d – 335g) delivered this judgment:

"This appeal therefore raises the question of the meaning of the words 'possession' and 'transfer' for the purposes of the 1968 Act and in the context of the facts found proved by the magistrates. In construing this Act it seems to me that we should keep in mind two principles of construction which may in practice be in apparent conflict. The first is that, if ambiguity arises, consideration may be given to the general intention of the Act and the mischief it seeks to prevent; and the second is that, as a penal statute, where more than one construction is possible, it should be construed in a sense favourable to an accused.

In my view the plain intention of the 1968 Act is to prevent a firearm from getting into the hands of an unauthorised and uncertificated person and to enable the relevant authority, in this case the police, properly to regulate and control the certification of the persons entitled to be in possession of such firearms. It is thus important to observe in my view that what is prohibited in s.3(2) is the sale or transfer of the gun itself, the legal nature of the transfer being prescribed by the definition of the word 'transfer' in s.57(4). [The respondent] has argued before us that the physical transfer of the gun must in the circumstances involve a transfer of some form of legal right and that the respondent Cotton parted with the possession of the shotguns within the ordinary and natural meaning of that phrase when he physically transferred the shotguns to Treadwell's house, not only for the duration of the holiday but also for some weeks thereafter until the police intervened on 11 September, and the fact that the arrangements involved that [T] should clean the guns before their return to Cotton reinforces his submissions. He argued that the converse of this proposition necessarily involved the respondent Treadwell having the shotguns in his possession. In the alternative he argued that if, in the light of the decision of this court in *Sullivan v. Earl of Caithness* . . ., the respondent [C] himself retained possession of the guns all the time on the basis that he had not in any way relinquished the right to possess, nonetheless custodial possession had been transferred to the respondent [T]. This argument involves the proposition that the word 'possession' can in law embrace two separate legal concepts, 'proprietary possession' and 'custodial possession'.

1–01–21   I therefore turn to consider *Sullivan v. Earl of Caithness*. That case was concerned with the question whether or not [Caithness], who at the material time lived in Oxfordshire, and who was the owner of certain guns he kept at his mother's apartment in Hampton Court Palace, was in 'possession' of the guns (unlawfully, since he had failed to renew the firearms certificate previously issued to him in respect of those guns). The contention on behalf of Lord Caithness was that since he lived in Oxfordshire and the guns were at his mother's apartment in Surrey, he was not in 'possession' of them.

1–01–22   In the course of giving the first judgment of the court . . . May J. said ([1976] 1 All E.R. 844 at 847, [1976] Q.B. 966 at 970):

'Looking at the context of the word "possession" in s.1 of the 1968 Act in the present case, I have no doubt that one can be in possession of a firearm even though one is at a place other than that at which the firearm physically is. To agree with the justices' decision in the present case would in my view effectively be to equate the word "possession" in s.1 with custody, and this I am satisfied would be wrong.'

After pointing out that the form of application for a certificate requires the appellant not only to state the address of his residence, but also the place where the firearm is to be kept, thus implying that the person to whom the certificate is issued may reside at a place other than the place at which the firearm is physically located, he continued . . .:

'In my opinion the purpose of s.1 of the 1968 Act and its ancillary provisions is to regulate and license not merely those who have physical custody of firearms, or who keep them in the place in which they live, but also those who have firearms under their control at their behest, even though for one reason or another they may be kept at their country cottage, at the local shooting range or indeed at Bisley. As a matter of construction, therefore, which must to some extent also be a matter of first impression, and looking at the context and what I believe to have been the intent of s.1 of the 1968 Act, it may well be, I think, that the owner of a firearm who does not at the relevant time have physical possession of it can nevertheless truly be said still to be in possession of it. In the present case, the respondent was at all material times the owner of the firearms. He could no doubt obtain them from his mother's flat at any time when he wanted them. She had the barest custody of them, not because she had any interest in them, but because her flat was safer than the respondent's home in Oxford. In these circumstances and on the admitted facts, in my judgment the respondent was at material times in Swalcliffe in possession of those firearms for the purposes of the 1968 Act, and consequently I think the justices were wrong and should on the facts as they found them have convicted the respondent.'

Thus this case is, in my view, clear authority for the **1–01–23** proposition that a person can be 'in possession' of a firearm at a time when he is physically not in control of it or is himself not physically at the place at which it is then situated. Cases such as this must depend on their own facts, but on the facts as found by the justices in this case in my opinion the respondent Cotton retained 'possession' in the *Sullivan v. Earl of Caithness* sense, which I will refer to as 'proprietary possession', at all times when the shotguns were at the house of the respondent Treadwell.

Does this finding therefore justify the conclusion reached by the justices that 'possession', if retained by Cotton, cannot have been transferred by him to the respondent Treadwell, contrary to s.3(2) and the consequent finding that, if not so transferred, then [T] cannot have been 'in possession' of the shotguns himself since such possession had not been transferred to him?"

His Lordship interpreted the meaning of "transfer" as defined by section 57(4) and continued at 336e:

1–01–24   "The definition of the word 'transfer' commences with the word 'includes' and, therefore, subject to the ejusdem generis rule, the definition is not exclusive or exhaustive. In my view on the facts of this case, and in particular that the shotguns were retained in [T's house] for a fortnight or so after the return of the respondents from holiday, and were still in the house when the police found them, and were to be cleaned by him before their return to [C], it seems to me that the proper conclusion is that [T] had more than the 'barest custody' which May J. in *Sullivan v. Earl of Caithness* found to be the position of Lord Caithness's mother at Hampton Court. . . .

1–01–25   As a matter of law, no doubt there is a distinction between 'custody' and 'possession', though in many cases, in my view, the former will necessarily involve the latter. 'Custody' and 'possession' are certainly equated in drugs cases where one person knowingly has custody of drugs for another. In my opinion, at least on the facts of this case, custody coupled with the knowledge of such custody must be equated with 'possession'. . . . [C] retained 'proprietary possession' in the sense adjudged in *Sullivan v. Earl of Caithness*. [T] had 'custodial possession'. Having regard to all the facts, for my part I am unable to accept the proposition that [T] had no interest at all except for the provision of his house as a place at which the shotguns were physically located. Accordingly, such custody could only arise by at least a custodial interest being transferred from one respondent to another and falls within the phrase 'lend and part with possession', whether read conjunctively or disjunctively. . . . If read conjunctively, it seems to me there must have been a lending in this transaction. However, if this be wrong, and even if custody could not, contrary to my view, be equated with 'possession', on the facts of this case the word 'includes' would be apt to include custody if the definition is construed ejusdem generis with the express words, since 'custody' by an unauthorised person is in my view clearly one of the mischiefs to which the 1968 Act is directed."

In his supporting judgment Hirst J. at 337g added:

"The definition of 'transfer' in s.57(4) is a very wide one, and in my judgment Cotton's actions in relation to these two shotguns . . . manifestly constituted a transfer within the scope of that definition. Having regard to the wording of s.3(2), it is immaterial whether or not Cotton himself retained possession, or at least a right to possession, of the two shotguns, though I agree with Stocker LJ that he did, in line with the decision of this court in *Sullivan v. Earl of Caithness.*

So far as Treadwell is concerned, the guns were in his **1–01–26** home and in the custody of [his] lodger, presumably his agent for this purpose, during the holiday, and thereafter remained there for several weeks until the police called and found them. Meantime [T] had responsibility for cleaning the guns. These elements of both custody, and, to a limited extent, control, of the two guns, quite clearly to my mind demonstrate that [T] was in possession of them. It is not, I think, correct to equate his position with that of Lord Caithness's mother in *Sullivan v. Earl of Caithness*, since their respective roles were by no means identical, and in any event the Divisional Court were not called upon to consider her position . . . apart from May Js comment that she had no more than 'the barest custody'.

In reaching these conclusions I am in no way deterred by the borderline examples cited by both counsel for the respondents. Cases of momentary delivery of a shotgun to another person in, for example, a temporary emergency or for the purpose of inspection, could hardly be said to have involved either a transfer by the deliveror or the taking of possession by the deliveree; equally, a spouse of servant temporarily entrusted with the custody of a shotgun by its owner would in normal circumstances be regarded as the owner's agent; there would thus be no transfer by the latter, nor acceptance of any more than the barest custody by the former, with no infringement of the 1968 Act in either case."

1–01–27   The issues considered in this judgment surfaced in the case of *Argo v. Carmichael,* 1990 J.C. 210; 1990 S.L.T. 296; 1990 S.C.C.R. 64. A's brother inherited three rifles following their grandfather's death and had added them to his firearms certificate, which at the time contained no requirements as to the place at which the weapons were to be kept. A did not possess a firearm certificate, but one of the rifles was stored in A's home, by A, on his brother's behalf. A assumed that his brother would ensure that the firearm certificate would be renewed as required, but this did not happen. When police called at A's home they were directed to the weapon by A, who admitted having no certificate and was charged with contravening section 1 of the Act.

Evidence showed that A viewed the gun as his brother's property but, nevertheless, he had locked the gun in a cupboard in his home and kept the bolt and firing pin (without which the gun was inoperable) in a safe for a considerable time. Only A and his mother had a key to this safe, though it was common knowledge where the gun was kept. Crucially, the sheriff, in his findings, held that A "was able to and did exercise control over the gun at the material time".

At trial it was argued on A's behalf that while he had knowledge of the weapon and access to it, this did not mean he had control of it. A was represented to be in a similar position to Lady Caithness in the *Sullivan* case, enjoying no more than "the barest custody". The sheriff founded upon A's responsible steps to secure the weapon and render it inactive and the key-holding arrangements as sufficient evidence of possession which, of course, was not licensed.

On appeal it was submitted that A's brother had proprietary control of the gun but that A did not have custodial possession. The court founded upon the nature and completeness of A's control of the gun and upheld the conviction. It is of note that no argument was advanced to suggest (following Hirst J. in *Hall v. Cotton* at 338) that A was merely temporarily entrusted with custody of the gun: no finding had been stated about the length of time the gun had been in A's home. We can infer that it had been there for too substantial a period to qualify as a brief exercise of agency and that the manner of its retention pointed to more than "the barest custody".

Requirement of certificate for possession of shotguns

2.—(1) Subject to any exemption under this Act, it is an offence **1–02–01** for a person to have in his possession, or to purchase or acquire, a shot gun without holding a certificate under this Act authorising him to possess shot guns.

(2) It is an offence for a person to fail to comply with a condition subject to which a shot gun certificate is held by him.

OBSERVATIONS

(a) The criteria governing the grant or renewal of shot gun **1–02–02** certificates are laid out in section 28(1) of the 1968 Act, as amended by section 3(1) of the 1988 Act. The 1988 Act introduced subsection (1A) into the earlier Act which now required applicants to show good reason for the possession, purchase or acquisition of a shot gun. The Firearms Consultative Committee in their Fourth Annual Report 1992–93 noted a marked decline in England and Wales in the number of shot gun and firearm certificates extant since the passage of the 1988 Act (para. 7.6): to what extent one event produced the other is not entirely clear. The corresponding provisions governing firearm certificates are found in section 27 of the 1968 Act, as amended.

(b) A rifle with a barrel more than 24 inches long, whose rifling **1–02–03** has been removed to produce a smooth-bore weapon, becomes a shot gun for certification purposes. This is so even if the weapon is still capable of firing firearm ammunition. The issue was decided in *R. v. Hucklebridge; Attorney General's Reference (No. 3 of 1980)* [1980] 1 W.L.R. 1284; [1980] 3 All E.R. 273; (1980) 71 Cr.App.R. 171 which, it should be noted, overturned an earlier majority ruling of the Queen's Bench Division, reported as *Creaser v. Tunnicliffe* [1977] 1 W.L.R. 1493; [1978] 1 All E.R. 569.

In *Hucklebridge* the court followed the dissenting judgment of Lord Widgery in the *Creaser* case two years before. The facts in *Hucklebridge* were that H possessed two Lee Enfield rifles but

held no section 1 certificate and was charged on counts of
contravening that section. Evidence led showed that the barrel
length of both guns was 25.25 inches: the barrel of one gun had
been reamed to produce a smooth-bore gun which could now
fire .410 shot gun ammunition and (with much loss of accuracy
and range) its original .303 rifle ammunition; the second gun
had also been altered to a smooth-bore and had been recham-
bered to fire shot gun cartridges and could still fire its original
.303 ammunition, again with a concomitant loss of accuracy and
range. Expert evidence was led as to whether the weapons
before the court were still rifles and subject to section 1 of the
Act, or shot guns requiring a shot gun certificate. The trial judge
directed an acquittal on the first count and ruled the second gun
was a section 1 firearm, at which point the accused plead guilty
to that charge. Following the Attorney General's reference both
sides appealed. The Lord Chief Justice repeated the terms of
sections 1(1) and (3) and 57(4) of the principal Act and the
salient facts from *Creaser* before adding ([1980] 1 W.L.R. 1284
at 1287H):

> "It seems to this court that what impression the weapon
> makes upon the court, namely, does it impress the court as
> being a rifle or does it impress the court as being a shot gun,
> is an immaterial consideration. What the court has to con-
> sider, and I do not apologise for repeating it, is the definition
> of section 1(3)(*a*).
>
> This court, with respect to the majority in *Creaser v.
> Tunnicliffe* [cited above], finds the reasoning of Lord Widgery
> C.J. compelling. If I may cite a passage from his judgment, at
> p. 1500: 'When one goes back to examine the circumstances
> in which a firearm may be possessed without a firearms
> certificate, which means going back to section 1 of the Act,
> one is immediately struck by the fact that the broad distinc-
> tion drawn between one firearm and another firearm is that
> the smooth-bore weapon (popularly called a shot gun) goes
> into one class, and all the rest go into another. Thus all the
> rifles are in a class described by section 1 of the Act. The
> reason must be clear enough. It is because the element of
> risk, danger and lethal quality which a rifle has when
> compared to a shot gun is very different. Parliament no doubt
> had in mind that people may have a legitimate excuse for
> holding shot guns, but not have any excuse for saying they

required a rifle. One looks [at section 1]. In my imagination I pick up one of these weapons and look at it. I say: has it got a smooth bore? Yes, because the rifling has gone. Is the barrel more than 24 inches in length? Yes, it is. Therefore it is a shot gun for the purposes of this Act. How is that approach to be faulted? It is said by some that this cannot be a shot gun. This Lee-Enfield with the rifling bored out does not look like a shot gun; one cannot shoot rabbits with it. That may be so. It still seems to me to satisfy the definition of a shot gun in the Act.'

With that passage this court respectfully agrees. As I say, it is not for us to express our view what the particular weapon might look like. That is not the problem. The question is, does it come within the exception as Parliament has set that exception."

The court rejected submissions for the Attorney General that the gun must still be composed of component parts which, at one time, must have combined to produce a section 1 weapon; the question to be addressed first was whether or not the article met the statutory description of a shot gun, and if it did then its component parts could be freely possessed without a certificate, unlike the component parts of either a section 1 firearm or a prohibited weapon (as defined in section 5, *infra*).

The Lord Chief Justice added (at 1289A):

"Finally Mr. Leary, in his concluding argument, was trying to impress us with the dangerous situation which may result if the Attorney-General's reference does not succeed and if the appeal against conviction on the other count does succeed. He was suggesting to us that that might open the floodgate to undesirable possessors of weapons which could take .303 cartridges and might be detrimental to law-abiding citizens. Some of course think that a shot gun is just as lethal a weapon as a rifle. In certain circumstances it would be. In any event if the holder or possessor of one of these modified weapons desires to discharge from the weapon, albeit inefficiently, a round of .303 ammunition, he will, we understand, have to possess a firearm certificate before he can obtain such ammunition. In any event even if that is not the case, it is not for this court to fly in the face of what we consider to be the plain words of an Act of Parliament."

The court quashed the conviction, ruling both weapons to be shotguns and therefore subject to the provisions of section 2, not section 1, of the Act. A reading of both sections confirms the Lord Chief Justice's understanding: ammunition for section 1 firearms can only be possessed by the holder of a firearm certificate, and in such quantities as the certificate specifies; shot gun ammunition can be purchased by anyone except those under the age of seventeen, and can be freely possessed by everyone except those whose previous convictions preclude such possession. (See 1–21–07 and sections 21 and 22(1)).

In contrast to the above judgment it should be appreciated that a weapon which has a rifled barrel of less than 24 inches in length, and whose rifling has been removed to produce a smooth-bore shot gun or even an air weapon, remains a section 1 firearm. See the Firearms (Amendment) Act 1988, sections 2(2) and 7(2).

The length of a firearm barrel is "measured from the muzzle to the point at which the charge is exploded on firing" as defined in section 57(6)(*a*) of the 1968 Act.

Business and other transactions with firearms and ammunition

1–03–01   **3.**—(1) A person commits an offence if, by way of trade or business, he—

    (*a*) manufactures, sells, transfers, repairs, tests or proves any firearm or ammunition to which section 1 of this Act applies, or a shot gun; or

    (*b*) exposes for sale or transfer, or has in his possession for sale, transfer, repair, test or proof any such firearm or ammunition, or a shot gun,

without being registered under this Act as a firearms dealer.

1–03–02   (2) It is an offence for a person to sell or transfer to any other person in the United Kingdom, other than a registered firearms dealer, any firearm or ammunition to which section 1 applies, or a shot gun, unless that other produces a firearm certificate authorising him to purchase or acquire it or, as the case may be, his shot gun certificate, or shows that he is by virtue of this Act entitled to purchase or acquire it without holding a certificate.

1–03–03   (3) It is an offence for a person to undertake the repair, test or proof of a firearm or ammunition to which section 1 of this Act applies, or of a shot gun, for any other person in the United Kingdom other than a registered firearms dealer as such, unless that other produces or causes to be produced a firearm certificate authorising him to have possession of the firearm or ammunition or, as the case may be, his shot gun certificate, or shows that he is by virtue of this Act entitled to have possession of it without holding a certificate.

(4) Subsections (1) to (3) above have effect subject to any exemption under subsequent provisions of this Part of this Act. **1–03–04**

(5) A person commits an offence if, with a view to purchasing or acquiring, or procuring the repair, test or proof of, any firearm or ammunition to which section 1 of this Act applies, or a shot gun, he produces a false certificate or a certificate in which any false entry has been made, or personates a person to whom a certificate has been granted, or makes any false statement. **1–03–05**

(6) It is an offence for a pawnbroker to take in pawn any firearm or ammunition to which section 1 of this Act applies, or a shot gun. **1–03–06**

OBSERVATIONS

(a) The objective of the section is to ensure that the records maintained by dealers in conjunction with police records provide a complete record of all holdings of firearms and ammunition. Section 3(1) restricts commercial dealings in firearms to dealers registered by the police in compliance with section 33 of the 1968 Act. The word "sell" is not statutorily defined in the Acts but "transfer" is (in section 57(4) of the 1968 Act) and is of sufficient breadth to strike at swaps, part-exchanges, and temporary loans between private individuals, as well as more commonplace commercial transactions, of section 1 ammunition and certificated firearms. (No certificate is necessary for possession of ammunition suitable for section 2 shot guns.) **1–03–07**

(b) It is implicit in the definition of "transfer" that the individual concerned has possession of the firearms or ammunition in question. Observe that sections 3(2)and (3) above apply to the United Kingdom, defined in the Interpretation Act 1978, Schedule 1 as Great Britain and Northern Ireland (this excludes the Channel Islands and the Isle of Man), even though by section 60(3), the 1968 Act did not extend to Northern Ireland: plainly the locus of any contravention of these subsections would have to be within Great Britain even if it related to firearms moved to, or received from, Northern Ireland. However, the point has not been judicially decided. **1–03–08**

The meaning of "transfer" was raised in *Hall v. Cotton* and in *R. v. Wilson* [1989] Crim. L.R. 146. See *supra*, at 1–01–19 and *infra*, at 2–02–02.

Conversion of weapons

1–04–01   **4.**—(1) Subject to this section, it is an offence to shorten the barrel of a shot gun to a length less than 24 inches.

1–04–02   (2) It is not an offence under subsection (1) above for a registered firearms dealer to shorten the barrel of a shot gun for the sole purpose of replacing a defective part of the barrel so as to produce a barrel not less than 24 inches in length.

1–04–03   (3) It is an offence for a person other than a registered firearms dealer to convert into a firearm anything which, though having the appearance of being a firearm, is so constructed as to be incapable of discharging any missile through its barrel.

1–04–04   (4) A person who commits an offence under section 1 of this Act by having in his possession, or purchasing or acquiring, a shot gun which has been shortened contrary to subsection (1) above or a firearm which has been [1 converted as mentioned in subsection (3) above] (whether by a registered firearms dealer or not), without holding a firearm certificate authorising him to have it in his possession, or to purchase or acquire it, shall be treated for the purposes of provisions of this Act relating to the punishment of offences as committing that offence in an aggravated form.

NOTE

(1) Inserted by the 1988 Act, section 23(1).

OBSERVATIONS

1–04–05   (a) Section 4(1) deals with the proscription of the sawn-off shot gun, a firearm favoured by criminals more for its ease of concealment and freer movement in confined spaces than for ballistic accuracy. Only registered firearms dealers can lawfully possess such a weapon, and that solely as a means of effecting repairs to a certificated shot gun. (Practically, it is inconceivable that the police would license the possession of a sawn-off shot gun by a member of the public.)

Council Directive 89/617 amended Council Directive 80/181, which specifies the metric units of measurement to be used instead of traditional imperial units and takes effect from

October 1, 1995. Some traditional measurements (for example, the pint for bottled milk and for beer) are exempted, but this concession has not been extended to firearms.

Accordingly, the metric conversion of 24 inches, namely 0.609m, will need to be incorporated in charges from that date; this calculation marginally understates the true figure (609.6mm).

The Directives are enacted by the Units of Measurement Regulations (S.I. 1994 No. 2867), which permit the use of imperial measurements only as supplementary indications.

(b) This section does not extend to the class of large capacity **1–04–06** smooth-bore weapons discussed in note (c) to section 1 above (see 1–01–13): these, it will be remembered, require a section 1 certificate, not a shot gun certificate, to be legally possessed. Accordingly, such weapons are not subject to the provisions of section 4. Instead they are dealt with in section 7(2) of the Firearms (Amendment) Act 1988. (The difference in treatment is cosmetic only; unlawful possession of either type of weapon attracts the same penalty.) Note that the penalty for contravening section 4(4) of the 1968 Act is found under the entry relating to section 1(1) at column 4 in the Table of Punishments found in Schedule 6 to the Act; the penalty for shortening a section 1 smooth-bore gun is contained in section 6(1) of the 1988 Act.

(c) Section 4(3) is directed against the illegal conversion of **1–04–07** imitation firearms into functioning weapons. Until the passage of the 1982 Act no certificate was needed to possess an imitation firearm capable of being readily converted into a firearm, provided no active steps had been taken to alter it to a working weapon. Section 1(2) of that Act brought readily convertible imitations within the scope of the licensing provisions created by section 1 of the principal Act; the statutory defence contained in section 1(5) of the 1982 Act applies only to the possession of unconverted imitations, and would provide no defence to an alleged contravention of section 4(3) above.

(d) In Scotland only: by section 50(2) a constable can arrest **1–04–08** without warrant any person he has reasonable cause to suspect of contravening section 4, and may enter any place to effect such arrest. General provisions governing England and Wales are contained in the Police and Criminal Evidence Act 1984, section 24(5) and (6) in the case of "arrestable offences" and section 116(2)(*b*) and Schedule 5, Part II, which refers to contraventions of sections 16–18 of the Firearms Act 1968 as being "serious arrestable offences".

Prohibition of certain weapons and control of arms traffic

Weapons subject to general prohibition

1–05–01   5.—(1) A person commits an offence if, without the authority of the [¹ Secretary of State], he has in his possession, or purchases or acquires, or manufactures, sells or transfers—

[²(*a*) any firearm which is so designed or adapted that two or more missiles can be successively discharged without repeated pressure on the trigger;

(*ab*) any self-loading or pump-action rifle other than one which is chambered for .22 rim-fire cartridges;

(*ac*) any self-loading or pump-action smooth-bore gun which is not chambered for .22 rim-fire cartridges and either has a barrel less than 24 inches in length or (excluding any detachable, folding, retractable or other movable butt-stock) is less than 40 inches in length overall;

(*ad*) any smooth-bore revolver gun other than one which is chambered for 9mm. rim-fire cartridges or loaded at the muzzle end of each chamber;

1–05–02   (*ae*) any rocket launcher, or any mortar, for projecting a stabilised missile, other than a launcher or mortar designed for line-throwing or pyrotechnic purposes or as a signalling apparatus;]

1–05–03   (*b*) any weapon of whatever description designed or adapted for the discharge of any noxious liquid, gas or other thing; and

1–05–04   [³(*c*) any cartridge with a bullet designed to explode on or immediately before impact, any ammunition containing or designed or adapted to contain any such noxious thing as is mentioned in paragraph (*b*) above and, if capable of being used with a firearm of any description, any grenade, bomb (or other like missile), or rocket or shell designed to explode as aforesaid.]

1–05–05   [⁴(1A) Subject to section 5A of this Act, a person commits an offence if, without the authority of the Secretary of State, he has in his possession, or purchases or acquires, or sells or transfers—

(*a*) any firearm which is disguised as another object;

(*b*) any rocket or ammunition not falling within paragraph **1–05–06**
(*c*) of subsection (1) of this section which consists in or
incorporates a missile designed to explode on or immediately before impact and is for military use;

(*c*) any launcher or other projecting apparatus not falling
within paragraph (*ae*) of that subsection which is
designed to be used with any rocket or ammunition
falling within paragraph (*b*) above or with ammunition
which would fall within that paragraph but for its being
ammunition falling within paragraph (*c*) of that
subsection;

(*d*) any ammunition for military use which consists in or **1–05–07**
incorporates a missile designed so that a substance
contained in the missile will ignite on or immediately
before impact;

(*e*) any ammunition for military use which consists in or
incorporates a missile designed, on account of its having
a jacket and hard-core, to penetrate armour plating,
armour screening or body armour;

(*f*) any ammunition which is designed to be used with a
pistol and incorporates a missile designed or adapted to
expand on impact;

(*g*) anything which is designed to be projected as a missile
from any weapon and is designed to be, or has been,
incorporated, in—

(i) any ammunition falling within any of the preceding
paragraphs; or

(ii) any ammunition which would fall within any of those
paragraphs but for its being specified in subsection
(1) of this section.]

(2) The weapons and ammunition specified in [⁵subsections **1–05–08**
(1) and (1A) of this section (including, in the case of ammunition, any missiles falling within subsection (1A) (*g*) of this
section] are referred to in this Act as "prohibited weapons" and
"prohibited ammunition" respectively.

(3) An authority given to a person by the [¹Secretary of State] **1–05–09**
under this section shall be in writing and be subject to conditions specified therein.

(4) The conditions of the authority shall include such as
the[¹Secretary of State], having regard to the circumstances of

each particular case, [¹thinks] fit to impose for the purpose of securing that the prohibited weapon or ammunition to which the authority relates will not endanger the public safety or the peace.

1–05–10 (5) It is an offence for a person to whom an authority is given under this section to fail to comply with any condition of the authority.

(6) The [¹Secretary of State] may at any time, if [¹he thinks] fit, revoke an authority given to a person under this section by notice in writing requiring him to deliver up the authority to such person as may be specified in the notice within twenty-one days from the date of the notice; and it is an offence for him to fail to comply with that requirement.

1–05–10 [⁶(7) For the purposes of this section and section 5A of this Act—

(a) any rocket or ammunition which is designed to be capable of being used with a military weapon shall be taken to be for military use;

(b) references to a missile designed so that a substance contained in the missile will ignite on or immediately before impact include references to any missile containing a substance that ignites on exposure to air; and

(c) references to a missile's expanding on impact include references to its deforming on or immediately after impact.]

NOTES

(1) Words substituted by the Transfer of Functions (Prohibited Weapons) Order 1968 (S.I. 1968 No. 1200).
(2) Words substituted by the Firearms Act 1988, section 1(2).
(3) Words substituted by the 1988 Act, section 1(3).
(4) Inserted by the Firearms Acts (Amendment) Regulations 1992 (S.I. 1992 No. 2823), regulation 3(1).
(5) Inserted by S.I. 1992 No. 2823, regulation 3(2).
(6) Inserted by S.I. 1992 No. 2823, regulation 3(3).

OBSERVATIONS

1–05–11 (a) As the Notes above suggest, section 5 of the Act has been extensively updated by the 1988 Act to prohibit the possession of automatic or pump-action weapons, larger calibre revolvers and a variety of rockets and rocket-delivered armaments; and by the 1992 Regulations which are intended to set similar minimum standards for firearms control throughout the European

Community and for the movement of firearms between member States.

(b) Since section 1 makes possession of a section 1 firearm or ammunition an absolute offence (see the discussion following 1–01–09) it is implicit that section 5 similarly creates an absolute offence. **1–05–12**

In *R. v. Bradish* [1990] 1 Q.B. 981; [1990] 2 W.L.R. 223; (1990) 90 Cr.App.R. 271 B had been arrested on a separate matter and taken to a police station. When searched he was found to have a spray canister labelled "Force 10 Super Magnum CS" and, on questioning, admitted it was a CS gas aerosol which he knew he should not have. The assistant recorder ruled this to be a prohibited weapon and, on appeal, a ruling was sought as to whether possession thereof did attract strict liability.

Auld J. delivered the judgment; references are to W.L.R., cited above. Having cited the terms of sections 5(1) and 57(1) he added at 225F:

> "In *R. v. Clarke (Frederick)* [1986] 1 W.L.R. 209, the Court of Appeal held that the words of section 57(1) are to be read into section 5(1). In that case, which concerned an incomplete sub-machine gun, the court held that it was nevertheless a prohibited weapon for two reasons, one of which was that the words of section 57(1)(*b*) were to be read into section 5(1)(*a*) with the result that it was an offence to possess any component part of a weapon designed or adapted for automatic fire. Whilst this appeal relates to an alleged offence under section 5(1)(*b*), which concerns weapons for the discharge of noxious liquid or gas, our decision as to whether the offence is absolute or requires mens rea covers all three categories in section 5(1)(*a*), (*b*) and (*c*). In the case of a firearm, the subject of section 5(1)(*a*), the question may arise in relation to some small part of an automatic weapon, perhaps not readily identifiable as such on its own.
>
> The Firearms (Amendment) Act 1988 has now, by section 1, considerably extended the categories of prohibited weapons falling within section 5. . .
>
> There is no authority on the question whether an offence under section 5 of the Act of 1968 is one of strict liability or requires mens rea. There is, however, authority on the same question in relation to the lesser offence under section 1(1)

of the Act which makes it an offence for a person to possess, purchase or acquire a firearm unless he or she is authorised to do so by a current firearm certificate."

1–05–13   His Lordship considered the *Warner* judgment and the more lucid interpretation of the statutory defence in the Misuse of Drugs Act 1971, section 28(3), afforded by *R. v. McNamara* (1987) 87 Cr.App.R. 246, a further drugs "container" case. *Warner* has been discussed briefly at 1–01–10, *supra*, but offers no practical guidance (and much confusion) to interpretation of the Firearms Act. The reasoning in *R. v. Howells* [1977] Q.B. 614; [1977] 2 W.L.R. 716; [1977] 3 All E.R. 417 (a case considered at 4–06–04, *infra*) and *R. v. Hussain*, cited at 1–01–09, *supra*, in regard to section 1 weapons was approved. The judgment continued, at 230G:

> "Having set out the principal authorities bearing on the question, we turn now to the assistant recorder's ruling and the arguments advanced before us in support of and against the appeal.
>
> The assistant recorder ruled: '. . . I can see no argument for distinguishing, in respect of this particular case, from section 1 and section 5. I, therefore, feel bound to follow the judgments of *R. v. Howells* and *R. v. Hussain*, which is that it is an offence of strict liability and the prosecution need not prove mens rea;. . . '
>
> The principal submission of [the appellant] is that this is a 'container' case of the sort considered by the House of Lords in [*Warner*] and that, therefore, the 'half-way house' approach adopted by Lord Pearce, Lord Reid and Lord Wilberforce in that case applies. He argues that once the prosecution have proved that a person was knowingly in possession of an item and that that item was in fact a prohibited weapon, it is a defence for him to show, on a balance of probabilities, that he neither knew nor suspected nor should be deemed to have known that it was a prohibited weapon. He added that, in practice, this defence will only be available in a 'container' case; that is, where the nature of the item is concealed by the container.
>
> In his submission that this is a 'container' case Mr Jenkins treats the canister as the container and the noxious gas the thing contained. He suggests that the court should not

assume that the defendant had read the marking on the canister . . . He distinguishes [*Howells* and *Hussain*] on the basis that they were not 'container' cases. He pointed out that in each case the nature of the weapon was evident to its possessor . . . both knew that they had a weapon of some sort, but they had made a mistake in law. . . .

We start with the presumption of statutory interpretation that Parliament intends there to be a mental element in offences of a truly criminal nature. However, that presumption can be rebutted, and it is conceded on behalf of the defendant that it is rebutted in the case of an offence under section 5 to the extent that all the prosecution have to do is prove that an accused knowingly had in his possession an article which was in fact a prohibited weapon. The only issue is whether, if the prosecution prove that, it is a defence for an accused to show on a balance of probabilities that he did not know and could not have been expected to know that the article was a prohibited weapon."

The court summarised the factors which import strict liability **1–05–14** to section 5 offences: (1) the words used in the section, (2) the comparable wording of section 1 which, it was recognised following *Howells* and *Hussain*, created an absolute offence and (3) the clear purpose of the Firearms Act to impose a tight control on the use of highly dangerous weapons; since section 1 involved strict liability, it had to be beyond a peradventure that section 5, dealing with yet "more serious weapons" and imposing more severe penalties, followed suit.

As to the question of the applicability of the *Warner* judgment **1–05–15** to a "container" case under section 5 of the Act (an approach which it had been submitted would raise a defence of ignorance as to the container's contents), the court rejected this line of argument and followed the strict construction taken by Lord Morris in *Warner* in preference to the "half-way house" adopted by Lords Pearce, Reid and Wilberforce in that case. The Firearms Act contained no provision which matched the statutory defence available to defendants in section 28(3) of the Misuse of Drugs Act. Additionally, neither section 1 nor section 5 of the Act had introduced any reference to the state of an accused's mind, although such provisions had been included elsewhere in the Act, while the tenor of the (then) recently introduced 1988 Act signalled a yet more restrictive approach to firearms possession.

Finally, at 232H his Lordship stated:

"... [T]he possibilities and consequences of evasion would be too great for effective control, even if the burden of proving lack of guilty knowledge were to be on the accused. The difficulty of enforcement, when presented with such a defence, would be particularly difficult where there is a prosecution for possession of a component part of a firearm or prohibited weapon, as provided for by sections 1 and 5 when read with section 57(1) of the Act of 1968. It would be easy for an accused to maintain, lyingly but with conviction, that he did not recognise the object in his possession as part of a firearm or prohibited weapon. To the argument that the innocent possessor or carrier of firearms or prohibited weapons or parts of them is at risk of unfair conviction under these provisions, there has to be balanced the important public policy behind the legislation of protecting the public from the misuse of such dangerous weapons. Just as the Chicago-style gangster might plausibly maintain that he believed his violin case to contain a violin, not a sub-machine gun, so it might be difficult to meet a London lout's assertion that he did not know an unmarked plastic bottle in his possession contained ammonia rather than something to drink.

Accordingly, we are of the view that, whether or not this case is regarded as a 'container' case, and even if the canister had not been clearly marked 'Force 10 Super magnum CS', this was an absolute offence, and it would have been no defence for the defendant to maintain that he did not know or could not reasonably have been expected to know that the canister contained CS gas. It follows that . . . section 5 creates an offence of strict liability. [The assistant recorder] was not asked to consider the further question that we have just resolved against the defendant, whether, if the prosecution established possession of the prohibited weapon, it was open to the defence to raise and to prove on a balance of probabilities that he did not know that he had a prohibited weapon.

1–05–16   We would add that, on the facts of this case, it is a surprising vehicle for the arguments of law that have been advanced to us on behalf of the defendant, even if we had accepted them. It is clearly not a 'container' case. As we have already observed, section 5(1)(*b*) refers to a "weapon . . . designed or adapted for the discharge of any noxious liquid, gas or other thing." It is the combination of canister and contents that makes the weapon; the noxious gas in this case cannot be regarded as the contents of a container in the sense that drugs were the contents of a box in [*Warner* and *McNamara*]. Given the clear marking on the canister of what it contained, we cannot see the beginnings of a defence for the defendant, even if one had existed in law, that he took possession of the canister without realising what it was."

The appeal was dismissed. Perhaps the analogy of an ammonia-filled plastic bottle was not ideal in the circumstances when the decision in *R. v. Titus* (see 1–05–17) is considered, but His Lordship amply underlined the pitfalls of applying an authority, like *Warner*, too readily.
(c) In *Ferguson v. H.M. Advocate*, 1991 S.C.C.R. 965, where the accused was found in possession of a CS gas canister during a football-related disturbance and appealed against a sentence of one year's detention, the court gave short shrift to suggestions that the canister might more properly be regarded, for the purposes of sentence, as an offensive weapon rather than a firearm and refused the appeal.
Subsection 5(1)(*b*) also covers stun guns which discharge a "noxious thing" namely a high voltage electric charge; see *Flack v. Baldry* [1988] 1 W.L.R. 393; [1988] 1 All E.R. 673; (1988) 87 Cr.App.R. 130. However, while section 5(1)(*b*) refers to a **1–05–17** weapon, rather than a firearm, designed or adapted for the discharge of any "noxious . . . thing" this has been held not to extend to a plastic detergent bottle filled with hydrochloric acid, since the bottle had not been designed as a weapon and no adaption of the article had occurred. Such an article would be an offensive weapon, in terms of the Prevention of Crime Act 1953, possession of which in a public place would attract a much less onerous penalty than section 5(1)(*b*) of the Firearms Act 1968 provides on conviction. See *R. v. Formosa; R. v. Upton* [1991] 2 Q.B. 1; [1990] 3 W.L.R. 1179; (1990) 92 Cr.App.R. 11. In *R. v. Titus* [1971] Crim.L.R. 279, in which five men were charged with contraventions of section 18 of the 1968 Act (possession of a firearm or imitation firearm with intent) with

regard to water pistols filled with ammonia, it was submitted as an objection to relevancy by defence counsel that the pistols were weapons, as defined in section 5(1)(*b*), designed or adapted for the discharge of a noxious liquid; the Crown in support of the charge libelled contended that the pistols had not been "designed" or "adapted", since the former phrase should refer to the function envisaged by the manufacturer, while "adapted" required more than simply filling the article with noxious contents. The appearance of the water pistols brought them within the scope of "imitation firearms" defined in section 57(4) of the Act, a situation which did not arise in *Titus*.

1–05–18 (d) The broad intention of this section is to keep out of the public's hands military weapons designed or adapted for continuous fire, or the component parts of such weapons.

Prohibited weapons do not evade the rigour of section 5 by being modified or restricted in their operation, or if they do not function as designed through some defect or fault. In *R. v. Hucklebridge* (cited above at 1–02–03) it had been held that a section 1 weapon, a rifle, would be categorised as a section 2 firearm (a shot gun) if its rifling was removed: no such conces-

1–05–19 sion extends to prohibited weapons. In *R. v. Pannell* [1982] Crim.L.R. 752, the appellant, who was a registered firearms dealer entitled to possess section 1 firearms and ammunition, had been charged with contravening section 5(1)(*a*) in respect of three Sterling carbines; these weapons had been designed for military use to fire automatically (by continuous trigger pressure) or one shot at a time. When recovered by the police, the trigger mechanisms had rods inserted enabling only single shots to be fired. Careful pressure on the triggers did achieve limited continuous automatic fire. The appellant (who had received an absolute discharge on being convicted) argued that section 5(1)(*a*) did not apply since the articles when seized by the police had been no more than component parts of firearms, and as such could be held under a section 1 certificate. While recognising that the weapons were in a dismantled state when seized, the court noted that the appellant had possession of all parts of each of the weapons; submissions that the court should look at their state only at the time when illegal possession was alleged were rejected. Each weapon had been designed to achieve continuous fire and nothing had been done to convert its character to something different.

It should be noted that this decision overturned that in *R. v.* **1–05–20**
Jobling [1981] Crim.L.R. 625, where a Bren machine gun,
designed to fire either single shots or continuous automatic fire,
but modified between its trigger and bolt to preclude automatic
fire, had been held not to be a firearm governed by section
5(1)(*a*). Even then, in *Jobling* it was stressed that a temporary or
intermittent fault in a weapon subject to section 5(1)(*a*), which
prevented its full operation, would not suffice to change its
character. On broadly similar facts to *Jobling*, the Scottish
Appeal Court followed the *ratio* in *Pannell*, noting that nothing
had been done to change the weapon to one of a different
character; only its efficiency had been impaired: see *Jessop v.
Stevenson*, 1988 S.L.T. 223; 1987 S.C.C.R. 655. In any event it
would equally have been true (though the court made no
finding) that the accused had possession of component parts of
a lethal or prohibited weapon as defined in section 57(1)(*b*) of
the 1968 Act, a line of reasoning followed in *R. v. Clarke
(Frederick)* [1986] 1 W.L.R. 209; [1986] 1 All E.R. 846; [1986]
Crim.L.R. 334.

The issue of whether adaptations to a weapon have been
sufficiently substantial to alter its character, as originally
designed, may at times be a fine one. The best that can be said is
that the courts will be slow to hold that such a weapon is not still
prohibited, and consideration might then focus on the question
of component parts raised above.

(e) Section 5(1A) prohibits the acquisition, purchase, posses- **1–05–21**
sion, sale or transfer of weapons (or the appropriate ammunition) listed in the section. There is no bar upon the manufacture
of such weapons or ammunition, so the approval of the Secretary of State is not needed by a manufacturer. However, once
the prohibited weapons or ammunition had been manufactured,
it would then be necessary to secure such approval to possess,
sell or transfer them.

Exemptions from requirement of authority under section 5

[¹5A.—(1) Subject to subsection (2) below, the authority of **1–05–22**
the Secretary of State shall not be required by virtue of
subsection (1A) of section 5 of this Act for any person to have in
his possession, or to purchase, acquire, sell or transfer, any
prohibited weapon or ammunition if he is authorised by a
certificate under this Act to possess, purchase or acquire that

weapon or ammunition subject to a condition that he does so only for the purpose of its being kept or exhibited as part of a collection.

(2) No sale or transfer may be made under subsection (1) above except to a person who—

    (*a*) produces the authority of the Secretary of State under section 5 for his purchase or acquisition or;

    (*b*) shows that he is, under this section or under the Schedule to the Firearms (Amendment) Act 1988 (museums etc.) entitled to make the purchase or acquisition without the authority of the Secretary of State.

(3) The authority of the Secretary of State shall not be required by virtue of subsection (1A) of section 5 of this Act for any person to have in his possession, or to purchase or acquire, any prohibited weapon or ammunition if his possession, purchase or acquisition is exclusively in connection with the carrying on of activities in respect of which—

    (*a*) that person; or

    (*b*) the person on whose behalf he has possession, or makes the purchase or acquisition,

is recognised for the purposes of the law of another member State relating to firearms, as a collector of firearms or a body concerned in the cultural or historical aspects of weapons.

(4) The authority of the Secretary of State shall not be required by virtue of subsection (1A) of section 5 of this Act for any person to have in his possession, or to purchase or acquire, any expanding ammunition or the missile for any such ammunition if—

    (*a*) he is authorised by a firearm certificate to possess, purchase or acquire ammunition which is designed to be used with a pistol; and

    (*b*) the certificate contains a condition prohibiting the use of expanding ammunition for purposes not authorised by the European weapons directive.

(5) The authority of the Secretary of State shall not be required by virtue of subsection (1A) of section 5 of this Act for any person to have in his possession any expanding ammunition or the missile for any such ammunition if—

    (*a*) he is entitled, under section 10 of this Act, to have a slaughtering instrument and the ammunition for it in his possession; and (*b*) the ammunition or missile in question is designed to be capable of being used with a slaughtering instrument.

(6) The authority of the Secretary of State shall not be required by virtue of subsection (1A) of section 5 of this Act for the sale or transfer of any expanding ammunition or the missile for any such ammunition to any person who produces a certificate by virtue of which he is authorised under subsection (4) above to purchase or acquire it without the authority of the Secretary of State.

(7) The authority of the Secretary of State shall not be required by virtue of subsection (1A) of section 5 of this Act for a person carrying on the business of a firearms dealer, or any servant of his, to have in his possession, or to purchase, acquire, sell or transfer, any expanding ammunition or the missile for any such ammunition if—

(*a*) the person carrying on that business is registered as a firearms dealer subject to a condition which prohibits the purchase or acquisition of any such ammunition or missile except for the purpose of making sales or transfers to persons whose purchases or acquisitions are authorised by subsection (4) above or this subsection; and

(*b*) the possession, purchase, acquisition, sale or transfer in question is in the ordinary course of that business.

(8) In this section—

(*a*) references to expanding ammunition are references to any ammunition which is designed to be used with a pistol and incorporates a missile which is designed to expand on impact; and

(*b*) references to the missile for any such ammunition are references to anything which, in relation to any such ammunition, falls within section 5(1A)(*g*) of this Act.]

NOTE

(1) Section inserted by the Firearms Acts (Amendment) Regulations 1992 (S.I. 1992 No. 2823) Regulation 3(4).

OBSERVATIONS

(a) The importance of uniform standards of firearms control **1–05–23** within Member States of the European Community is amply illustrated by the terms of subsection (3) above, which contain the only definition in the regulations of the term "collector". Compliance with the European weapons directive has created, so far as prohibited weapons, at least, are concerned, a situation which is potentially more permissive and confusing than the Firearms (Amendment) Act 1988 allowed. Section 17(3) of that Act allowed a visitor to obtain a visitor's firearm permit (in lieu of a firearm or shot gun certificate) from the police, subject to their right to refuse an application where there was reason to believe that possession of the weapons or ammunition in issue would represent a danger to the public safety or peace. Permits did not extend to section 5 weapons or ammunition. Section 5(6) of the 1968 Act empowers the Secretary of State to revoke an authority to possess prohibited weapons previously granted under section 5(1A). The Regulations, however, do not incorporate within the Firearms Acts any means by which the Secretary of State can control the activities in Great Britain of collectors of prohibited weapons and ammunition who visit from other member States.

(b) The possession of expanding ammunition is generally prohibited by section 5(1A)(*g*) of the Act as amended. Note that section 5(7) further refines the earlier subsection.

The 1968 Act exempted licensed slaughterhouse proprietors (or persons appointed by in that regard) from compliance with the Firearms Acts' certification requirements so far as slaughtering instruments were concerned. The provisions of section 5A(5) now explicitly permit such proprietors to possess expanding ammunition for use in these instruments.

Power to prohibit movement of arms and ammunition

1–06–01   **6.**—(1) The Secretary of State may by order prohibit the removal of firearms or ammunition—

(*a*) from one place to another in Great Britain; or

(*b*) . . .

(*c*) for export from Great Britain,

unless the removal is authorised by the chief officer of police for the area from which they are to be removed, and unless such other conditions as may be specified in the order are complied with.

[[1](1A) The Secretary of State may by order prohibit the removal of firearms or ammunition from Great Britain to Northern Ireland unless—

(*a*) the removal is authorised by the chief officer of police for the area from which they are to be removed and by the Chief Constable of the Royal Ulster Constabulary; and

(*b*) such conditions as may be specified in the order or imposed by the chief officer of police or the Chief Constable are complied with.]

(2) An order under this section may apply—   1–06–02

(*a*) either generally to all such removals, or to removals from and to particular localities specified in the order; and

(*b*) either to all firearms and ammunition or to firearms and ammunition of such classes and descriptions as may be so specified; and

(*c*) either to all modes of conveyance or to such modes of conveyance as may be so specified;

but no such order shall prohibit the holder of a firearm certificate from carrying with him any firearm or ammunition authorised by the certificate to be so carried.

(3) It is an offence to contravene any provision of—   1–06–03

(*a*) an order made under this section; or

(*b*) an order made under section 9 of the Firearms Act 1920 (the former enactment corresponding to section 18 of the Firearms Act 1937 and this section); or

(*c*) any corresponding Northern Irish order, that is to say an order made under the said section 9 as extending to Northern Ireland or under any enactment of the Parliament of Northern Ireland repealing and re-enacting that section, prohibiting the removal of firearms or ammunition from Northern Ireland to Great Britain.

(4) An order under this section shall be made by statutory instrument and may be varied or revoked by a subsequent order made thereunder by the Secretary of State.

NOTE

(1) Subsection (*b*) was repealed by section 20(3) of the 1988 Act which, by section 20(2), inserted subsection (1A) above. The Firearms (Removal to Northern Ireland) Order 1990 (S.I. 1990 No. 2621) prohibits the removal from Great Britain to Northern Ireland of section 1 firearms or ammunition unless the chief officer of police in the area from which the items are to be removed and the Chief Constable of the R.U.C. give authority and the conditions imposed by both officers are met.

OBSERVATION

1–06–04 Despite the military and political situation in Northern Ireland, which has prevailed almost as long as the 1968 Act itself, it is of note that there are no cited reports arising from the above section. Contravention of section 6(3) attracts only three months' imprisonment and/or a level 3 penalty on the standard scale. By contrast, if the circumstances of removal of items to Northern Ireland were ruled to be contributions of property towards acts of terrorism or to proscribed organisations, whether for consideration or not, potential penalties would be much more severe. Contraventions of sections 9 or 10 of the Prevention of Terrorism (Temporary Provisions) Act 1989 incur summary penalties of up to 6 months' imprisonment and/or the statutory maximum fine; on indictment imprisonment up to 14 years and/or fine without limit could be imposed.

Special exceptions from sections 1 to 5

Police permit

1–07–01 **7.**—(1) A person who has obtained from the chief officer for the area in which he resides a permit for the purpose in the prescribed form may, without holding a certificate under this Act, have in his possession a firearm and ammunition in accordance with the terms of the permit.

(2) It is an offence for a person to make any statement which he knows to be false for the purpose of procuring, whether for himself or for another person, the grant of a permit under this section.

OBSERVATION

1–07–02 The power to grant a permit under this section is distinct from the granting of firearm or shot gun certificates empowered by section 26 of the 1968 Act. A decision by the chief officer of police to refuse to grant (or renew) such a certificate is subject to appeal as laid out in section 44 of and Schedule 5 to the Act. By contrast, no appeal procedure governs what is essentially a discretionary power vested in the hands of chief officers of police. Although it is not expressly stated, it follows from the terms of section 5, *supra*, that the grant of such a permit to possess prohibited weapons and ammunition would still be contingent upon the Secretary of State's authorisation.

Authorised dealing with firearms

8.—(1) A person carrying on the business of a firearms dealer **1–08–01** and registered as such under this Act, or a servant of such a person may, without holding a certificate, have in his possession, or purchase or acquire, a firearm or ammunition in the ordinary course of that business.

(2) It is not an offence under section 3(2) of this Act for a person—

(*a*) to part with the possession of any firearm or ammunition, otherwise than in pursuance of a contract of sale or hire or by way of gift or loan, to a person who shows that he is by virtue of this Act entitled to have possession of the firearm or ammunition without holding a certificate; or

(*b*) to return to another person a shot gun which he has lawfully undertaken to repair, test or prove for the other.

OBSERVATIONS

(a) Firearms dealers obtain that status by registering with the **1–08–02** chief officer of police for their area in accordance with section 33 of the principal Act; they are statutorily required to detail every place in that area where the business of firearms dealer will be conducted. So in *R. v. Bull* [1994] Crim.L.R. 224, where B, a firearms dealer, stored ammunition in a friend's barn (a place not specified in the register), B was charged with contravening section 1(1) of the Act. Initially B argued that such possession was covered by the general provisions of section 8 and that no additional certificate was necessary. B was convicted, the court ruling that such possession could not be viewed as occurring in the ordinary course of business. On appeal it was submitted for B that the exemption under section 8 applied to a person, not to a place, and, accordingly, a registered firearms dealer would be exempt from the certification provisions of the Firearms Acts. The Crown argued that section 8 fell to be read in conjunction with section 33 and not in isolation; the concept of "place of business" was critical to the policing of the Acts.

The court dismissed the appeal and held that to benefit from the special exemption afforded to firearms dealers from the certification requirements of sections 1 to 5 of the 1968 Act, dealers must register every place where their business was to be conducted; only possession of firearms and ammunition in pursuance of the ordinary course of business was permitted by section 8.

1–08–03 The importance of accurate records was highlighted in *Star-avia Ltd v. Gordon* [1973] Crim.L.R. 298 when separate informations laid against the managing director of a company and the company itself alleging contravention of section 39(2) were dismissed (the latter on appeal) due to ambiguities in the records maintained by the responsible police authority.

1–08–04 (b) In *Woodage v. Moss* [1974] 1 W.L.R. 411; [1974] All E.R. 584 the question was briefly considered of whether the accused (who had taken a firearm into his possession having arranged to deliver it to a registered firearms dealer he knew) could be regarded as a servant of the dealer and thus exempted from the certification provisions of the Acts under section 8. The court ([1974] 1 W.L.R. 411 at 416C), in finding against the respondent, stated: "There was no obligation on [him] to carry out that request, he received no remuneration for it, and it was simply a means which he adopted of satisfying the request made by the dealer and doing, as I think, a good turn to the unknown man."

Carriers, auctioneers, etc.

1–09–01 **9.**—(1) A person carrying on the business of an auctioneer, carrier or warehouseman, or a servant of such a person, may, without holding a certificate, have in his possession a firearm or ammunition in the ordinary course of that business.

(2) It is not an offence under section 3(1) of this Act for an auctioneer to sell by auction, expose for sale by auction or have in his possession for sale by auction a firearm or ammunition without being registered as a firearms dealer, if he has obtained from the chief officer of police for the area in which the auction is held a permit for that purpose in the prescribed form and complies with the terms of the permit.

(3) It is an offence for a person to make any statement which he knows to be false for the purpose of procuring, either for himself or for another person, the grant of a permit under subsection (2) of this section.

1–09–02 (4) It is not an offence under section 3(2) of this Act for a carrier or warehouseman, or a servant of a carrier or warehouseman, to deliver any firearm or ammunition in the ordinary course of his business or employment as such.

OBSERVATION

Carriers are exempted from the need to possess a firearm certificate while carrying firearms or ammunition in the course of business. That exemption, it is submitted, would not extend to the carriage of prohibited weapons since a section 5 authority granted by the Secretary of State would be needed; the only exception to this general rule is found in section 58(1) of the 1968 Act and deals with the carriage of firearms only to and from the two designated proof houses for the purposes of proof.

Slaughter of animals

10.—(1) A person licensed under [[1]section 39 of the Slaugh- **1–10–01** terhouses Act 1974] or [[2]section 15 of the Slaughter of Animals (Scotland) Act 1980] may, without holding a certificate, have in his possession a slaughtering instrument and ammunition therefor in any slaughterhouse or knacker's yard in which he is employed.

(2) The proprietor of a slaughterhouse or knacker's yard or a person appointed by him to take charge of slaughtering instruments and ammunition therefor for the purpose of storing them in safe custody at that slaughterhouse or knacker's yard may, without holding a certificate, have in his possession a slaughtering instrument or ammunition therefor for that purpose.

NOTES

(1) Words substituted by the Slaughterhouses Act 1974, Sched. 3, para. 5.
(2) Words substituted by the Slaughter of Animals (Scotland) Act 1980, s.23 and Sched. I, para. 3.

OBSERVATIONS

(a) The general prohibition on the possession, purchase, acquisi- **1–10–02** tion, sale or transfer of ammunition or missiles which expand on impact does not apply to those licensed to operate slaughter-houses or those appointed by such persons. See section 5A(5), *supra*.
(b) "Slaughtering instrument" is statutorily defined in section 57(4) of the 1968 Act. See *infra*, at 4–05–04.

Sports, athletics and other approved activities

11.—(1) A person carrying a firearm or ammunition belong- **1–11–01** ing to another person holding a certificate under this Act may, without himself holding such a certificate, have in his possession that firearm or ammunition under instructions from, and for the use of, that other person for sporting purposes only.

(2) A person may, without holding a certificate, have a firearm in his possession at an athletic meeting for the purpose of starting races at that meeting.

1–11–02　　(3) A member of a [¹ . . .] cadet corps approved by the Secretary of State may, without holding a certificate, have in his possession a firearm and ammunition when engaged as a member of the [¹ . . .] corps in, or in connection with, drill or target practice.

(4) A person conducting or carrying on a miniature rifle range (whether for a rifle club or otherwise) or shooting gallery at which no firearms are used other than air weapons or miniature rifles not exceeding .23 inch calibre may, without holding a certificate, have in his possession, or purchase or acquire, such miniature rifles and ammunition suitable therefor; and any person may, without holding a certificate, use any such rifle and ammunition at such a range or gallery.

1–11–03　　(5) A person may, without holding a shot gun certificate, borrow a shot gun from the occupier of private premises and use it on those premises in the occupier's presence.

(6) A person may, without holding a shot gun certificate, use a shot gun at a time and place approved for shooting at artificial targets by the chief officer of police for the area in which that place is situated.

NOTE

(1) Words deleted by the 1988 Act, s.15(7).

OBSERVATIONS

1–11–04　(a) Section 11(4) exempts the operator of miniature rifle ranges or shooting galleries from the certification provisions of the Acts. Although the calibre of rifles whose use without certificate is explicitly stated, no such clarity applies to air weapons; however, reference to section 57(4), which in turn refers the reader to section 1(3)(*b*) of the 1968 Act, shows that only air weapons which have not been declared specially dangerous can be freely possessed as a result of the subsection's exemption.

1–11–05　(b) The provisions originally contained in section 11 relating to rifle clubs and miniature rifle clubs were modified by the 1988

Act and are in section 15 thereof. In *R. v. Wilson (Maxim)* [1989] Crim.L.R. 901, the appellant was charged with contravening section 1(1)(*b*) of the 1968 Act. W held a firearms certificate and whilst he was abroad, the police in a search of his home found a quantity of ammunition in excess of the amount permitted him by his certificate. W claimed that the ammunition had been accumulated for a private shoot a month earlier which had been cancelled due to adverse weather; it was submitted for W that the express provisions of section 11(3) (since replaced in regard to rifle clubs by section 15(1) of the 1988 Act) provided a defence and that there would be an interval after such a shoot when lawful possession of any unused ammunition in excess of the authorised figure would be permissible. The submission was rejected at trial and, on appeal, it was held that irrespective of the legitimacy of possession for any shorter period, the lapse of one month was clearly excessive since any engagement in target shooting had long since ceased. Whether a *locus poenitentiae* can be inferred by sections 11(3) or 15(1) of the 1968 and 1988 Acts respectively, or the length of any interval, remains undecided: equity suggests that such a defence should be open.

(c) Section 16 of the 1988 Act also provides that supervised use **1–11–06** of borrowed firearms on a certificate holder's premises, and the purchase of ammunition by the borrower for the purpose of shooting there, can be exempted from the provisions of section 1 of the principal Act.

Theatre and cinema

12.—(1) A person taking part in a theatrical performance or a **1–12–01** rehearsal thereof, or in the production of a cinematograph film, may, without holding a certificate, have a firearm in his possession during and for the purpose of the performance, rehearsal or production.

(2) Where the [¹Secretary of State is] satisfied, on the application of a person in charge of a theatrical performance, a rehearsal of such a performance or the production of a cinematograph film, that [²a prohibited weapon] is required for the purpose of the performance, rehearsal or production, [¹he] may under section 5 of this Act, if [¹he thinks] fit, not only authorise that person to have possession of [²the weapon] but also authorise such other persons as he may select to have possession of it while taking part in the performance, rehearsal or production.

NOTES

(1) Inserted by the Transfer of Functions (Prohibited Weapons) Order 1968 (S.I. 1968 No. 1200).
(2) Words substituted by the 1988 Act, s.23(2).

OBSERVATION

Given the plethora of imitation firearms widely available today it is questionable how necessary the section's provisions are now. Note that the concession made does not extend to possession of either section 1 or section 5 ammunition.

Equipment for ships and aircraft

1–13–01   13.—(1) A person may, without holding a certificate,—

(*a*) have in his possession a firearm or ammunition on board a ship, or a signalling apparatus or ammunition therefor on board an aircraft or at an aerodrome, as part of the equipment of the ship, aircraft or aerodrome;

(*b*) remove a signalling apparatus or ammunition therefor, being part of the equipment of an aircraft, from one aircraft to another at an aerodrome, or from or to an aircraft at an aerodrome to or from a place appointed for the storage thereof in safe custody at that aerodrome, and keep any such apparatus or ammunition at such a place; and

(*c*) if he has obtained from [¹a constable] a permit for the purpose in the prescribed form, remove a firearm from or to a ship, or a signalling apparatus from or to an aircraft or aerodrome, to or from such place and for such purpose as may be specified in the permit.

(2) It is an offence for a person to make any statement which he knows to be false for the purpose of procuring, either for himself or for another person, the grant of a permit under subsection (1)(*c*) of this section.

NOTE

(1) Inserted by the 1988 Act, s.23(3).

OBSERVATIONS

1–13–02   (a) References to ships, vessels or boats in the Acts are extended to include hovercraft by the Hovercraft (Application of Enactments) Order 1972 (S.I. 1972 No. 971).

(b) In *R. v. Singh* [1989] Crim.L.R. 724 it was held that a flare **1–13–03** launcher was a firearm, while flares, being explosively charged, could constitute ammunition. S had misappropriated these items from Army signalling kit while serving in the Territorial Army. At his trial, expert evidence was led by both sides as to whether the launcher "cup" fulfilled the statutory definition of a firearm in section 57(12), *viz.* a lethal barrelled weapon. The Court of Appeal held that that issue was properly a jury question under suitable direction from the trial judge.

Persons temporarily in Great Britain

14.—. . . **1–14–01**

NOTES

(1) Section repealed by the 1988 Act, s.23(8). The current provisions relating to visitors' permits are found in s.17 of that Act.

Holder of Northern Irish certificate

15.—Section 2(1) of this Act does not apply to a person **1–15–01** holding a firearm certificate issued in Northern Ireland authorising him to possess a shot gun.

Prevention of crime and preservation of public safety

Possession of firearm with intent to injure

16.—It is an offence for a person to have in his possession any **1–16–01** firearm or ammunition with intent by means thereof to endanger life [1. . .], or to enable another person by means thereof to endanger life [1. . .], whether any injury [. . .] has been caused or not.

NOTE

(1) Words deleted (England and Wales) by the Criminal Damage Act 1981, s.11(7) and Schedule thereto; the words "serious injury to property" still apply in Scotland: see observation (c) at 1–16–08 below.

OBSERVATIONS

(a) This section raises several problems of construction. Most **1–16–02** obviously, does danger to life include the life of the accused? In

R. v. Norton (Rex) [1977] Crim.L.R. 478 the defendant, who lawfully possessed a 12-bore shot gun, had previously attempted suicide and had a history of depression. Following an argument with his wife he took the gun and threatened to kill himself. He fired several shots at the ceiling and walls then placed the gun to his mouth, but after pleas from his wife, he left the house, climbed an adjacent scaffold, fired more shots in the air then fell to the ground to his severe injury. He was charged with contravening section 16. It was submitted on his behalf that there was no criminality in attempting to take his own life: the Crown had to prove intent to endanger others' lives. The submission was upheld. (Presumably it was not felt that the damage caused to property was serious; no argument was advanced on this aspect.)

It will be noted that N was certificated to possess a shot gun but could properly be charged under section 16. If the use to which the firearm is put is not one allowed by the certificate, then there is nothing to prevent a prosecution. However, it has to be conceded that proving the necessary criminal intent to satisfy the parameters of section 16 would be doubly difficult where possession of the firearm or ammunition in question had begun in conformity with a firearm or shot gun certificate. Note, too, that the section refers to "any firearm or ammunition": that phrase covers air weapons and their ammunition as well as certificated weapons.

1–16–03   The next question is whether section 16 creates an absolute offence. In *R. v. Georgiades* [1989] 1 W.L.R. 759; [1989] Crim.L.R. 574, the Crown conceded that possession of a firearm with intent to endanger life might, in rare circumstances, be lawful. G, who was a heroin addict and dealer, confronted police officers with a loaded shot gun when they called at his flat to arrest his brother. In his defence G (who had only days before been acquitted of shooting another man in circumstances he claimed were accidental) alleged that he had loaded the guns in his control to defend himself against what he took to be an attack upon himself and was acting in self defence. At G's trial, his counsel had conceded that a plea of self defence could not succeed in view of the terms of section 16. G appealed against conviction.

Despite the concession made by the Crown at the appeal, and the Court of Appeal's judgment that the question of self defence should have been left to the jury, it is submitted that this view is flawed.

For a plea of self defence to succeed there has to be a reasonable apprehension of imminent danger, no practicable means of avoiding or escaping that danger, and a degree of retaliation reasonably matching the perceived threat. These are elements for a jury to consider in conjunction with a recognition that all these factors had to be addressed by an accused in the heat of a moment.

It is difficult to reconcile these tests with the language of **1–16–04** section 16, which refers to "possession" and to "intent". Both terms import an element of contemplation and planning which is entirely inappropriate to self defence situations. For example, in a further prosecution under section 16, *R. v. Bentham; R. v. Baillie; R. v. Simpson* [1973] 1 Q.B. 357; [1972] 3 W.L.R. 398; [1972] 3 All E.R. 271, Cairns L.J. stated ([1972] 3 W.L.R. 398 at 403E):

> "We cannot accept that the only intent which falls within the section is an intent immediately and unconditionally to endanger life. The intent with which a man wounds another or detonates an explosive is an intent which accompanies the act, but possession is not an act done at a particular moment; it is a continuing state of things and in our view the intent to endanger life is something which may last as long as the possession lasts. It cannot therefore be limited to an intent to endanger life immediately. Nor do we see any reason why it should be limited to an unconditional intent. It would indeed in most cases be impossible to establish an unconditional intent to endanger life until the moment before a firearm was fired. The mischief at which the section is aimed must be that of a person possessing a firearm ready for use, if and when occasion arises, in a manner which endangers life."

[Note that the word "intention", not "intent", is used in other reports of this judgment.]

For the concept of possession, which is central to the oper- **1–16–05** ation of the Firearms Acts, to make sense, it has to mean more than a physical propinquity: it is more akin to the way in which possession is treated under the Misuse of Drugs Act 1971 than, say, the Prevention of Crime Act 1953. The sort of immediate physical possession, readily within reach, which characterises offences against the Prevention of Crime Act does arise in the Firearms Acts, but not in section 16 above: it was the failure to grasp this essential which led to the decision in *Georgiades*, described above.

1–16–06   Self defence could be a valid defence to certain of the charges specified in section 18 of and Schedules 1 and 2 to the Act, but this is because the section, by use of the phrase "have with him", echoes precisely the form of physical propinquity necessary to commit, rather than to intend to commit, an offence. A special defence of self defence would surely only come into play when there had been an *actus* necessitating an aggressive response. Section 16 does not require that life be endangered by use of a firearm at all. It need only be established that possession was, at some point, with the intent to endanger life; use of a firearm would only be evidence of that intent. See *R. v. East* [1990] Crim.L.R. 413.

1–16–07   (b) Section 6(1)(*b*) of the Criminal Damage Act 1981 empowers a justice of the peace, on receipt of evidence on oath that any person has in his custody, under his control, or on his premises anything which there is reasonable cause to believe has been used, or is intended to be used, to destroy or damage property in a way likely to endanger the life of another, to grant warrant to a constable to search for and seize that thing. Section 6(1)(*a*) of the same Act grants similar powers in relation to the damage, or prospective damage to property where there is no danger to life. It will be appreciated that the distinction between these offences and that in section 16 of the Firearms Act above may well be a narrow one.

1–16–08   (c) It is ironic that the original reference in the Act to "serious injury to property" which has been deleted in relation to England and Wales by the 1981 Act above, is still in force in relation to Scotland. The phrase has no direct meaning in Scots criminal law, the common law crime of malicious mischief being the nearest equivalent. While repetition of the statutory terms of section 16 would constitute a relevant charge in Scottish criminal proceedings, it has to be said that the concept introduced by this phrase would be more likely to confuse than clarify.

In all likelihood a Scottish prosecutor would libel common law charges of malicious mischief, or culpable and reckless conduct, or assault (depending upon the precise facts of the case) if any active steps such as discharge of a firearm had occurred and damage or danger to life had resulted. Alternatively, breach of the peace might be libelled if the use of a firearm had only been threatened verbally, without the gun being presented, or if its use had only caused alarm.

The suspicion that section 16 was drafted with little regard to its application beyond England and Wales is hard to resist. (The provisions of the Criminal Damage Act mentioned above do not apply to Scotland.)

Distinctively Scottish problems surfaced in *Urquhart v. H.M.* **1–16–09** *Advocate,* 1987 S.C.C.R. 31. U was charged with assaulting a woman by threatening her with a loaded shot gun and with contravening section 16 above. Two witnesses gave evidence of the accused's use of the gun to threaten the complainer but did not concur on the exact locus of the incident and it appears that this may have caused the jury to return a not proven verdict on the assault charge. There was no dispute that U had possessed the weapon for some while and had it with him in the complainer's house on the occasion libelled. It was argued on U's behalf before the Court of Appeal that there was insufficient evidence upon which the jury could infer U's intent to endanger life. The Lord Justice-Clerk at 35 stated:

> "We are not satisfied that a finding of guilty in respect of [a charge of contravening section 16 of the Act] is in any way inconsistent with the jury finding the first charge not proven, because the evidence of the witnesses who spoke to the events which are the subject of the first charge was available to the jury to be considered along with the other evidence in the case from the point of view of determining whether the necessary inference of intention could be drawn."

Possession of firearm with intent to cause fear of violence

[**16A.**—It is an offence for a person to have in his possession **1–16–10** any firearm or imitation firearm with intent —

(*a*) by means thereof to cause, or

(*b*) to enable another person by means thereof to cause,

any person to believe that unlawful violence will be used against him or another person.]

NOTE

(1) Inserted by the Firearms (Amendment) Act 1994, s.1(1).

OBSERVATIONS

Like section 16 above, this new provision is a preventative measure. Once the fact of possession of a firearm is evident, the nature of the intent behind that possession will have to be established. The nature of this section suggests that such possession will occur from the inception of a scheme directed against another person to the point when an attempt at that crime is launched. Problems of proof, particularly in instances when the possession of the firearm is certificated for lawful purposes, may well be considerable: the most likely source of evidence will be the accused's own utterances to others, including any admissions on arrest.

It is suggested that another person's belief as to the reasons behind the accused being in possession of a firearm will not itself suffice to bring liability home to an accused; there has to be some evidence of the accused's intent such as to render that belief credible. Following *R. v. Morris; R. v. King* ([1984] Crim.L.R. 422, discussed more fully at 4–05–18) the witness's impression at the time of the incident as to the nature of the imitation firearm, rather than its appearance when seen in the forensic calm of a court later, is the evidence which jurors should be directed to consider. If the jury is satisfied that the witness's impressions were reasonable at the time in regarding an article as an imitation firearm, and that it otherwise fulfils the statutory definition in section 57(4) of the Act of an imitation firearm, then they have sufficient evidence to convict an accused.

Use of firearm to resist arrest

1–17–01 17.—(1) It is an offence for a person to make or attempt to make any use whatsoever of a firearm or imitation firearm with intent to resist or prevent the lawful arrest or detention of himself or another person.

1–17–02 (2) If a person, at the time of committing or being arrested for an offence specified in Schedule 1 to this Act, has in his possession a firearm or imitation firearm, he shall be guilty of an offence under this subsection unless he shows that he had it in his possession for a lawful object.

(3)[1]. . .

1–17–03 (4) For the purposes of this section, the definition of "firearm" in section 57(1) of this Act shall apply without paragraphs (*b*) and (*c*) of that subsection, and "imitation firearm" shall be construed accordingly.

(5) In the application of this section to Scotland, a reference **1–17–04** to Schedule 2 to this Act shall be substituted for the reference in subsection (2) to Schedule 1² . . .

NOTES

(1) Repealed by the Theft Act 1968, s.33(3) and, Sched. 2, Pt. III.
(2) Words deleted as in (1) above.

OBSERVATIONS

(a) Section 17(2) above was extended to include assaults upon a **1–17–05** prisoner custody officer acting in pursuance of prisoner escort arrangements, or performing custodial duties at a contracted-out prison which involved the use of a firearm by the Criminal Justice Act 1991, section 90(1) and (2).

(b) The terms of sections 17(2) and 18(1) relating to the **1–17–06** prevention of a lawful arrest, although similar superficially, contain several critically important differences. Although it is by no means obvious, the words "shall be construed accordingly" which appear in section 17(4) have the effect of confining the operation of section 17 to firearms and those imitation firearms capable of discharging a shot, bullet or other missile as stipulated in section 57(1) of the Act. A contravention of section 17 can occur even if the weapon in question is not loaded, and it will be noted that the phrase "make any use whatsoever", which appears in section 17(1), provides the broadest possible scope for interpretation.

It will be seen that the Firearms Act 1982, section 1(4)(*b*), defines readily convertible and converted imitation firearms by reference to section 57(1) of the 1968 Act, but since section 17(4) above does not refer to the 1982 Act at all, it has to be the case that the operation of section 17 is limited to firearms and converted imitations.

Section 17(2) and (5) strikes at possession of such firearms **1–17–07** both at the time of committing a Schedule offence and at the time of arrest for such an offence. Observation (a) to section 16 1–16–05, *supra*) noted that "Possession", as applied in the Firearms Acts, covers situations of knowledge and control of the relevant weapons and ammunition, but does not necessarily require immediate physical proximity to them. Accordingly, these subsections are contravened if it can be shown that at the time of committing a Schedule offence, an accused had control of a firearm even though the firearm was not used in connection with that offence.

1–17–08   In contrast section 18 goes a stage further and deals with situations where a firearm, or any sort of imitation firearm, is carried on the person, or within immediate reach, during the commission of an indictable crime, or in Scotland a Schedule 2 offence (attempted crimes excepted).

The distinction between possession and having a firearm with one was succinctly considered in *R. v. Kelt* [1977] 1 W.L.R. 1365; [1977] 3 All E.R. 1099. The phrase "have with him" recurs frequently in sections 16 to 24 of the 1968 Act and denotes an active form of possession. *Kelt* is an important judgment and accordingly is quoted at some length.

Kelt and another man took part in the robbery of a security guard. Kelt presented a sawn-off shot gun while his accomplice used a pair of bolt-cutters to cut the chain on the guard's wrist secured to a money bag. Kelt subsequently admitted his use of the gun and, at the time of his arrest, was in a house in which the police found what the accused himself described as a robber's kit — the gun, woollen hats, masks, a bottle of ammonia, bolt cutters and ammunition. Kelt claimed to be looking after the kit for a friend. He was charged with, and convicted of, robbery and contravention of section 18 of the Act, and received 10 years' imprisonment for robbery and two years concurrent for the firearms offence. (As Scarman L.J. was to note, the appeal against the section 18 conviction therefore had a "certain academic flavour".)

Delivering judgment, Scarman L.J. stated ([1977] 1 W.L.R. 1365 at 1366E):

> "The defendant appeals against his conviction under section 18 of the Firearms Act 1968 of the offence of having with him a firearm with intent to commit an indictable offence. He submits through [counsel] that that section is to be interpreted on the basis that 'having with him' means 'carrying': alternatively, in case that should be wrong, that 'having with him' is to be distinguished from 'possession' and that the learned judge in summing up the case to the jury failed to give an adequate or indeed any direction as to the distinction between possessing a firearm and having a firearm with him."

After a review of the evidence described above, the judgment continued (at 1367F):

"[Counsel for the defendant] submits that upon this evidence there was no 'carrying of the firearm' and that 'having a firearm with him', where those words are used in the section, means carrying. The submission was overruled and the matter was left to the jury. In the course of the summing up the trial judge, as it seems to this court, allowed the jury to think that there was no distinction between possession and 'having a firearm with him'.

[Counsel's] second submission was that if such were the direction which the judge gave to the jury, then that also was wrong in law. We look first at the submission that the offence created by section 18 is one of carrying with criminal intent.

Section 18 appears in that part of the 1968 Act concerned with the prevention of crime and the preservation of public safety. A number of sections in that part of the Act create a number of offences and in order to construe section 18 properly, it is necessary, in our judgment, to have in mind the scheme of those offence-creating sections. They are sections 16 to 24 inclusive. It will be observed in regard to these sections that the draftsman had in mind throughout that there was a clear distinction between possession and having a firearm with one."

His Lordship narrated the terms of these sections briefly, adding at 1368D:

"There is an indication that the sections which make it an offence to "have a firearm with him" in certain circumstances were intended to deal with carrying firearms. As [counsel for the defendant] submits, the indication comes from the marginal notes. Each section which creates an offence for a person to have a firearm with him has a marginal note which includes the word 'carrying'. Where this phrase is used in other criminal statutes, one finds also the same marginal note. For example, in the Prevention of Crime Act 1953, it is an offence for a person without lawful authority or reasonable excuse to have with him in a public place an offensive weapon and the marginal note reads 'Prohibition of the Carrying of Offensive Weapons.'

1–17–09   It used to be thought that one could have no regard to marginal notes in studying the meaning of an Act of Parliament. It is still law that one may not use a marginal note for the purpose of interpreting an Act, but the House of Lords made it clear in [*Director of Public Prosecutions v. Schildkamp* [1971] A.C. 1; [1970] 2 W.L.R. 279; [1969] 3 All E.R. 1640], that regard may be had to a marginal note, not to interpret the Act of Parliament, but as an indication of the mischief with which the Act is dealing. . . . There can be no doubt but that the main subject [of section 18] is that of carrying firearms with criminal intent, and the presence of a marginal note is a useful indication that this is the main subject. But that does not mean that the marginal note is of any value in determining the scope of the section, which is the problem with which the court at this moment is concerned."

At 1369C the judgment continued:

"[Counsel for the Crown] submitted that the section cannot be confined merely to carrying a firearm. He indicates that section 18 is very general in the way it is drafted. It is not limited for instance to having a firearm in a public place, and it is wide enough to cover any situation, whether it be on private premises or a public place, where a man may properly be said to have a firearm with him.

We think that [this submission] is sound, and that it must be a matter of fact and degree for a jury to determine whether, in all the circumstances, the accused person does have with him a firearm. This firearm was found in the kitchen of the house where the defendant was living. [He] was arrested in the kitchen and it was in the kitchen that this gun was found. Plainly therefore there was evidence here which, subject to a proper direction by the judge when summing up, could have formed the basis of a verdict of guilty of the offence charged.

But one thing is clear in our judgment: the legislature has drawn a distinction between a person who has a firearm with him and a person who is in possession of a firearm. Some of the offences created by the sections to which I have referred are offences of possession, others are offences of having with one a firearm. This cannot be merely a semantic distinction, it must be a distinction of substance. The legislature must have had in mind that, in regard to those offences where it is an offence for the person to have with him a firearm, there must be a very close physical link and a degree of immediate control over the weapon by the man alleged to have the firearm with him . . . . We have come to the conclusion that it is necessary when summing up a case in which an offence under section 18 is alleged, for the judge to make it clear to the jury that possession is not enough, that the law requires the evidence to go a stage further and to establish that the accused had it with him. Of course the classic case of having a gun with you is if you are carrying it. But, even if you are not carrying it, you may yet have it with you, if it is immediately available to you. But if all that can be shown is possession in the sense that it is in your house or in a shed or somewhere where you have ultimate control, that is not enough."

Having regard to the misdirection by the trial judge, the conviction under section 18 was quashed.

(c) In *R. v. Guy* (1991) 93 Cr.App.R. 108, the accused, who had **1–17–10** a firearm in his possession at the time of carrying out a robbery, was charged with contravening section 17(2) of the 1968 Act. On appeal it was objected that robbery was not an offence specified in Schedule 1 and conviction on that count should be quashed. The Court refused the appeal on the grounds that while robbery was admittedly not a Schedule 1 offence itself, anyone convicted of robbery must, of necessity, have committed the crime of theft which was specified in the Schedule.

(d) Inclusion of the word "lawful" in subsections (1) and (2) **1–17–11** introduces the possibility of a defence that the firearm was used for a lawful purpose including the prevention of an unlawful arrest.

(e) Paragraphs 4 and 6 of Schedule 6, Part II to the 1968 Act **1–17–12** provide that the penalties specified in the Act for contravening sections 17(1) and (2) shall be in addition to any penalty imposed for the original offence which gave rise to the arrest. It is submitted that as a matter of law this has to mean that the sentence imposed for breach of this section, where conviction for the original offence has also occurred, should be a consecutive one. Certainly the Scottish courts have until recently passed *cumulo* sentences with no apparent regard to the requirement to impose consecutive sentences for contraventions of section 17.

Perhaps this duty could have been more clearly stipulated; one has to look to a Schedule to the Act for a fundamental sentencing provision (which might have been better incorporated into the main text of the section) and the fine print of that Schedule has a considerable impact upon the section's provisions.

The few reported cases available indicate that the courts have had some difficulty in applying consecutive sentences when contraventions of section 17 have been established. Although it may be felt that the Schedule's provisions are missionary in their clarity, a number of factors can be seen to have vexed the courts.

First, the mandatory provisions of the Schedule are at odds with the well-understood principle in criminal sentencing that where charges have arisen out of the same incident, or formed part of one transaction (as they obviously do in the case of section 17(2) convictions) then concurrent sentences should follow. Secondly, it may be felt that conviction of an offence which involved the use, or potential use, of a firearm will itself attract such a condign sentence as to render any additional penalty nugatory. Furthermore, it has to be said that libelling a section 17(2) charge in addition to the Schedule 1 or 2 contravention might be construed by some as double jeopardy.

Yet there can be no doubt that Parliament expressly signalled that the use of a firearm in furtherance of a crime fell to be regarded as a serious aggravation and that sentences should reflect that view. Equally, it could be argued that a failure by the prosecutor to include a section 17(2) charge in the libel might be taken as a concession that no firearm was used in the commission of the crime.

In *R. v. Clarke and McGinn* [1981] Crim.L.R. 346, both accused pleaded guilty to a number of charges of armed robbery at building society offices, and had received consecutive sentences for the firearms offences libelled. Adopting the "one transaction" approach, the Court of Appeal held it to be bad practice both to libel the robbery counts and the firearms charges on one indictment and to impose consecutive sentences upon such a libel. Significantly, the court did not consider the sentencing guidelines laid down by Widgery L.C.J. in *R. v. Faulkner* [1972] 56 Cr.App.R. 394, a case which centered upon the imposition of a consecutive sentence for contravening section 18 of the Act in the course of a conspiracy. This case is discussed at 1–18–09, *infra*.

It will be remembered that the additional penalty provisions contained in Part II of Schedule 6 applied only to contraventions of section 17.

This judgment was approved and applied in *R. v. French* [1982] 75 Cr.App.R. 1, and Lane L.C.J. upheld the practice of libelling more than one count arising from the same factual circumstances. It is only fair to observe that the critical commentary annexed to the *Clarke and McGinn* judgment in the *Criminal Law Review* (cited above) correctly stated the law.

Reported Scottish judgments are rarer still on this point, but **1–17–13** in *Willetts and Davidson v. H.M. Advocate*, 1991 S.C.C.R. 976, sentences of 18 months' detention for assault and robbery and 6 months consecutive for contravening section 17 were upheld on appeal. The accused were 15 and 16 years old at the time of the offences, and social inquiry reports had recommended community service and probation. The court did not comment upon the consecutive element of the sentences.

The issue was expressly considered in *Chalmers v. H.M. Advocate*, 1994 S.C.C.R. 651, though this is not evident from the case report which concentrates upon matters of sufficiency. C had been convicted of armed robbery and of contravening section 17(2) and appealed against sentences of eight years' imprisonment for the robbery and two years' consecutive imprisonment for the statutory offence. Dealing with this aspect of the appeal the Lord Justice-General stated:

"So far as the appellant's sentence of two years [for] having the shotgun at the time of the robbery, that does not appear to us to be excessive either. It must be remembered that it is a very serious offence for a person to have a firearm in his possession at the time of committing a robbery. That has been recognised as such by Parliament, which has laid down that the punishment to which a person is liable for this offence is to be an additional punishment. The only point is whether the Court should make a discount for the fact that this [two year sentence], must be served consecutively. Now the fact that it has to be served consecutively is something which arises from the directions of Parliament, and we are not persuaded that a discount should be made from the sentence which would otherwise be appropriate, even although, as is inherent in the charge, the firearm was being used for the furtherance of the same assault and robbery for which the appellant was being sentenced on the other charge."

This approach was not followed by the Lord Justice-General in a subsequent appeal against sentence, *Dewar v. H.M. Advocate*, 1995 G.W.D. 12–686, a case mainly concerned with comparative sentences. (To date the case has only been digested; reference here is to the unpublished judgment.)

D had pled guilty to a charge of armed robbery and to related firearms offences, one of which was a section 17(2) charge. He had a prior analgous conviction which had attracted eight years' imprisonment. His co-accused went to trial on these charges and an earlier armed robbery; he had previously been convicted of assault and assault to severe injury some three years before and had served four years' imprisonment. When sentenced D received 15 years' imprisonment and S received 12 years. No consecutive sentences were imposed for contravening section 17(2), a point taken up by the Crown at the appeal, following the earlier *Chalmers* judgment.

The Lord Justice-General stated:

"In [*Chalmers*] the sheriff imposed consecutive sentences on this interpretation of paragraph 6, but this was not taken as a point of appeal in the appeal against sentence and was not fully argued. We wish to make it clear that nothing that was said in that case should be taken as indicating that the court has decided that the sentence imposed on a charge under [section 17(2)] requires to be consecutive to the sentence for the other offence. We are aware that practice has varied in this matter, and that it is not uncommon for the sentences to be ordered to be served concurrently as was done in this case. This approach may be justified on the view that the sentence on the other charge, especially if it is for a common law offence, also reflects the use of a firearm, and that what paragraph 6 requires is no more than that a separate sentence be imposed in regard to the offence under section 17(2). Whether that is something which the court is entitled to do will require to be determined at a later date after full argument in an appropriate case."

The appeal was refused.

Given the serious consequences which flow from a literal reading of paragraph 6 (the only tenable approach which can be adopted unless the paragraph is reduced to the level of tautology), the lack of a settled and coherent interpretation of its meaning is unedifying.

It should not be forgotten that the real impact of a consecutive sentence, which falls to be served at the conclusion of the sentence imposed for the original offence, is in its effect upon any period of remission of sentence: remission will only be calculated upon the later (consecutive) element of sentence and not upon the sentence imposed for the offence designated in Schedules 1 or 2 to the 1968 Act.

A failure of the High Court to impose such a consecutive **1–17–14** sentence can be found in *H.M. Advocate v. McVey* (January 19 1994, unreported) a case in which an appeal against conviction and sentence was marked after, and notwithstanding, the *Chalmers* judgment. Understandably, the appeal against sentence was later abandoned, but *McVey* remains an interesting example of the complexities inherent in the application of section 17(1) and (2).

McV had been convicted, after trial, of numerous contraventions of section 1 of the 1968 Act, attempted murder of a police officer, contravening section 17(1) by use of a firearm to resist arrest and contravening the Police (Scotland) Act 1967 section 41(1)(*a*) by struggling violently with all these officers.

The facts were that the accused left his home in a vehicle which was followed by a number of unmarked police vehicles through Glasgow. When the car stopped at traffic lights the police officers rapidly surrounded the car; the officers wore bright fluorescent armbands marked "Police" and identified themselves as police officers. The accused, sitting in the front passenger seat drew his pistol and fired one shot at the nearest officer, on his nearside, before the gun jammed. Although he persisted in pulling the trigger his efforts to discharge further shots at the same officer were unsuccessful and a struggle then ensued as the police on both sides of the car tried to wrest the pistol from him. Following conviction for the above offences, McV received two sentences of twelve years' imprisonment, one of five years' imprisonment and two periods of two years' imprisonment, all concurrent; no additional sentence was imposed for the section 17 contravention described.

The grounds of appeal argued that the same set of facts were used to support the convictions of attempted murder and contravening section 17(1) in what was clearly one incident and, in any event, only one bullet had been discharged.

Leaving aside the evidence that McV had fired directly at one officer and repeatedly tried, without success, to fire his (by now) jammed pistol at the same officer and others when being arrested, the question remains whether this is a case of "double jeopardy" and, if so, whether that is fatal to the conviction.

It is difficult to see what meaning section 17 of the Act has unless the same *species facti* can be adduced for the original offence and that statutory contravention. In this case McV had used his pistol in an attempt to murder the officer, whereby he had contravened section 17(2) of the Act, since attempted murder, as an aggravated form of assault, falls within Schedule 2; he had, by the same token, used the weapon to resist lawful arrest, an action which offended against section 17(1) of the 1968 Act and against section 41(1)(*a*) of the Police (Scotland) Act 1967. Nonetheless it must be emphasised that no charge was preferred of contravening section 17(2) in relation to either of the Schedule 2 offences of attempted murder or contravening the Police (Scotland) Act, though such a charge attracts an even more severe maximum penalty than would a conviction under section 17(1).

It might be argued that if there was "double jeopardy" in McV's case it arose in relation to the simultaneous libelling of a charge of resisting arrest contrary to the Firearms Act and the Police (Scotland) Act.

The fundamental point remains; having been convicted of the section 17(1) offence, McV, in resisting arrest for "any other offence committed by him" (to quote the terms of paragraph 4 of Part II of Schedule 6 to the Act), should have received an additional (consecutive) not a concurrent sentence.

1–17–15   It has to be conceded, however, that the provisions of section 17 and Part II of the Schedule above are anything but clear, particularly since both subsections (1) and (2) can be deployed in circumstances involving the use of a firearm to resist arrest.

Possibly the only task more formidable than that facing the draftsman of such charges in an indictment is that confronting a trial judge required to direct a jury as to the meaning of section 17 and to explain the array of alternative verdicts falling to be considered in consequence of paragraphs 4 and 5 of the Schedule mentioned above.

Even when these alternatives are perceived, some caution is needed before applying them. Although section 17(1) includes a reference to the use or attempted use of a firearm to prevent the arrest of an accused or some other person, paragraph 4 specifies an additional penalty only for resisting the arrest or detention of himself for another offence committed by the accused.

Paragraph 5 of Part II of Schedule 6 allows that even if acquitted of contravening section 17(1), a jury may still convict an accused of the crime of possession of a firearm or imitation firearm or when arrested for such a crime: so while section 17(1) militates against the use of a firearm (or imitation firearm) in defiance of any lawful arrest (and paragraph 4 restricts the operation of additional penalties yet further as was discussed above), section 17(2) can only be applied when the offence committed and leading to the accused's arrest is one specified in Schedule 1 (in England and Wales) or Schedule 2 (in Scotland) of the Act.

Although there is room for debate about the precise application of section 17, it is manifest that its provisions deserve clearer expression.

Carrying firearm with criminal intent

18.—(1) It is an offence for a person to have with him a **1–18–01** firearm or imitation firearm with intent to commit an indictable offence, or to resist arrest or prevent the arrest of another, in either case while he has the firearm or imitation firearm with him.

(2) In proceedings for an offence under this section proof that **1–18–02** the accused had a firearm or imitation firearm with him and intended to commit an offence, or to resist or prevent arrest, is evidence that he intended to have it with him while doing so.

(3) In the application of this section to Scotland, for the **1–18–03** reference to an indictable offence there shall be substituted a reference to any offence specified in paragraphs 1 to 18 of Schedule 2 to this Act.

OBSERVATIONS

(a) The section strikes at the use, or the carrying, or the **1–18–04** immediate ability to use, a firearm or imitation firearm in pursuance of a crime. (The weapon need not be loaded, a matter which, in any event, it may not always be possible to prove.)

Difficulty can arise over the effect of "intent" where it appears in subsection (1); intent might normally be regarded as a current indication of a future course of action. However, study of Schedule 2, which applies only to Scotland, shows that attempts at crimes in Scotland are specifically excluded; one can sense why counsel in *Kelt, supra* turned to the Act's marginal notes as an aid to construction.

1–18–05 In fact it is the words "have with him", as distinct from the more usual phrase "possession" employed in the Act, which signal that this is to be regarded as a crime achieved by the active use, or intention to resort to the use, of a firearm in pursuance of a criminal objective. "Have with him" typically applies to the carrying of a firearm in the course of a crime, but is by no means confined to such circumstances. In *R. v. Pawlicki; R. v. Swindell* [1992] 1 W.L.R. 827; [1992] 3 All E.R. 902, the decision in *Kelt* was followed and refined. P drove a car containing three sawn-off shot guns to an auctioneer's premises in Bradford. P parked the car, entered the premises and stood near S, presumably unaware that the police had advance intelligence of a planned robbery and were waiting inside. Both men were arrested and the car was searched as a result of which three guns, two sets of handcuffs, a roll of masking tape and a set of keys were recovered. At trial P's explanation of these items was as memorable as it was improbable; the articles were a chance accumulation, the guns being for restoration, the tape to dress an injury to his dog and the handcuffs to enliven sexual intercourse with his wife.

A search of their houses showed that keys found in the car fitted locks in S's home, including the locks of a cupboard containing two shot guns, while ammunition suitable for one of these guns was found in P's home. A key in S's possession was discovered to fit the handcuffs mentioned earlier, but during police interviews S claimed not to recognise the various house keys and was generally evasive.

1–18–06 Convictions of contravening section 18 followed and both men appealed, claiming insufficient evidence of a joint criminal enterprise and arguing further that they had not had with them the three guns at the time of their arrest, these being in a locked car some 50 yards distant.

Delivering judgment, Steyn L.J. ([1992] 1 W.L.R. at 831D), **1–18–07**
having noted the value of the *Kelt* decision, stated:

"We do not, however, consider that the court in *R. v. Kelt*
intended to lay down that for the words 'to have with him a
firearm' should be read as 'to have immediately available a
firearm' .... One can be confident that Scarman L.J. in
[*Kelt*] did not have in mind such a substitution. Read in
context, and particularly in the light of the examples given,
the court was merely intending to highlight the element of
propinquity which is a necessary ingredient of section 18(1)
but not of offences of possession under the Act of 1968. ...

A literalist approach may have led to section 18 being
interpreted as applying only to the carrying of firearms. That
approach was rejected in [*Kelt*]. It seems to us implicit in that
decision that the words 'to have with him a firearm' must
derive their colour from the purpose of [the Act]. That
purpose, in broad terms, is to combat the use of the firearms
in and about the commission of crime and to protect public
safety. ... It is submitted that a distance of 50 yards between
the men and the guns placed the men beyond the ambit of
section 18(1). If that proposition is accepted, the Act of 1968
is less effective than one would have expected. It seems to us
that a court ought to try to make sense of the statute and its
purpose. If this purposive approach is adopted, it will still be
necessary to consider the element of propinquity. But the
emphasis must not be so much on exact distances between
the criminals and their guns but rather on the accessibility of
those guns, judged in a common sense way in the context of
criminals embarking on a joint enterprise to commit an
indictable offence.

In our judgment the separation in terms of space of [the
accused] from the guns, which they agreed to bring on the
planned robbery, does not mean that for the purpose of
section 18(1) they did not have the guns with them. It is
sufficient that the guns were readily accessible to them at a
time when they were about to commit the robbery."

The appeal was refused. Since Swindell did not give evidence
we can only guess at the explanation he would have offered to
explain his possession of the handcuffs' key.

(b) In *R. v. Houghton* [1982] Crim.L.R. 112 it was held that it **1–18–08**
was not necessary that the criminal intent be formed before a

firearm (or imitation firearm) was used. H hired a taxi and fell asleep during the journey. On being awoken by the driver at the destination (which unfortunately for H was near a police station) H drew an imitation firearm from a shoulder holster and said to the driver "Where do you want it?". On arrest, H claimed to have been too drunk to remember the event or to form the *mens rea* necessary to contravene the Theft Act 1968 or the Firearms Act, section 18(1). His appeal was refused and, from the brief report, it is clear that efforts to equate section 18 with case authorities under the Prevention of Crime Act 1953 were unsuccessful; section 18 covers both the carrying of firearms with intent and their actual use whereas the 1953 Act, as its title says, is a preventative measure only and is directed against possession, rather than the ultimate use of offensive weapons.

1–18–09 (c) The practice to be adopted by courts in England and Wales in sentencing contraventions of sections 17 and 18 is expressed in *R. v. Faulkner (John Alistair)* (1972) 56 Cr.App.R. 594. F had been convicted of conspiracy to commit theft, having articles for theft, police assault, use of a firearm to resist arrest and having no firearm certificate which attracted concurrent sentences totally three years; a sentence of three years' imprisonment for assault occasioning actual bodily harm and carrying a firearm with intent was to run concurrently with one other and consecutive to all other charges. F appealed against the imposition of a consecutive sentence. Before the single judge it was argued that the consecutive elements of sentence were inappropriate as all offences "formed part of one transaction". This argument was not entertained by Lord Widgery C.J. who held (at 596):

> ". . . as regards the sentences being consecutive, it should be recognised now that where an offender carries a firearm, with intent, when pursuing his criminal intention, he can expect and will receive a sentence of imprisonment consecutive to that which would otherwise be imposed upon him and this will be attributed to the use of the firearm. . . . Therefore in this case where the second sentence of three years was made consecutive and was one relating to the carrying of a firearm, this Court would wish to stress that that was a perfectly proper approach to the problem, and one which should be followed."

The sentence imposed earlier was not modified. However it **1–18–10** should be noted that in *R. v. McGrath (Sean)* (1986) 8 Cr.App.R.(S.) 372; [1987] Crim.L.R. 143 it was stressed that consecutive sentences arose because of the aggravated nature of such offences and were not statutorily required by Schedule 6, Part II in the case of contraventions of section 17(2). Parliament had required a separate additional penalty to be imposed for the firearms offence, and while a consecutive penalty would be the norm, regard should always be paid to the totality of the sentence imposed.

Carrying firearm in a public place

19.—A person commits an offence if, without lawful authority **1–19–01** or reasonable excuse (the proof whereof lies on him) he has with him in a public place a loaded shot gun or loaded air weapon, or any other firearm (whether loaded or not) together with ammunition suitable for use in that firearm.

OBSERVATIONS

(a) Following Note (a) to Section 18 above, the words "have **1–19–02** with him" denote that the offence here is that of carrying a loaded shot gun or air weapon, or any other firearm (loaded or not) in a public place. So in the case of a validly certificated firearm an offence would only arise if such a firearm together with its ammunition was being carried in public in circumstances not permitted by the certificate. See *Ross v. Collins* [1982] Crim.L.R. 368, where a ferry owner who had a valid shot gun certificate fired at ducks from his ferry on the Thames, an activity not explicitly permitted in his certificate.

The onus of proving lawful authority or reasonable excuse would only pass to the accused once the prosecution had made out the factors specified in the paragraph above.

(b) This section makes it patent that all air weapons are to be **1–19–03** regarded as firearms, a fact not immediately evident from the statutory definition of a "firearm" contained in section 57(1) of the 1968 Act. The point was raised in *Brannan v. Crowe,* 1992 S.C.C.R. 795, a prosecution under section 20 of that Act. The court emphasised that an air weapon is a firearm within the meaning of the Act even when exempted from its certification provisions.

(c) For the purposes of the Act, a statutory definition of a loaded shot gun or loaded air weapon is found in section 57(6)(*b*), *infra*.

1–19–04 (d) "Public place" is defined at section 57(4), *infra*, in familiar statutory terms; the same definition appears, for example, in the Prevention of Crime Act 1953, section 1. In this context see *Anderson v. Miller* (1977) 64 Cr.App.R. 178. The appellants, who were registered firearms dealers, kept a loaded revolver under their shop counter for protection and were held to have contravened the section. Although the area behind the shop counter was closed to the public and could not *ex facie* be regarded as a public place, the Queen's Bench Divisional Court held that the shop formed a single unit and, as the public had access within it, the shop was indeed a public place for the purpose of the Firearms Act.

This approach had been followed earlier that year in *Cawley v. Frost* [1976] 1 W.L.R. 1207, which dealt with offences under the Public Order Act 1936 following a pitch invasion during a match within a football ground.

1–19–05 The case of *McLeod v. McLeod*, 1982 S.C.C.R. 130, which centred upon the status of the foreshore in Scots common law, remains a curiosity.

McL was charged with contravening section 19 at a public place, "the shore front, Beach Park, Irvine, Cunninghame". Evidence established that he had fired a shot gun for recreational purposes at targets below the high tide mark at Irvine, a Clyde coast town. The Crown recognised that title to the foreshore was part of the regalia of the Crown (*i.e.* vested in the monarch) and that the locus was a public place within the meaning of the Act. It was argued that section 19 applied in these circumstances since the Act had not excluded such land from its provisions.

The sheriff accepted that the foreshore was a place to which the public in Scotland enjoyed access for recreational purposes (including shooting). However, she was satisfied, as a matter of statutory construction, that nothing in the Act expressly or impliedly bound the Crown by its terms: since the accused's use of the land was entirely innocent and did not, at the time, interfere with others' use thereof she acquitted the accused.

The unusual factual background in this case limits its application even in Scotland. The decision would not apply in English law given the much more restricted rights of public access to the foreshore.

(e) It should be stressed that possession of a firearm certificate **1–19–06** does not itself constitute lawful authority for the possession of a firearm in a public place. In *R. v. Jones (Terence Michael), The Times,* August 19, 1994, the appellant, who had held a firearm certificate, had been charged with contravening section 19. Apparently unknown to him, his certificate was no longer valid. Several issues as summarised in the Court of Appeal arose from these facts.

First, would a valid firearm certificate provide the necessary lawful authority for the carrying of a firearm in a public place? Secondly, if a valid certificate was such authority for carrying the firearm, could a mistaken belief on the appellant's part that his certificate was a valid one, then amount to a reasonable excuse?

Lastly, if no authority arose from possession of a certificate, could J, as the holder of an invalid certificate, found upon mistaken beliefs on his part (that he held a current certificate and was thereby entitled to carry firearms in public) as a reasonable excuse for breach of the statute?

Consideration of sections 1 and 2 of the 1968 Act indicated that possession of weapons which were subject to these sections could only begin to be lawful if the possessor held a relevant certificate; but that did not constitute authority for anything more than was specified in the certificate issued by the police. Their Lordships founded upon the decision in *Ross v. Collins* (cited above, at 1–19–02) and noted that neither section 1 nor section 2 made any reference to possession in a public place. Accordingly, the holder of a firearm or shot gun certificate would only have authority to carry such weapons in a public place when that was expressly stated in the body of his certificate.

That said, if the holder of a valid certificate under the Act purported to have had a mistaken belief of facts which if true would have constituted a lawful authority, then it would be a matter for a jury, suitably directed, to assess whether the accused had established that he had held such beliefs and then to consider whether they were satisfied that these beliefs constituted a reasonable excuse.

In J's case, since the certificate he had held was not valid and could not, even if valid, provide a basis for authority to carry a firearm in public, then a defence of reasonable excuse was not available to him.

Trespassing with firearm

1–20–01   **20.**—(1) A person commits an offence if, while he has a firearm [¹or imitation firearm] with him, he enters or is in any building or part of a building as a trespasser and without reasonable excuse (the proof whereof lies on him).

(2) A person commits an offence if, while he has a firearm [¹or imitation firearm] with him, he enters or is on any land as a trespasser and without reasonable excuse (the proof whereof lies on him).

(3) In subsection (2) of this section the expression "land" includes land covered with water.

NOTE

(1) Words inserted by the Firearms Act 1994, s.2(1).

OBSERVATIONS

1–20–02 A "trespasser" is not defined in the Act, so common law principles have to be applied. The clearest instance of trespass would occur where a person's presence on the land (or in the building) was wholly unauthorised. Inevitably more complex situations arise when an individual with a limited authority to be there, say to exercise a right of way, goes beyond the scope of his right while carrying a firearm.

Usually the carrying of a firearm would serve as an indication of the purpose of the trespass (commonly to poach), but even if the possession of the firearm was entirely incidental, section 20 would have been contravened.

1–20–03   In *Ferguson v. McPhail,* 1987 S.C.C.R. 52, F had the authority of a shooting syndicate to control vermin on their behalf on land leased from the Forestry Commission; it was implicit that this allowed him to shoot for that purpose. Neither he nor syndicate members were entitled to shoot deer, but F was found on the land carrying a loaded rifle equipped with a telescopic sight, binoculars and a gralloching knife (a tool specifically designed for disembowelling deer). The rifle was held to be of a calibre normally used for shooting deer.

At the appeal against conviction the Lord Justice-General stated (at 55):

"In our judgment it is as plain as plain can be that a person who has authority to enter land for one purpose becomes a trespasser if he enters the land for another purpose. And on this occasion the appellant, as the sheriff has found, entered the land for a totally different purpose well outwith the limits of his authority to do so, and to that extent [the appeal] fails."

Reviewing the equipment found in F's possession the Lord Justice-General added at 56:

"In these circumstances it is difficult to quarrel with the sheriff's inference that the purpose of the appellant's presence on the land was to be deduced from an examination of the equipment which he had with him at the time . . . to shoot deer with the loaded rifle he carried, and in these circumstances he was entitled, upon a proper construction of section 20(2), to hold that he was there as a trespasser with the rifle".

Note that here the court paid some heed to the way in which **1–20–04** the weapon was loaded as a means of assessing F's intentions. However, section 20, unlike section 19, does not require that the firearm be loaded; its mere possession during a trespass is enough to offend against section 20.

Possession of firearms by persons previously convicted of a crime

21.—(1) A person who has been sentenced [[1]to custody for **1–21–01** life or] to preventative detention, or to imprisonment or to corrective training for a term of three years or more [[1]or to youth custody [[2]or detention in a young offenders institution] for such a term], or who has been sentenced to be detained for such a term in a young offenders institution in Scotland, shall not at any time have a firearm or ammunition in his possession.

(2) A person who has been sentenced [3]. . . to imprisonment **1–21–02** for a term of three months or more but less than three years [[4]or to youth custody [[2]or detention in a young offender institution] for such a term], or who has been sentenced to be detained for such a term in a detention centre or in a young offender institution in Scotland [[5]or who has been subject to a secure training order], shall not at any time before the expiration of the period of five years from the date of his release have a firearm or ammunition in his possession.

1–21–03　[⁵(2A) For the purposes of subsection (2) above, "the date of his release" means —

　　(*a*) in the case of a person sentenced to imprisonment with an order under section 47(1) of the Criminal Law Act 1977 (prison sentence partly served and partly suspended), the date on which he completes service of so much of the sentence as was by that order required to be served in prison;

　　(*b*) in the case of a person who has been subject to a secure training order —

　　　(i) the date on which he is released from detention under the order;

　　　(ii) the date on which he is released from detention ordered under section 4 of the Criminal Justice and Public Order Act 1994; or

　　　(iii) the date halfway through the total period specified by the court in making the order,

whichever is the later.]

1–21–04　(3) A person who —

　　(*a*) is the holder of a licence issued under section 53 of the Children and Young Persons Act 1933 or section 57 of the Children and Young Persons (Scotland) Act 1937 (which sections provide for the detention of children and young persons convicted of serious crime, but enable them to be discharged on licence by the Secretary of State); or

　　(*b*) is subject to a recognizance to keep the peace or to be of good behaviour, a condition of which is that he shall not possess, use or carry a firearm, or is subject to a probation order containing a requirement that he shall not possess, use or carry a firearm; or

　　(*c*) has, in Scotland, been ordained to find caution a condition of which is that he shall not possess, use or carry a firearm;

shall not, at any time during which he holds the licence or is so subject or has been so ordained, have a firearm or ammunition in his possession.

1–21–05　[⁶(3A) Where by section 19 of the Firearms Act (Northern Ireland) 1969, or by any other enactment for the time being in Northern Ireland and corresponding to this section, a person is prohibited in Northern Ireland from having a firearm or ammunition in his possession, he shall also be so prohibited in Great Britain at any time when to have it in his possession in Northern Ireland would be a contravention of the said section 19 or corresponding enactment];

(4) It is an offence for a person to contravene any of the foregoing provisions of this section.

(5) It is an offence for a person to sell or transfer a firearm or ammunition to, or to repair, test or prove a firearm or ammunition for, a person whom he knows or has reasonable ground for believing to be prohibited by this section from having a firearm or ammunition in his possession.

(6) A person prohibited under subsection (1), (2) [[6](3) or (3A)] of this section from having in his possession a firearm or ammunition may apply to [[7] the Crown Court] or in Scotland, in accordance with Act of Sederunt to the Sheriff for a removal of the prohibition; and if the application is granted that prohibition shall not then apply to him.   **1–21–06**

(7) Schedule 3 to this Act shall have effect with respect to the courts with jurisdiction to entertain an application under this section and to the procedure appertaining thereto.

NOTES

(1) Inserted by the Criminal Justice Act 1982, s.77 and Sched. 14, para. 24(*a*).
(2) Inserted (England and Wales) by the Criminal Justice Act 1988, s.123(6) and Sched. 8, paras. 6 and 16.
(3) Words deleted by the Act last-mentioned, sections 123(6), 170(2) and Sched. 8, para. 16.
(4) Inserted by the 1982 Act above, s.77 and Sched. 14, para. 24(*b*).
(5) Inserted by the Criminal Justice and Public Order Act 1994 (c.33), Sched. 10, para. 24.
(6) Inserted by the Criminal Justice Act 1972 (c.71), s.29 and 67(*a*).
(7) Words substituted by the Courts Act 1971, s.56(2) and Sched. 9, Pt. II.

OBSERVATIONS

(a) The rigour of this section is not generally appreciated, least **1–21–07** of all by police officers, the persons mainly responsible for its enforcement. Those subject to its provisions by reason of having served a requisite term of imprisonment cannot possess any sort of firearm or ammunition. Accordingly, the section applies not only to certificated weapons and ammunition, and prohibited firearms and ammunition, but to shot gun ammunition (which does not require a firearms certificate and can be freely possessed) and to all air weapons and ammunition for same.

1–21–08   Given the preventive nature of this section it is surprising that
its terms do not extend to imitation firearms except, of course,
converted or readily convertible imitations which are subject to
the provisions of section 1 anyway. It also seems that possession
of de-activated weapons by those persons subject to section 21's
provisions would not be unlawful: the Firearms (Amendment)
Act 1988, section 8, enacts that such weapons shall cease to be
firearms, a concession, despite good intentions, which was ill-
advised.

1–21–09   Police powers to enforce the operation of section 21 are
defined in section 50 of the Act as arrest without warrant and a
power of entry, again without warrant, to any place for the
purpose of securing such an arrest.

1–21–10   (b) The prohibition against possession of firearms or ammunition by those sentenced to a term of imprisonment does not
extend to persons convicted of crimes and detained in psychi-
atric hospitals on account of mental disorder. Similarly, the
Mental Health Acts do not contain any limitation upon possession of firearms or ammunition by persons compulsorily
detained under these Acts.

1–21–11   (c) The effect of *cumulo* sentences, where an individual receives
a series of consecutive sentences totalling three years or more,
would be to bring him within the ambit of the prohibitions
contained in section 21. The section focuses upon the term of
imprisonment imposed, so it follows that implementation of a
suspended sentence would necessarily be included in the calculation. See *Davies v. Tomlinson* [1980] 71 Cr.App.R. 279.

Equally, however, the imposition of a suspended sentence
would not be sufficient to make section 21 operate: see *R. v.
Fordham* [1970] 1 Q.B. 77; [1969] 3 W.L.R. 317; [1969] 3 All
E.R. 532.

1–21–12   (d) Section 21(6) provides a mechanism, on application, for
dispensing with section 21's provisions. It is a concession likely
to be granted sparingly, and note that it only removes the
disqualification; it would still be necessary for a successful
petitioner to apply to the chief constable for the area in which
he lived for a firearm or shot gun certificate if he wanted to
possess such weapons.

(e) On release from such a term of imprisonment or detention a
person liable to the provisions of section 21 has this specifically
drawn to his attention by means of a notice which he is required

to sign and acknowledge. Little evidential use is made of this in proceedings.

Acquisition and possession of firearms by minors

22.—(1) It is an offence for a person under the age of seventeen **1–22–01** to purchase or hire any firearm or ammunition.

[[1](1A) Where a person under the age of eighteen is entitled, **1–22–02** as the holder of a certificate under this Act, to have a firearm in his possession, it is an offence for that person to use that firearm for a purpose not authorised by the European weapons directive.]

(2) It is an offence for a person under the age of fourteen to **1–22–03** have in his possession any firearm or ammunition to which section 1 of this Act applies, except in circumstances where under section 11(1), (3) or (4) of this Act [[2]or section 15 of the Firearms (Amendment) Act 1988] he is entitled to have possession of it without holding a firearm certificate.

(3) It is an offence for a person under the age of fifteen to **1–22–04** have with him an assembled shot gun except while under the supervision of a person of or over the age of twenty-one, or while the shot gun is so covered with a securely fastened gun cover that it cannot be fired.

(4) Subject to section 23 below, it is an offence for a person **1–22–05** under the age of fourteen to have with him an air weapon or ammunition for an air weapon.

(5) Subject to section 23 below, it is an offence for a person **1–22–06** under the age of seventeen to have an air weapon with him in a public place, except an air gun or air rifle which is so covered with a securely fastened gun cover that it cannot be fired.

NOTES

(1) Inserted by S.I. 1992, No. 2823, reg. 4.
(2) Inserted by Firearms (Amendment) Act 1988, s.23(4).

OBSERVATIONS

(a) It will rapidly be apparent that sections 22 to 24 of the **1–22–07** principal Act contain a hotchpotch of provisions dealing with the possession by, or supply to, young people of firearms and ammunition. Seemingly arbitrary age restrictions abound.

So far as subsection (1) above is concerned, it will be noted that Schedule 6, Part II of the Act enacts provisions to deal with situations where offences listed in Schedule 1 to the Magistrates' Courts Act 1980 are libelled against a person aged 17 in conjunction with an offence against either section 17(1) or (2) of the Firearms Act 1968. While Schedule 1 offences committed by such a youth could only be tried summarily, when a section 17 firearms charge is added the Firearms Act provides that the court shall then proceed as if the listed offence is triable only on indictment. To complicate matters further, section 24 of the 1980 Act above stipulates that a person aged under 18 years must, unless charged with homicide or falling within the exceptions contained in section 24(1)(*a*) or (*b*) of that Act, be tried summarily. Accordingly, despite the provisions contained in Schedule 6, Part II to the Firearms Act 1968 (doubtless the fruits of considerable effort on the draftsman's part) the reality is that such a youth would almost inevitably be tried summarily for both offences.

Given the terms of both Schedule 6, Part II and section (1A) above, it is a pity that the provisions of section 68 of the Criminal Justice Act 1991, which amended the age of 17 years to 18 years in some statutes, did not extend to the Firearms Act.

1–22–08 (b) Subsection (1) does not prevent a person aged 17 or less from possessing a firearm. However, the cumulative effect of sections 22(1) and (2) and 24(2) means that no person under 14 years can possess a section 1 firearm or ammunition except in the controlled circumstances permitted in section 11(1), (3) and (4); no person less than 15 years old can have an assembled shot gun in public except when supervised by an adult or when it is secured against use; and no one under 17 years old can use an air weapon in public places.

1–22–09 It will also be noted that while section 22 imposes these absolute restrictions by reason of age upon the possession or use of firearms by young people, all those who are of age will still require to obtain a firearm or shot gun certificate from the chief constable for any weapon except a low-powered air pistol or rifle.

1–22–10 (c) From previous comments it will be seen that section 22 distinguishes several distinct relationships between the young person and different categories of firearm. Subsection (1) has already been discussed: subsection (2) ranges wider by barring possession of section 1 firearms or ammunition, while subsections (3) to (5) employ the phrase (already discussed in the context of *R. v. Kelt* at 1–17–08) "have with him". While this phrase does not automatically preclude possession of a firearm, that, to all intents, is the practical effect.

(d) Section 51(4) of the Act provides that any summary **1–22–11** prosecution can be initiated within four years from the date of commission of the offence. In England and Wales any such prosecution more than six months after the incident must proceed on the express authority of the Director of Public Prosecutions.

The only offences which are subject to the ordinary six month **1–22–12** time-bar provisions contained in section 127(1) of the Magistrates' Courts Act 1980 (in England and Wales) and section 331 of the Criminal Procedure (Scotland) Act 1975 are those which relate specifically to air weapons and contraventions of section 22(3) of the Firearms Act. Hence where the Act refers to "firearms" (a phrase which includes air weapons) any offence proceeded with summarily will be subject to the four-year period; only when a direct reference is made to an air weapon and the offence is prosecuted summarily will the six-month limitation apply.

(e) Subsection (1A) was introduced by the 1992 Regulations **1–22–13** cited above, to give effect to the EC Directive on the Control of the Acquisition and Possession of Firearms. The authorised purposes are: use as a slaughtering instrument; sporting purposes; shooting vermin or, in the case of estate management, other wildlife; competition purposes and any target shooting not already authorised by reason of being conducted for competition purposes.

Exceptions from s.22(4) and 5

23.—(1) It is not an offence under section 22(4) of this Act for a **1–23–01** person to have with him an air weapon or ammunition while he is under the supervision of a person of or over the age of twenty-one, but where a person has with him an air weapon on any premises in circumstances where he would be prohibited from having it with him but for this subsection, it is an offence —

(*a*) for him to use it for firing any missile beyond those premises; or

(*b*) for the person under whose supervision he is to allow him so to use it.

1–23–02 (2) It is not an offence under section 22(4) or (5) of this Act for a person to have with him an air weapon or ammunition at a time when —

> (*a*) being a member of a rifle club or miniature rifle club for the time being approved by the Secretary of State for the purposes of this section or [¹section 15 of the Firearms (Amendment) Act 1988] he is engaged as such a member in or in connection with target practice; or
>
> (*b*) he is using the weapon or ammunition at a shooting gallery where the only firearms used are either air weapons or miniature rifles not exceeding .23 inch calibre.

NOTE

(1) Substituted by the Firearms (Amendment) Act 1988, s.23(4).

OBSERVATIONS

1–23–03 (a) Section 23(2) extends the exemptions applied to certificated firearms and ammunition, when used for sports, athletics and other approved purposes, in section 11(3) and (4) to air weapons and ammunition. In these controlled circumstances a person under 14 years old could have an air weapon and ammunition with him while supervised by an adult of 21 years or more.

Section 22(5) bans the carrying of air weapons (whether loaded or not) in public by those aged under 17 years unless such weapons are properly secured. By contrast, as section 19 provides, those over 17 years old are only precluded from carrying loaded air weapons in public.

The concession enacted in section 23(2), it is submitted, permits those members of rifle, or miniature rifle, clubs under 17 years old to carry properly secured air weapons and suitable ammunition in public while operating as a club member or in connection with target shooting.

1–23–04 (b) Section 23(1) envisages two situations; first a person less than 14 years under adult supervision having with him an air weapon or its ammunition; secondly the misuse of such an air weapon by firing it beyond "the premises".

Interpretation of this subsection has to be undertaken with a measure of caution, given the dearth of authorities.

It is argued that the supervisor referred to in section 23(1) not only must be over 21 years of age, but has to be an individual whose previous convictions do not make him liable to the provisions of section 21. This reading rests on the proposition that while the young person will have the weapon or ammunition with him, the supervisory role of the adult means that the adult would, *de facto*, be in possession thereof: section 21 precludes possession of any firearm or ammunition.

While it is patent that subsection (1)(*b*) can render a supervising adult liable in the event that the weapon is fired beyond the premises by the youth, it is by no means clear whether the adult's guilt arises both in cases of commission and omission. It is submitted that we have to adopt the purposive approach of Steyn L.J. in *R. v. Pawlicki; R. v. Swindell* (cited at 1–18–05 *supra*) and "try to make sense of the statute and its purpose", and that forces the conclusion that acts of dereliction of supervision and acts of incitement would be equally odious.

Finally, it will be noted that section 23(1)(*a*) defines an offence of firing "beyond the premises". The statutory definition of premises, in section 57(4) of the Act, includes land. If, while meant to be supervised on private property, the youth fired his air weapon beyond the confines of the property, an offence would be committed.

Supplying firearms to minors

24.—(1) It is an offence to sell or let on hire any firearm or **1–24–01** ammunition to a person under the age of seventeen.

(2) It is an offence —

    (*a*) to make a gift or lend any firearm or ammunition to which section 1 of this Act applies to a person under the age of fourteen; or

    (*b*) to part with the possession of any such firearm or ammunition to a person under that age, except in circumstances where that person is entitled under section 11(1), (3) or (4) of this Act [¹or section 15 of the Firearms (Amendment) Act 1988] to have possession thereof without holding a firearm certificate.

(3) It is an offence to make a gift of a shot gun or ammunition for a shot gun to a person under the age of fifteen.

(4) It is an offence —

    (*a*) to make a gift of an air weapon or ammunition for an air weapon to a person under the age of fourteen; or (*b*) to part with the possession of an air weapon or ammunition for an air weapon to a person under that age except where by virtue of section 23 of this Act the person is not prohibited from having it with him.

(5) In proceedings for an offence under any provision of this section it is a defence to prove that the person charged with the offence believed the other person to be of or over the age mentioned in that provision and had reasonable ground for the belief.

NOTE

(1) Inserted by the 1988 Act, s.23(4).

Supplying firearm to person drunk or insane

1–25–01   **25.**—It is an offence for a person to sell or transfer any firearm or ammunition to, or to repair, prove or test any firearm or ammunition for, another person whom he knows or has reasonable cause for believing to be drunk or of unsound mind.

OBSERVATION

Possession of a firearm in a public place while drunk (Scotland) is an offence under the Civic Government (Scotland) Act 1982, s.50(5). Note that the definition of "firearm" in that statute is extended to include crossbows.

PART II

FIREARM AND SHOT GUN CERTIFICATES; REGISTRATION OF FIRE-
ARMS DEALERS

*Grant, renewal, variation and revocation of firearm and shot gun
certificates*

Application for, and grant of, certificates

26.—(1) An application for the grant of a firearm or shot gun 2–01–01
certificate shall be made in the prescribed form to the chief
officer of police for the area in which the applicant resides and
shall state such particulars as may be required by the form.

(2) Rules made by the Secretary of State under section 53 of
this Act may—

    (*a*) require any application for a certificate to be accom-
        panied by [¹ up to four photographs] of the applicant;

    (*b*) require the verification in the prescribed manner of any
        prescribed particulars and of the likeness of any such
        photograph to the applicant.

  [²(*c*) require any application for a certificate to be accom-
        panied by a statement by the person verifying the matters
        mentioned in paragraph (*b*) above to the effect that he
        knows of no reason why the applicant should not be
        permitted to possess a firearm.]

(3) Subject to the special provision made for shot gun
certificates by section 28(3) below, a certificate shall, unless
previously revoked or cancelled, continue in force for three
years [³   ] from the date when it was granted or last renewed,
but shall be renewable for a further period of three years,
[³   ] by the chief officer of police for the area in which the
holder resides, and so on from time to time; and the foregoing
provisions of this section apply to the renewal of a certificate as
they apply to a grant:

    Provided that, subject to the power of renewal conferred by
this subsection, a certificate granted or last renewed in
Northern Ireland shall not continue in force for a period
longer than that for which it was so granted or last renewed.

    [⁴(3A) The Secretary of State may by order provide that
subsection (3) above shall have effect as if the references to

three years were references to such period as is specified by the order.

(3B) An order made under subsection (3A) above shall apply only to certificates granted or renewed after the date on which the order comes into force.

(3C) The power to make orders under subsection (3A) above shall be exercisable by statutory instrument and any statutory instrument containing such an order shall be subject to annulment in pursuance of a resolution of either House of Parliament.]

2–01–02 (4) A person aggrieved by the refusal of a chief officer of police to grant or to renew a certificate under this Act may in accordance with section 44 of this Act appeal against the refusal.

(5) It is an offence for a person to make any statement which he knows to be false for the purpose of procuring, whether for himself or any other person, the grant or renewal of a certificate under this Act.

NOTES

(1) Words inserted by the Firearms (Amendment) Act 1988, s.9.
(2) Words inserted by the 1988 Act, s. 10.
(3) Deletion effected by the Firearms (Amendment) Act 1992, s. 1(1)(*a*).
(4) Subsections inserted by the 1992 Act, s. 1(1)(*b*).

OBSERVATIONS

2–01–03 (a) A public consultation paper was published in 1992 seeking views on the establishment of a central national firearms licensing board. It was felt that such a body would bring greater consistency to decisions about the grant or renewal of certificates; however, operating costs were estimated to be "substantially more" than cost estimates for the current system administered by police forces, whose role in enforcing the Act would necessarily remain. (*Hansard*, Parliamentary Written Answer 44, July 21, 1994).

(b) It is noted that the Secretary of State proposes, using the powers in section 26(3A), to increase the currency of firearm and shot gun certificates from three to five years. The relevant orders took effect on January 1, 1995.

Orders raising the fees for the grant of firearm certificates and the grant, or renewal, of shot gun certificates were laid before Parliament in Autumn 1994. The prime effect will be to raise the costs of shot gun certificates substantially, albeit, certificates would last five, instead of the current three, years. Fees for game licences will not be charged in future. The justification for these rises is stated to be the increased level of costs necessitated by the more rigorous checks introduced by the 1988 Act, particularly in the case of applications for shot gun certificates. (*Hansard*, Parliamentary Written Answer 45, July 21, 1994.)

(c) The strictness of the residency qualification is illustrated by **2–01–04** *Burditt v. Joslin* [1981] 3 All E.R. 203, an appeal to the Divisional Court from an earlier decision of the Crown Court which had upheld refusal, by the Chief Constable of Warwickshire, of an application by B for a firearm certificate. B was a serving officer in the British Army in Germany and owned a property in Rugby; the property was let by B to a tenant and it was agreed that B had no right of occupancy, and no other residence in the county. In every other respect B was undoubtedly a fit and proper person to hold a certificate, but the Chief Constable argued that he had no jurisdiction upon which he could grant B's application since B did not reside in Warwickshire.

Delivering judgment (at 204d), Donaldson L.J. stated:

"It is said by counsel for Colonel Burditt that [section 26] must receive a wide construction, that it has only an administrative purpose, namely to identify which chief constable shall deal with an application for a firearm certificate and that all the very necessary precautions and limitations on the right to bear arms are contained in s27, which provides for conditions to be inserted in firearms certificates and so on.

I think there is force in that submission, but I cannot get away from the fact that Parliament has decided that in general no one shall possess a firearm in this country unless they are authorised in accordance with the procedures laid down by Parliament. It follows that [B] and anybody else in his position has to bring himself within some authorisation procedure. Parliament could have said that anybody who has a residential base in this country, or anybody who owns property in this country, shall be entitled to apply to the chief officer of police where that property is situated. But what it has said is that the application must be to the chief officer of police for the area in which applicant [*sic*] resides, and it must follow from that that the only people who can apply are people who are actually residing in this country.

Again I would accept that people can have two residences. An obvious example is somebody who has a weekend cottage in the country and a mid-week flat in London. He resides in both of them.

But if Colonel Burditt is to succeed in this case the sections have to have a wider meaning than that. It is not even sufficient to say 'ordinarily resides' because at the time of the application he did not ordinarily reside in Rugby. What counsel suggested was that 'resides' in this context means... 'the place with which you have a residential connection at the present time or have had such a connection in the past coupled with an intention to reside at that place in the future'. . .

I am not averse to applying a broad construction in order to remedy any deficiencies in an Act of Parliament which would be apparent if one applied a narrow construction. But there are, I think, limits to the extent to which there can be judicial amendment of Acts of Parliament, and . . . it would go beyond the accepted limits to hold (and this decision as far as I am concerned is entirely confined to this) that somebody resides at an address for the purpose of s26 at a time at which that address is let to others and therefore he has no right to occupy it."

The appeal was dismissed; leave to appeal was granted.

2–01–05   It may also be noted that *Sullivan v. Earl of Caithness*, cited at 1–01–19, *supra*, touched upon the mixed issue of residence and possession of a firearm.

2–01–06   (d) The rules referred to in section 26(2) are to be found in the Firearms Rules 1989 (S.I. 1989 No. 854), the Firearms (Amendment) Rules 1992 (S.I. 1992 No. 2824), the Firearms (Scotland) Rules 1989 (S.I. 1989 No. 889) and the Firearms (Scotland) Amendment Rules 1992 (S.I. 1992 No. 2821). The earlier rules set out the forms to be used in applications for the grant, renewal or variation of certificates and the registration of firearms dealers; the later rules prescribe additional conditions to which certificates may be subject.

(e) Section 26(4) relates only to the refusal by the chief constable to grant an application for a firearm or shot gun certificate. The variation of a certificate's conditions by the chief constable is dealt with in section 29, while his power to revoke a certificate is contained in section 30: see *infra*.

Special provisions about firearm certificates

27.—(1) A firearm certificate shall be granted by the chief **2–02–01** officer of police if he is satisfied that the applicant has a good reason for having in his possession, or for purchasing or acquiring, the firearm or ammunition in respect of which the application is made, and can be permitted to have it in his possession without danger to the public safety or to the peace:

Provided that a firearm certificate shall not be granted to a person whom the chief officer of police has reason to believe to be prohibited by this Act from possessing a firearm to which section 1 of this Act applies, or to be of intemperate habits or unsound mind, or to be for any reason unfitted to be entrusted with such a firearm.

[¹(1A) For the purposes of subsection (1) above a person under the age of eighteen shall be capable of having a good reason for having a firearm or ammunition in his possession, or for purchasing or acquiring it, only if he has no intention of using the firearm or ammunition, at any time before he attains the age of eighteen, for a purpose not authorised by the European weapons directive.]

(2) A firearm certificate shall be in the prescribed form and shall specify the conditions (if any) subject to which it is held, the nature and number of the firearms to which it relates [²including if known their identification numbers] and, as respects ammunition, the quantities authorised to be purchased [²or acquired] and to be held at any one time thereunder.

(3) This section applies to the renewal of a firearm certificate as it applies to a grant.

NOTES

(1) Subsection (1A) inserted by S.I. 1992 No. 2823, reg. 4(2).
(2) Words inserted by the 1988 Act, s.23(5).

OBSERVATIONS

(a) In *R. v. Wilson* [1989] Crim.L.R. 146, the appellant, who was **2–02–01** a registered firearms dealer, transferred possession of firearms to three customers in part exchange, or on loan while their weapons were undergoing repairs. Each of the customers had lodged a similar firearm with W, who noted details of the transactions in his register and informed the police as required. However, his customers' certificates were not varied to permit possession of the replacement weapons.

W was charged with selling or transferring firearms to persons who had not (since they could not have) produced certificates authorising their purchase or acquisition of the particular weapons, a contravention of section 3(2) of the Act. He argued that each weapon exchanged or traded in was of a similar type and calibre to those detailed in his customers' certificates and that as the police had been notified, he had fulfilled the requirements of the Act.

His appeal against conviction was refused; the Act refers to specific, identifiable, firearms being detailed on applications and certificates. Even where a weapon identical to that already possessed is acquired, and the old weapon has been given up by the certificate holder, an application for variation of the certificate would have to be made first.

2–02–03 (b) Subsection (1A) employs the double negative to quite stunning effect: it might have been simpler to say that until the age of 18 years is attained a person can only be granted a firearm certificate to possess, purchase or acquire a firearm or ammunition to which this section applies if his use thereof (until that age is attained) is for a purpose authorised by the European weapons directive.

Those purposes are listed at 1-22-13, *supra*.

Special provisions about shot gun certificates

2–03–01   28.—[[1](1) Subject to subsection (1A) below, a shot gun certificate shall be granted, or as the case may be, renewed by the chief officer of police if he is satisfied that the applicant can be permitted to possess a shot gun without danger to the public safety or to the peace.

(1A) No such certificate shall be granted or renewed if the chief officer of police—

(*a*) has reason to believe that the applicant is prohibited by this Act from possessing a shot gun; or

(*b*) is satisfied that the applicant does not have a good reason for possessing, purchasing or acquiring one.

2–03–02   (1B) For the purposes of paragraph (*b*) of subsection (1A) above an applicant shall, in particular, be regarded as having a good reason if the gun is intended to be used for sporting or competition purposes or for shooting vermin; and an application shall not be refused by virtue of that paragraph merely because the applicant intends neither to use the gun himself nor to lend it for anyone else to use.]

[²(1C) A person under the age of eighteen shall be regarded **2–03–03** for the purposes of paragraph (*b*) of subsection (1A) above as not having a good reason for possessing, purchasing or acquiring a shot gun, if it is his intention to use the shot gun, at any time before he attains the age of eighteen, for a purpose not authorised by the European weapons directive.]

(2) A shot gun certificate shall be in the prescribed form and shall—

    (*a*) be granted or renewed subject to any prescribed conditions and no others; and

    (*b*) specify the conditions, if any, subject to which it is granted or renewed.

[³(2A) A shot gun certificate shall specify the description of the shot guns to which it relates including, if known, the identification numbers of the guns.]

(3) Notwithstanding section 26(3) of this Act, a shot gun certificate issued before the expiration of six months from the date of the commencement of this Act shall continue in force for such period from that date or from the date when it is granted, whichever is the later, as may be specified in the certificate by the chief officer of police (being a period of not less than one year but not more than five years).

NOTES

(1) Substituted by the 1988 Act, s.3(1).
(2) Inserted by S.I. 1992 No. 2823, reg. 4(3).
(3) Inserted by 1988 Act, s.3(2).

OBSERVATIONS

The 1988 Act introduced a much less permissive approach to **2–03–04** the grant of applications for shot gun certificates; until then the criteria governing the grant of firearm certificates and those affecting shot gun certificates were radically different. Now, despite the apparent concession made in section 28(1B), the plain fact is that obtaining a shot gun certificate is a more elaborate, and costly, procedure than before.

In the light of the decision in *R. v. Wilson* (discussed at 1–03– **2–03–05** 08, *supra*) it is worth noting that section 4 of the 1988 Act enacts formal requirements covering transfers of shot guns while section 5 has introduced measures to restrict sales of shot gun ammunition suitable for section 1 shot guns (see 1–01–13, *supra*) to persons who have lawful authority under the Act.

2–03–06 Unlike section 1 ammunition, which can only be possessed by those persons licensed to do so, shot gun ammunition can be freely possessed without holding a shot gun certificate. The only persons whose possession of section 2 (shot gun) ammunition is restricted are those who are subject to the provisions of sections 21 and 24 above by reason of previous convictions or age.

Variation of firearm certificates

2–04–01 **29.**—(1) The chief officer of police for the area in which the holder of a firearm certificate resides may at any time by notice in writing vary the conditions subject to which the certificate is held, except such of them as may be prescribed, and may by the notice require the holder to deliver up the certificate to him within twenty-one days from the date of the notice for the purpose of amending the conditions specified therein.

2–04–02 (2) A firearm certificate may also, on the application of the holder, be varied from time to time by the chief officer of police for the area in which the holder for the time being resides; and a person aggrieved by the refusal of a chief officer of police to vary a firearm certificate may in accordance with section 44 of this Act appeal against the refusal.

(3) It is an offence for a person to make any statement which he knows to be false for the purpose of procuring, whether for himself or another person, the variation of a firearm certificate.

OBSERVATIONS

2–04–03 (a) The possible penalty for failure to comply with a section 29(1) requirement is revocation of the certificate: see section 30(1)(*b*). However, the Act does not specify whether compliance with such a requirement would be fulfilled by delivery of the certificate to the address from which the requirement was issued or, for example, by delivery to a police office within the jurisdiction of the chief constable. The Firearms Rules and Firearms (Scotland) Rules specify the formats of application forms and certificates; in Note 10 to the firearm application form it is stipulated that applications should, unless otherwise advised by the police, be made to one's local police station. For the avoidance of doubt any notice should clearly stipulate the place to which the certificate has to be returned.

2–04–04 (b) Note that the Act does not provide an appeal procedure for those aggrieved by the terms of an amendment made by the chief constable to a firearm certificate: appeal is only available when the police have refused a holder's application for variation of a certificate.

(c) Subsection (3) applies most obviously to applicants for certificates and to those who provide references as a countersignatory on such an application.

Revocation of certificates

30.—(1) A firearm certificate may be revoked by the chief 2–05–01 officer of police for the area in which the holder resides if—

    (*a*) the chief officer is satisfied that the holder is prohibited by this Act from possessing a firearm to which section 1 of this Act applies or is of intemperate habits or unsound mind, or is otherwise unfitted to be entrusted with such a firearm; or

    (*b*) the holder fails to comply with a notice under section 29(1) of this Act requiring him to deliver up the certificate.

(2) A shot gun certificate may be revoked by the chief officer 2–05–02 of police if he is satisfied that the holder is prohibited by this Act from possessing a shot gun or cannot be permitted to possess a shot gun without danger to the public safety or to the peace.

(3) A person aggrieved by the revocation of a certificate 2–05–03 under subsection (1)(*a*) or (2) of this section may in accordance with section 44 of this Act appeal against the refusal.

(4) Where a certificate is revoked by the chief officer of police under this section, he shall by notice in writing require the holder to surrender the certificate; and it is an offence for the holder to fail to do so within twenty-one days from the date of the notice:

    Provided that, if an appeal is brought against the revocation, this section shall not apply to that revocation unless the appeal is abandoned or dismissed, and shall then apply with the substitution, for the reference to the date of the notice, of a reference to the date on which the appeal was abandoned or dismissed.

OBSERVATIONS

(a) This section now has to be read in conjunction with section 2–05–04 12 of the 1988 Act which has, understandably, imported a greater sense of urgency into the revocation of certificates and surrender of weapons. It will be seen that these more recent provisions apply only in cases arising from section 30(1)(*a*) or (2). The requirements of any notice should be clearly expressed to avoid any plea of misunderstanding being tendered by a certificate holder.

Whereas the powers contained in the principal Act were limited to requiring surrender of the certificate, section 12, more sensibly in the circumstances, provides for surrender of the certificate held along with any firearm or ammunition. It has been remarked previously that shot gun ammunition can normally be freely possessed, *i.e.* without the need for any sort of certificate; nevertheless it seems odd that no power has been given to the police to require the surrender of such ammunition when its possessor is regarded as a danger to public safety or to the peace.

2–05–05   Only cases of alleged breaches of section 29(1) remain subject to the unmodified provisions of section 30 of the principal Act.

2–05–06   The 1988 Act, section 12 enacts that pending a resolution of an appeal against revocation of a certificate on the grounds specified in section 30(1)(*a*) or (2), the weapons and relevant ammunition shall be retained by the police. Further provisions govern the disposal of weapons and ammunition following upon refusal of such an appeal.

2–05–07   (b) This section has generated a substantial volume of case authorities in both English and Scottish courts. However, only in very recent years can it be said that the courts in both jurisdictions have been of one accord in its interpretation.

Reported cases have focused on two main themes: first, the factors which the police may properly take into account when deciding whether to grant or revoke certificates or a dealer's registration; secondly, the precise role and powers of the courts when appeals under section 44 of the Act have to be judicially considered.

(I) THE ROLE OF THE POLICE

2–05–08   The parameters governing revocation or refusal of certificates are contained in section 30(1) and (2) and are necessarily specific to individual applicants—a recipe for wounded pride, and, at times, inadvisable litigation. It has been contended that the grounds for revocation of a certificate had to be based upon evidence, or reasonable anticipation, of violent behaviour on the part of the holder. While superficially this might seem to reflect the objectives of the statute, the courts have held that the police can consider applicants' suitability much more broadly.

In *Ackers v. Taylor* [1974] 1 W.L.R. 405; [1974] 1 All E.R. 771 **2–05–09** the court rejected submissions that a chief constable's consideration of applications must be restricted to finding evidence of a threat of violent use of a weapon.

A and three companions had been found in a vehicle with their shot guns, several dogs and a number of freshly-shot pheasants. None of the men had a licence to kill game and were prosecuted in the magistrates' court for contravening the Game Licences Act 1860. Following their conviction the chief constable invoked section 30(2) of the Firearms Act 1968, revoking all licences, a decision which they successfully appealed against at King's Lynn Crown Court. The police conceded that there was no evidence that the men were of a violent disposition: that court, in its judgment, equated the construction of section 30(2) "without danger... to the peace" with its own formula "without danger of violent crime or crime involving the risk of violence". On appeal by the chief constable the Queen's Bench Division negatived such a narrow construction.

Delivering his judgment, Ashworth J. ([1974] 1 W.L.R. 405 at **2–05–10** 410B) stated:

> "I am absolutely satisfied that the judge was wrong in taking the narrow view which he expressed in his judgment, namely, that some notion of violence or prospective violence must be established before a chief officer of police can revoke a certificate. In other words 'danger... to the peace' in section 30(2) does not involve the concept of violence being used with the gun by the holder of the certificate."

Noting that it was only this narrow construction of the Act **2–05–11** that had impelled the lower court to find against the police, his Lordship expounded the principles which the police should apply in considering refusal or revocation of applications.

At 410E he continued:

> "For my part I attach importance to the wording of section 30(2)... namely, 'cannot be permitted to possess a shot gun

without danger... to the peace'. It seems to me that those
words make it quite plain that the possession of the shot gun
and matters affecting it are not only material but essential for
consideration when the matter of revocation comes up to be
decided. It must be danger to the peace arising out of the
possession, or use, or misuse of the shot gun which the chief
officer of police must consider. It is the nature of the danger
to the peace which is contemplated.

Secondly I would say... that it would be wrong to limit
section 30(2), as the judge limited it, to the possibility of the
misuse of the shot gun in circumstances of violence. Thirdly, I
believe, for my part, that the best approach to the understanding of this subsection is to regard it as forming part of
the equipment given to police officers for the preservation of
good order in public. [In *R. v. Queen's County Justices* (1882)
10 L.R. Ir. 294 at 301] what the judge referred to was 'a
branch of preventative justice, in the exercise of which
magistrates are invested with large judicial discretionary
powers for the maintenance of order and the preservation of
the public peace.' Translating that and altering those words as
appropriate to a chief officer when considering revocation of
a certificate, I think that they may afford him valuable
assistance.

2–05–12   Therefore he should consider, when he is deciding whether a
certificate should be revoked on the ground of danger to the
public peace, whether there is danger that the gun may be
misused in such a way that good order is disturbed or that
there is a risk of that happening. But I would go further in
endeavouring to assist. To my mind poaching such as was
taking place on the occasion when these men were caught is in
every sense of the word a disturbance of the public peace. It
might indeed be said to be a possible source of violence, but I
would put it on a much broader ground, that the carrying of a
gun on a poaching expedition does involve a breach of good
order and a danger to the peace in that sense of the word,
and. . . I would suggest that chief officers of police should have
in mind that this preventive remedy entrusted to them is
intended to be used partly to prevent danger to the public
safety and partly to prevent danger to the public peace which
may perhaps be expressed as involving disturbance to good
order. . . I would for my part be prepared to entrust a very

wide discretion, so long as the discretion is exercised in connection with the use or possession of a gun."

The obligation stated above, in relation to section 30(2) cases, **2–05–13** to consider only conduct arising from the misuse of a shot gun has itself been criticised as too narrow. In *Chief Constable of Essex v. Germain* [1991] C.O.D. 385, it was stipulated that the general conduct of the holder might be such as to give grounds for belief that when carrying the gun with him, or simply having it in his possession, he might constitute a danger to the public or to the peace. In Germain's case the chief constable had regarded drink-driving convictions as disclosing an irresponsible and uncontrolled character unfitted to possess a shot gun certificate.

The same stance has been adopted in several Scottish cases, **2–05–14** some of which are of note on the question of the scope of the courts' powers to review police decisions under section 30 and will be mentioned again later. In *Luke v. Little*, 1980 S.L.T. (Sh. Ct.) 138 Luke, a shot gun certificate holder, had been convicted of drink-driving for the third time and this impelled the chief constable to revoke his shot gun licence, repeating the terms of section 30(2), and allowing 14 days for any representations to be made.

The police treated Luke's drink-related convictions as evidence of his disregard for the public safety and as an indication that, as a personality, he could no longer be entrusted with a shot gun. Luke appealed and argued that there was no equation between his conduct with a gun and his disregard for the Road Traffic Act.

The sheriff was asked to hold that the chief constable had exercised his discretion unreasonably, a view which the sheriff manifestly rejected, noting that "preventive justice" required the police to gauge the likelihood of future misconduct by Luke with a gun. He added (at 139):

"This estimation will, in all probability, not be linked to his **2–05–15** behaviour with a gun but to his behaviour elsewhere, and the [police] equation of irresponsibility with a car with irresponsibility with a gun seems quite sound. It also follows from this approach that a licence-holder's behaviour should be monitored to see if the original estimate of his likely behaviour should be monitored in the light of the latest information available."

However, in *Spencer Stewart v. Chief Constable of Kent* (1989) 89 Cr.App.R. 307S, the holder of a shot gun certificate which had been granted despite previous convictions some years before for assault, was convicted during the currency of his certificate of handling stolen goods; this last conviction caused the police to revoke his certificate. S, who was also a prominent clay pigeon shooter, successfully appealed against this. The judge noted the previous convictions of the accused who, she observed, "has a very easily roused temper when he thinks that he is in the right". However while noting the Ackers decision she added (at 310):

> "Now, the only difference between 1985, when the licence was granted and today is the handling charge, and whilst I am satisfied that the defendant may still be associating with criminals, I cannot see that there is any indication from that of the risk to the peace—and of course committing criminal offences is a risk to the peace but I cannot see that it arises out of his possession or misuse of the shot gun."

The appeal was allowed reluctantly, and the Chief Constable appealed to the Divisional Court where *Luke v. Little* (cited above) was considered.

Bingham L.J. at 313 noted:

> "If therefore an applicant or holder of a licence is given to the commission of offences which, however serious, do not involve the slightest risk or likelihood of use of a shot gun, then that, in my judgment, as in that of the learned judge, is not a ground for refusing or revoking a licence... What [*Luke v. Little*] does not, in my view, support at all is the suggestion that any form of criminal behaviour, irrespective of whether it is likely to lead to the commission of any crime involving the use of a shotgun is sufficient ground for revocation of a licence."

His Lordship noted that there had been no suggestion that the judge had ignored or overlooked any evidence and no attack on her conclusions as to fact; one is left to ponder the outcome had the judge decided that S's easily roused temper (mentioned in her report) taken with the other facts in the case was reason enough to refuse him a certificate.

In *Howson v. Chief Constable, Fife Police*, 1994 G.W.D. 3-154 **2–05–16** it was held that once a sheriff has given due consideration to the grounds upon which a chief constable revoked a shot gun certificate and upheld that decision, it is not essential to express his views on the assertions of the holder or give reasons as to how they failed to meet the police case. The police had revoked H's shot gun certificate because of two proven instances in which he had brandished his gun aggressively and uttered threats against other people—grounds so clearly indicative of a danger to public safety as to defy contradiction.

The court has to issue a determination of the appeal and has **2–05–17** to apply it own discretion to the facts; so in *R. v. Acton Crown Court, ex p. Varney* [1984] Crim.L.R. 683 where the Crown Court upheld the decision of the police commissioner to revoke V's certificate, but there was no written judgment available explaining the grounds except a brief minute by the clerk concurring in that decision, the Queen's Bench Division quashed the decision.

It has been well established that courts in England and Wales **2–05–18** have the power to reconsider the evidence which gave rise to decisions by the police to revoke certificates; Scottish courts long held themselves able to intervene only where capricious or arbitrary conduct by the chief constable could be established.

Indeed, *in extremis* some Scottish courts went so far as to rule **2–05–19** that the Act vested an absolute discretion in the hands of the police and that the sheriff court had no role in ensuring that principles of natural justice were adhered to when the police considered refusal or revocation of certificates.

In considering the case for revocation or refusal of certificates under section 30, it is submitted that the police must be seen to proceed in accordance with those principles and that the court of first instances (the Crown Court or sheriff court) has a duty to ensure that this has been done, irrespective of the grounds of appeal to be argued before it.

True, the Act lays down no specific mechanism for intimating **2–05–20** to a holder that a section 30 revocation is under consideration, and in *Jarvis v. Chief Constable, Strathclyde Police*, 1976 S.L.T. (Sh. Ct.) 66, it was held that the Act placed no such obligation upon the police under section 30. The sheriff found support for this narrow construction from the fact that such express provisions did, by contrast, exist elsewhere in the Act—section 38(1) stipulates "reasonable notice" be given by police to firearms dealers who it is proposed to de-register. Ingenious as such a reading may be, it does not resolve the issue at all: section 38(1) requires notice to be given to a dealer before any action is taken to revoke his certificate but the section is as silent as section 30 as to what information (if any) is to be given to a person when his licence is revoked, or when an appeal is lodged against such a decision. The court in *Jarvis* was referred to an earlier case, *Cunning v. Chief Constable of Fife*, 1975 S.L.T. (Sh. Ct.) 18, in which it had been held that considerations of natural justice did arise as a result of which evidence was heard at a proof to scrutinise the chief constable's decision.

In *Cunning* the sheriff stated at 21:

2–05–21

"Where a public officer has power to deprive a person of his liberty or property, the general principle is that it is not to be done without his being given an opportunity of being heard and of making representations on his own behalf—per Lord Denning, M.R, in *Schmidt v. Secretary of State for Home Affairs* [1969] 2 Ch. 149, at p. 170. I see no valid distinction between a tangible right of property and the intangible right created by the certificates in the present case. Although the revocation may be regarded as an executive or administrative act, the decision to revoke must, in my opinion, be considered in a judicial spirit. This involves giving the appellant an opportunity to defend himself against the complaints upon which revocation is considered. . . .

In the present case I am satisfied that justice demanded that the appellant be informed of the reasons why his certificates might be revoked; and that he be given an opportunity to show cause why they should not be revoked. In view of the questions of character and credibility involved, an oral hearing would probably have been necessary in the present case."

2–05–22 The sheriff undertook such a hearing and recalled the earlier revocation. He properly declined to order the re-issue of the certificates since he was empowered only to hear appeals against the decision of the chief constable. It may be observed that the sheriff made scarcely a reference to the Firearms Act in his judgment, and significantly made no reference at all to the then leading Scottish authority of *Kaye v. Hunter*, 1958 S.C. 208, an appeal upon similar grounds under the Firearms Act 1937.

The grounds for revocation of a shot gun certificate are stated in section 28(1) and (1A) and are more limited than those in section 27(1) governing revocation of a firearm certificate: had, for example, the appellants in the *Germain* or *Luke* cases held firearm rather than shot gun certificates, they would certainly have fallen foul of the proviso in relation to "intemperate habits".

The Act, as Lord Widgery remarked in his dissenting judg- **2–05–23** ment in *Creaser v. Tunnicliffe* [1977] 1 W.L.R. 1493; [1978] 1 All E.R. 569 at 573c (a view later approved in *R. v. Hucklebridge* [1980] 1 W.L.R. 1284) draws a broad distinction between section 1 and section 2 weapons "because the element of risk, danger and lethal quality which a rifle has when compared to a shot gun is very different."

It is difficult, however, to justify a similar distinction when assessing the fitness (or otherwise) of persons to possess a firearm rather than a shot gun; sections 27 and 28 focus upon the qualities (or defects) of individuals and it is arguable that the tests to be applied by the police should be the same whether the application is for a shot gun or firearm certificate.

Jackson v. Chief Constable, Tayside Police, 1993 S.C.L.R. 160 **2–05–24** is possibly the most bizarre of these cases. J senior had had his firearm and shot gun certificates revoked as a result of recent previous convictions. An application was then made by his son, the appellant, for certificates for the same weapons at the same address. The chief constable plainly regarded this as a back-door method for J senior to resume use of the weapons despite the earlier revocations, and stated no objection to the applicant as such, except that J junior was likely to fall under the domineering influence of his father. In those circumstances J junior was held by the police to be unfitted to hold certificates.

The sheriff scrutinised this decision and came to the same **2–05–25** view, carefully adding at 162B that if the appellant "were to be living in his own house, away from his father, an application from him might meet with a different response." The terms of the judgment make clear that the sheriff heard evidence and made his own assessment of the application, an approach which the Scottish courts (with a few notable exceptions) had long held to be *ultra vires*.

It is noted that the Jackson decision pre-dated the addition to **2–05–26** the 1968 Act of section 28(1C) above. It is doubtful that Jackson junior was proposing to use the weapons for a purpose specified in the European weapons directive; that would now be a valid reason for refusal of certificates in the case of an applicant less than 18 years old.

(II) THE ROLE OF THE COURTS

2–05–27   It was observed above that English and Scottish courts had until recently diverged in interpreting the extent of their powers to review police decisions taken under section 30. Much energy was devoted in both jurisdictions to establishing whether appeals under the Act were to the court in its administrative or judicial capacities, an exercise which all too often obscured the issues the parties themselves had raised in appeal.

2–05–28   The Scottish courts, following the dubious precedent of *Kaye v. Hunter*, cited above, held themselves to be executing an administrative function with no remit to consider the factual basis of police decisions, and only able to intervene where it could be shown that the police had acted capriciously or arbitrarily in administering section 30. Until the five-judge decision of the Court of Session in *Rodenhurst v. Chief Constable, Grampian Police*, 1992 S.L.T. 104, the courts in the two jurisdictions had held themselves to have entirely different powers of review under the Act.

2–05–29   *Kaye* was an appeal under the 1937 Firearms Act against a police decision to refuse the appellant a firearm certificate. In terms of the Act the appellant had appealed first to the sheriff against refusal in an action which was dismissed as incompetent; the sheriff noted that English practice had no bearing and that his decision in what he regarded as an administrative matter was final. Kaye appealed to the First Division of the Court of Session in an action which the chief constable contended was incompetent.

Delivering judgment, Lord President Clyde (at 210) stated:

> "The distinction between appeals to the Sheriff in his administrative capacity and in his judicial capacity is a familiar one, and, while he is final in the former, his decision is subject to review in the latter. An almost infinite variety of statutory provisions on this matter can be found from a consideration of various Acts of Parliament where appeals to the Sheriff have been enacted, and there is no single criterion

which can be regarded as the conclusive test of whether it is the administrative or judicial capacity of the Sheriff which is being invoked. It is, consequently, misleading to search for precise analogies from other statutes, for each one must be considered on its own terms."

Lord Clyde referred to the relevant provision of the Act and to the Act of Sederunt which specified the procedures to be followed before adding (at 211):

"It seems to me that in these circumstances what is contemplated by the Legislature is not an open appeal in which the Sheriff acting in his judicial capacity must adjudicate between rival claims to the grant or refusal of a certificate, and in the end must, therefore, himself require to decide whether the applicant had good reasons for having a firearm from a consideration of the evidence led before him... What is contemplated under this section is that the Sheriff should only interfere with what the Chief Constable has done if he is persuaded on appeal that there has been a capricious or arbitrary exercise... of a discretion which the statute has entrusted to [the Chief Constable] and to him alone. The Sheriff is given no power to grant or withhold a certificate, as he would have been given if his jurisdiction in a judicial capacity had been invoked."

Following this reasoning the court approved the sheriff's 2–05–30 reasoning and ruled any further appeal incompetent. The decision failed to consider precisely how the sheriff could respond if he found that the chief constable had acted capriciously or arbitrarily; in that situation he was clearly empowered to overrule the police decision and grant a certificate despite the absence of express provisions in the Act. This was the approach, under the same statute, taken in courts south of the border.

Earlier it was observed that, in *Cunning*, the sheriff had 2–05–31 embarked on just the sort of proof Lord Clyde's judgment had rejected, and scarcely referred to the *Kaye* decision at all. A yet bolder approach was taken by the sheriff in *Hamilton v. Chief Constable of Strathclyde Police*, 1978 S.L.T. (Sh. Ct.) 69 by dint of distinguishing the *Kaye* judgment as inapplicable to appeal procedure under the Firearms Act 1968 (the statutory successor to the 1937 Act) and following the *ratio* in an English case,

Kavanagh v. Chief Constable of Devon and Cornwall [1974] Q.B.
624; [1974] 2 W.L.R. 762; [1974] 2 All E.R. 697, a leading
interpretation of the Act.

The sheriff noted the apparent anomalies that appeals in
England or Wales could go to the House of Lords but no further
than a sheriff in Scotland, and that Scottish courts (bound by
Kaye) could not consider the merits of the disputed application,
results which he doubted had been contemplated by the legislature. Further, Sheriff Stewart founded strongly upon the fact
that he was required to issue a written determination, a point
which in the case of *Arcari v. Dunbartonshire County Council*,
1948 S.L.T. 438; 1948 S.C. 62, had been noted by Lord President
Cooper as helpful in discerning if a judgment was judicial,
rather than administrative, in nature.

2–05–32   The sheriff's preference for the reasoning in *Arcari* rather
than that in *Kaye* was echoed in *Rodenhurst* (cited at 2–05–28,
above). This judgment succinctly overruled Lord Clyde's judgment, but of equal interest was the fact that the court examined
the material placed before the lower courts.

R had appealed to the sheriff against the chief constable's
revocation of his shot gun certificate, and was upheld. The chief
constable in turn appealed to the sheriff principal, who can
function as a forum for civil appeals. The sheriff principal held
this appeal to be incompetent, but helpfully indicated that on
the merits he would have reversed the lower court's decision; his
verdict as to competency was itself appealed by the police to the
Court of Session, it being argued that the court had wrongly
held itself bound by the *Kaye* judgment.

2–05–33   Having overruled *Kaye*, the court moved on to consider the
factual basis for the chief constable's original revocation; on
being advised that the parties at the original appeal had
incorrectly proceeded on an understanding that R had been
convicted of six offences, whereas he had actually been convicted of three, the court concluded that the chief constable had
based his decision upon a material misapprehension. Accordingly, while the chief constable's pleas-in-law were upheld, the
original decision of the sheriff (for what it was by then worth)
was upheld on the merits!

2–05–34   Although the factors which may properly be taken into
account by the chief constable have been mentioned, and often
formed the subject matter of appeals, it is surprising to note that

until *Kavanagh* (cited at 2–05–31 above) no consideration appears to have been given to the standard of proof applying to deliberations under the Act by the police or the courts. Indeed, it was well into a Crown Court appeal hearing that this problem surfaced.

The chief constable had refused applications for a shot gun certificate and a firearm dealer's registration to K, who appealed. Near the end of the chief constable's case, the court asked the parties whether or not it was bound by the rules of criminal evidence when deliberating, a question which perforce turned attention to the standard of evidence which could legitimately be heeded by the chief constable in his own consideration of applications. The question was referred to the High Court, and Cusack J. gave a judgment (reported at [1973] 3 W.L.R. 415) whose terms were later approved by the Court of Appeal.

His Lordship stated ([1973] 3 W.L.R. 415 at 419D):

"The decision [the chief constable] took was an administrative decision and a decision as to which the statute allowed him a discretion. For my part I do not think it is useful to consider whether the proceedings on appeal are civil or criminal. The [Act] in fact provides a code for dealing with matters relating to the licensing and possession of firearms which is in many ways to be regarded as self-contained. It would, however, be very strange if the question of civil or criminal jurisdiction were to be decided simply by reference to the nature of the tribunal to which the appeal lies. . . . What I think is of greater importance is to consider what function the Crown Court has on appeal under [the Act]. It clearly has to consider the matter from the beginning afresh, but it would be very strange if, in dealing with the appeal, the question whether a certificate should be issued or a dealer should be registered should be dealt with on one basis by the Chief Constable and have to be dealt with on a completely different basis by the tribunal to which the appeal lies.

The Crown Court has to apply its own discretion in exactly the same way as, in the first instance, the chief constable would have to apply his discretion. . . . If the Crown Court had to conduct its investigation on an entirely different basis from [the chief constable], then there would really be two standards applying as to whether or not a certificate should be issued or a dealer should be registered. I take the view that this procedure under the Firearms Act 1968, and I am simply dealing with the procedure by way of appeal under that Act, is something to which the ordinary rules of evidence applicable to criminal trials need not apply. The Crown Court is at liberty to take into consideration all the matters which the chief constable was at liberty to take into consideration. If in fact some of those matters are hearsay and are not supported by the evidence of witnesses in the Crown Court, of course it will be for that court to consider carefully what weight is to be attached to the evidence which is put before it in that fashion."

2–05–35 While the judge opined that evidence could be led in the ordinary way and be subjected to cross-examination, it is notable that in his Court of Appeal judgment, Lord Denning M.R. indicated ([1974] 2 W.L.R. at 766C):

"Hearsay can be permitted where it can fairly be regarded as reliable. No doubt [the court] must act fairly. They should give the party concerned an opportunity of correcting or contradicting what is put against him. But it does not mean that he has to be given a chance to cross-examine. It is enough if they hear what he has to say. . . . In an appeal under [the Act] it seems to me essential that the Crown Court should have before it all the material which was before the chief officer of police. After all, the chief officer is the person to give the decision in the first instance. Under section 27 it is he who is to be 'satisfied'. Under section 34 he may refuse if he is 'satisfied' of what is said there. It is plain that he can take into account any information that he thinks fit. He need not hold any hearing. He can decide on paper. If he refuses and the applicant appeals to the Crown Court, then the Crown Court must see whether or not the chief officer was right in refusing. [It] ought to know the material that was before him and what were the reasons which operated on his mind. It can also consider any other material which may be placed before it. In the end it must come to its own decision. . .".

The Court of Appeal upheld the lower courts' view that all matters which had influenced the Chief Constable in reaching his decision, irrespective of their probative value, could be taken into consideration in any appeal proceedings.

Certificate for prohibited weapon

31.—(1) A chief officer of police shall not refuse to grant or **2–06–01** renew, and shall not revoke, a firearm certificate in respect of a prohibited weapon or prohibited ammunition if the applicant for the certificate is for the time being authorised by the [¹Secretary of State] under section 5 of this Act to have possession of that weapon or ammunition.

(2) Where an authority of the [¹Secretary of State] under that section to have possession of, or to purchase or acquire, a prohibited weapon or prohibited ammunition is revoked, the firearm certificate relating to that weapon or ammunition shall be revoked or varied accordingly by the chief officer of police by whom it was granted.

NOTE

(1) Substituted by the Transfer of Functions (Prohibited Weapons) Order 1968 (S.I. 1968 No. 1200), arts. 2 and 3.

OBSERVATION

Note that the Chief Constable has no discretion over the issue **2–06–02** or revocation of certificates granted under this section. Grants are entirely outwith the ordinary licensing regime but it seems anomalous that a power of variation of a certificate (mentioned in subsection (2)) is vested in the police when the Secretary of State has already revoked it. The intention may be to enable elements of a certificate to be varied, but the section does not vest a power of variation in the Secretary of State's hands.

Fee for certificate and exemption from paying it in certain cases

[¹**32.**—(1) Subject to this Act, there shall be payable—   **2–07–01**
   (*a*) on the grant of a firearm certificate a fee of [£56];
   (*b*) on the renewal of a firearm certificate a fee of £46;
   (*c*) on any variation of a firearm certificate (otherwise than when it is renewed at the same time) so as to increase the number of firearms to which the certificate relates, a fee of £26;
   (*cc*) on the replacement of a firearm certificate which has been lost or destroyed a fee of £9;

(*d*) on the grant of a shot gun certificate a fee of [£43];

(*e*) on the renewal of a shot gun certificate a fee of [£18]; and

(*f*) on the replacement of a shot gun certificate which has been lost or destroyed a fee of £8.]

2–07–02   (2) No fee shall be payable on the grant to a responsible officer of a rifle club, miniature rifle club, [² pistol club], or cadet corps approved for the purpose by the Secretary of State, of a firearm certificate in respect of firearms or ammunition to be used solely for target practice or drill by the members of the club or corps, or on the variation or renewal of a certificate so granted, [² but in the case of a club whose approval is limited to target practice with specified types of rifles or pistols this subsection shall apply only to a certificate in respect of rifles or pistols of those types].

(3) No fee shall be payable on the grant, variation or renewal of a firearm certificate if the chief officer of police is satisfied that the certificate relates solely to and, in the case of a variation, will continue when varied to relate solely to—

(*a*) a firearm or ammunition which the applicant requires as part of the equipment of a ship; or

(*b*) a signalling apparatus, or ammunition therefor, which the applicant requires as part of the equipment of an aircraft or aerodrome; or

(*c*) a slaughtering instrument, or ammunition therefor, which the applicant requires for the purpose of the slaughter of animals.

[³(3A) No fee shall be payable on the grant, variation or renewal of a firearm certificate which relates solely to and, in the case of variation, will continue when varied to relate solely to a signalling device,which, when assembled and ready to fire, is not more than eight inches long and which is designed to discharge a flare, or to ammunition for such a device.]

2–07–03   (4) No fee shall be payable—

(*a*) on the grant or renewal of a firearm certificate relating solely to a firearm which is shown to the satisfaction of the chief officer of police to be kept by the applicant as a trophy of war; or

(*b*) on any variation of a certificate the sole effect of which is to add such a firearm as aforesaid to the firearms to which the certificate relates, if the certificate is granted, renewed or varied subject to the condition that the applicant shall not use the firearm.

NOTES

(1) Section 32's derivation is now rather involved. Except for the most recent alteration of fees introduced by the Firearms (Variation of Fees) Order and the Firearms (Variation of Fees) (Scotland) Order, respectively S.I. 1994 No. 2615 and 1994 No. 2652, art. 3 of which amended the fees in subs. (1)(*a*), (*d*) and (*e*), the last major reform of fees was made in 1990 by S.I. 1990 No. 290 and (S) 1990 No. 325.

    In addition the 1988 Act, s.11(3), provided that the fee for a coterminous certificate, *i.e.* a combined fee where the applicant held both a firearm certificate and a shot gun certificate, would be restricted to £5 when application could be made for them to run, and expire, of even date.

(2) Inserted by the 1988 Act, s.15(8).

(3) Section 32(3A) was introduced by S.I. 1978 No. 360 and amended by S.I. 1990 No. 290 and S.I. 1990 No. 325. Article 4 of the 1994 Orders cited above gives continued effect to the subsection.

OBSERVATIONS

(a) The fees now chargeable as a result of the two Orders above **2–07–04** are as follows—

Grant of firearm certificate	£56
Renewal of firearm certificate	£46
Variation of firearm certificate	£26
Grant of shot gun certificate	£43
Renewal of shot gun certificate	£18
Registration as Firearm dealer	£118
Renewal of firearm dealer certificate	£50
Home Office Club Approval	£84
Visitor's firearm or shot gun permit	£12
Visitors' group permit (six or more persons)	£60
Fee for a co-terminous certificate	£5

Source: Home Office News Release July 20, 1994

(b) Trophies of war are exempted from the fee structure only if **2–07–05** the chief constable is satisfied that the weapon will not be used. There are no reported authorities but it is likely that the police would be entitled to approach applications for such certificates as they would applications under sections 27 and 28. Furthermore, only a limited range of war trophies would be likely to be eligible for such a licence; the majority of military armaments are prohibited weapons as defined in sections 5 and 5A of the principal Act and would first require the authority of the

Secretary of State to be possessed or acquired. The only exceptions to this generality are licensed museums or approved collectors.

2–07–06 [¹32A.—(1) Where a person is granted, or is the holder of, a certificate under this Act, he shall be entitled to be issued by the chief officer of police for the area in which he resides with—

    (*a*) a document ("a European firearms pass") containing the required particulars; and

    (*b*) a document stating that, for the purposes of Article 7 of the European weapons directive, the holder of the certificate has the agreement of the United Kingdom authorities, for so long as the certificate remains in force, to any purchase or acquisition by him in another member State of any firearm or ammunition to which the certificate relates;

and an application for the issue of a document falling within paragraph (*a*) or (*b*) above may be made at the same time as any application for a certificate the grant of which will entitle him to the issue of the document or subsequently while the certificate is in force.

2–07–07 (2) Where—

    (*a*) a person who resides in Great Britain is proposing to purchase or acquire any firearm or ammunition in another member State;

    (*b*) that person is not for the time being the holder of a certificate under this Act relating to that firearm or ammunition;

    (*c*) the firearm falls within category B for the purposes of Annex I to the European weapons directive or the ammunition is capable of being used with such a firearm; and

    (*d*) that person satisfies the chief officer of police for the area where he resides that he is not proposing to bring that firearm or ammunition into the United Kingdom,

the chief officer of police may, if he thinks fit, issue that person with a document stating that, for the purposes of Article 7 of the European weapons directive, that person has the agreement of the United Kingdom authorities to any purchase or acquisition by him in another member State of that firearm or ammunition.

2–07–08 (3) For the purposes of subsection (1) above the required particulars, in relation to a person issued with a European firearms pass, are—

(*a*) particulars identifying that person;
(*b*) particulars identifying every firearm which—
  (i) that person has applied to have included in a European firearms pass; and
  (ii) is a firearm in relation to which a certificate granted to that person is for the time being in force;
(*c*) a statement in relation to every firearm identified in the pass as to the category into which it falls for the purposes of Annex I to the European weapons directive;
(*d*) the date of the issue of the pass and the period from its issue for which the pass is to be valid;
(*e*) the statements required by paragraph (*f*) of Annex II to that directive (statements as to travel in the member States with the firearms identified in the pass).

(4) For the purposes of this section the particulars of the **2–07–09** firearms to which a shot gun certificate relates which are to be contained in a European firearms pass by virtue of subsection (3)(*b*) above are—
  (*a*) a description of the shot guns to which that certificate relates; and
  (*b*) any identification numbers specified in or entered on that certificate in pursuance of section 28(2A) of this Act or in consequence of any person's compliance, in accordance with section 4(2) of the Firearms (Amendment) Act 1988 (formalities on transfer of shot guns), with any instructions contained in the certificate;
and, accordingly, references in this Act to a firearm identified in such a pass shall include references to any shot gun of a description specified in that pass.

(5) A European firearms pass shall contain space for the making of entries by persons authorised to do so under the law of any member State.

(6) The period specified in a European firearms pass as the period for which it is to be valid shall be whichever is the shorter of the following—
  (*a*) the period until the earliest time when a certificate relating to a firearm identified in the pass expires; and
  (*b*) the maximum period for the duration of that pass.

(7) For the purposes of subsection (6) above the maximum **2–07–10** period for the duration of a European firearms pass is—

(*a*) in the case of a pass identifying only a firearm or firearms stated in the pass to fall within category D for the purposes of Annex I to the European weapons directive, ten years; and

(*b*) in any other case, five years.]

NOTE

(1) Section inserted by Firearms Acts (Amendment) Regulations 1992 (S.I. 1992 No. 2823), reg. 5.

OBSERVATIONS

2–07–11 (a) Regulation 5 above implements the requirement of Council Directive No. 91/477, Article 1.4 for the issue by Member States of a European Firearms Pass (henceforth referred to as an E.F.P.). In the U.K. the administration of the E.F.P. scheme is the responsibility of the police locally. There is no fee charged for the issue of such a pass.

Annex I to the Directive divides firearms (shot guns are included within this definition) into four categories: the Annex is reproduced at 5–07–01, *infra*. The possession of such a pass indicates that its holder has obtained the prior consent of the authorities (an "Article 7 authority") for his purchase or acquisition of a category B firearm, or ammunition for same, to be made in another Member State. Those in possession of an appropriate domestic firearm or shot gun certificate can seek an E.F.P. by subsection (1) and will then be authorised to import weapons or ammunition, as specified in the E.F.P., into the U.K. Subsection (2) provides for the purchase or acquisition of such items within the E.C. when it is not intended to bring them into the U.K. and can be sought by residents of Great Britain (a significant distinction) who do not hold a certificate under the Act. Understandably the police have to be satisfied that the items will not be brought into the U.K. and also have to deem it appropriate to issue an Article 7 authority. The police cannot refuse to issue an E.F.P. to holders of certificates under the Act but can refuse applications made under subsection (2). Whether by accident or design, there is no appeal procedure under the Act against such a refusal: section 44 of the 1968 Act does not currently extend to section 32 above.

(b) An E.F.P. referring to category D firearms (any shot gun without a magazine) can last up to ten years; passes for all other categories can be of up to five years' duration.

[¹**32B.**—(1) On an application for the renewal by a chief **2–07–12** officer of police of a certificate under this Act relating to a firearm identified in a European firearms pass, the holder of the certificate may apply to the chief officer of police for the renewal of the pass.

(2) Where— **2–07–13**

    (*a*) a certificate relating to a firearm identified in a European firearms pass is to expire without being renewed; but

    (*b*) a certificate relating to another firearm identified in that pass will continue in force after the other certificate expires,

the holder of the pass may apply to the chief officer of police for the area in which he resides for the renewal of the pass subject to the deletion of the reference to any firearm to which the expiring certificate relates.

(3) Where, on an application to a chief officer of police under subsection (1) or (2) above—

    (*a*) the pass in question is produced to him; and

    (*b*) a certificate relating to a firearm identified in the pass is renewed or will continue in force after the time when the pass would (apart from its renewal) have ceased to be valid,

he shall renew that pass, subject to any appropriate deletion, from that for whichever is the shorter of the periods specified in section 32A(6)(*a*) and (*b*) of this Act.

(4) Where a European firearms pass ceases to be valid **2–07–14** without being renewed under this section, the chief officer of police for the area in which the person to whom it was issued resides may, by notice in writing, require that person, within twenty-one days of the date of the notice, to surrender the pass to him.

(5) It is an offence for any person to fail to comply with a notice given to him under subsection (4) above.]

NOTE

(1) The derivation of this section is identical to section 32A above.

[¹**32C.**—(1) Where— **2–07–15**

    (*a*) a certificate relating to a firearm identified in a European firearms pass or a certificate in respect of which an Article 7 authority has been issued is varied, revoked or cancelled under this Act;

(*b*) the Secretary of State gives notice that any European firearms pass needs to be modified by the addition or variation of any such statement as is mentioned in section 32A(3)(*e*) of this Act; or

(*c*) the holder of a European firearms pass applies to have particulars of another firearm added to the pass,

it shall be the duty of the chief officer of police for the area in which the holder of the pass or authority resides to make such variations of the pass or authority as are appropriate in consequence of the variation, revocation, cancellation, notice or application or, where appropriate, to cancel it.

(2) For the purpose of performing his duty under subsection (1) above the chief officer of police for the area in which any person who is or has been the holder of any certificate resides may, by notice in writing, require that person, within twenty-one days of the date of the notice, to produce or surrender to him any European firearms pass or Article 7 authority issued to that person.

2–07–16   (3) Where a person is for the time being the holder of an Article 7 authority issued under section 32A(2) of this Act by the chief officer of police for any area, the chief officer of police for that area may, if he thinks fit, at any time—

(*a*) revoke that authority, and;

(*b*) by notice in writing require that person, within twenty-one days of the date of the notice, to surrender that authority to him.

(4) Where a firearm identified in a European firearms pass which is for the time being valid, is lost or stolen, the holder of the pass shall immediately—

(*a*) inform the chief officer of police for the area in which he resides about the loss or theft; and

(*b*) produce the pass to that chief officer for him to endorse particulars of that loss or theft on the pass.

2–07–17   (5) Where a firearm to which an endorsement under subsection (4) above relates is returned to the possession of the holder of the pass in question, the chief officer of police for the area in which that person resides may, on the production to him of that pass, make such further endorsement on that pass as may be appropriate.

(6) It is an offence for any person to fail to comply with a notice given to him under subsection (2) or (3) above or with

any obligation imposed on him by virtue of subsection (4) (*a*) or (*b*) above.

(7) Any reference in this section to the variation of a certificate includes a reference to the making of any entry on a shot gun certificate in pursuance of the requirement under section 4(2) of the Firearms (Amendment) Act 1988 (formalities on transfer of shot guns) to comply with instructions contained in the certificate.]

NOTE

(1) The derivation of this section is identical to section 32A above.

Registration of firearms dealers

Police register

33.—(1) For purposes of this Act, the chief officer of police **2–08–01** for every area shall keep in the prescribed form a register of firearms dealers.

(2) Except as provided by section 34 of this Act, the chief officer of police shall enter in the register the name of any person who, having or proposing to have a place of business in the area, applies to be registered as a firearms dealer.

(3) In order to be registered, the applicant must furnish the **2–08–02** chief officer of police with the prescribed particulars, which shall include particulars of every place of business at which he proposes to carry on business in the area as a firearms dealer and, except as provided by this Act, the chief officer of police shall enter every such place of business in the register.

(4) When a person is registered, the chief officer of police shall grant or cause to be granted to him a certificate of registration.

(5) A person for the time being registered shall, [¹on or before the expiration of the period of three years from the grant of the certificate of registration for the time being held by him]—

    (*a*) surrender his certificate to the chief officer of police; and

    (*b*) apply in the prescribed form for a new certificate;

and thereupon the chief officer of police shall, subject to sections 35(3) and 38(1) below, grant him a new certificate of registration.

NOTE

(1) Amended by the 1988 Act, s.13(1).

OBSERVATION

2–08–03 The importance of registering every place of business is highlighted in *R. v. Bull*, cited and discussed at 1–08–02 *supra*. Only by being so registered do firearms dealers escape certification requirements which would otherwise apply to their possession of firearms and ammunition. See also *Staravia Ltd v. Gordon*, cited and discussed at 1–08–03.

Grounds for refusal of registration

2–09–01   34.—(1) The chief officer of police shall not register an applicant as a firearms dealer if he is prohibited to be so registered by order of a court in Great Britain made under section 45 of this Act, or by order of a court in Northern Ireland under section 8(5) of the Firearms Act 1920 or any enactment of the Parliament of Northern Ireland amending or substituted for that section.

    [[1](1A) The chief officer of police may refuse to register an applicant unless he is satisfied that the applicant will engage in business as a firearms dealer to a substantial extent or as an essential part of another trade, business or profession.]

2–09–02   (2) Subject to subsection (3) below, the chief officer of police may refuse to register an applicant, if he is satisfied that the applicant cannot be permitted to carry on business as a firearms dealer without danger to the public safety or to the peace.

    (3) In the case of a person for the time being authorised by the [[2](Secretary of State] under section 5 of this Act to manufacture, sell or transfer prohibited weapons or ammunition, the chief officer of police shall not refuse to enter his name in the register on the ground that he cannot be permitted to carry on business as a firearms dealer without danger to the public safety or to the peace.

2–09–03   (4) The chief officer of police, if he is satisfied that a place of business notified to him under section 33(3) of this Act by an applicant for registration is a place at which the person cannot be permitted to carry on business as a firearms dealer without danger to the public safety or to the peace, may refuse to enter that place of business in the register.

2–09–04   (5) A person aggrieved by the refusal of a chief officer of police to register him as a firearms dealer, or to enter in the register a place of business of his, may in accordance with section 44 of this Act appeal against the refusal.

NOTES
(1) Inserted by the 1988 Act, s.13(2).
(2) Amended by S.I. 1968 No. 1200, arts. 2 and 3.

OBSERVATIONS

Contrast the provisions of subsections (2) and (4); the former **2–09–05** clearly relates to the character of the applicant and the same considerations as are applied to firearm and shot gun certificate holders by section 30 above would prevail. Subsection (4) refers to the premises in which the business would operate and, it is suggested, that the phrase "place of business" used in section 33(3) will be broadly construed, applying to stores just as much as retail premises.

Bull apart, there are no reported cases on this topic, but it could well be the case that factors other than the security of the building might properly be considered by the police; for example the proximity of proposed ammunition stores to chemical stores or location in a high crime area.

Fee for registration and renewal thereof

35.—(1) Subject to this Act, on the registration of a person as **2–10–01** a firearms dealer there shall be payable by him
[¹a fee of £118.]
[²(1A) If the chief officer of police for the area in which the applicant has applied to be registered is satisfied—
  (*a*) that the only place of business in respect of which the application is made is at a game fair, trade fair or exhibition, agricultural show or an event of a similar character, and
  (*b*) that the applicant's principal place of business is entered in the register for another area,
the fee payable shall be [³£12].]

(2) No fee shall be payable if the chief officer of police for the **2–10–02** area in which the applicant has applied to be registered is satisfied that the only place of business in respect of which the application is made—
  (*a*) has become situated in that area because of an alteration in the boundary of the area and was previously entered in the register for another area; or
  (*b*) is one to which the applicant proposes to transfer the business previously carried on by him at a place entered in the register for another area.

[⁴(3) Before a person for the time being registered as a firearms dealer can be granted a new certificate of registration under section 33(5) of this Act, he shall pay a fee of £50.]

NOTES

(1) Inserted (England & Wales) by S.I. 1994 No. 2615, art. 6(*a*) and (Scotland) by S.I. 1994 No. 2652, art. 5 and Sched. 2, Pt. I of each.
(2) Subsection (1A) added (England & Wales) by S.I. 1986 No. 986 and (Scotland) by S.I. 1986 No. 996, art. 7 of each.
(3) Sum amended by art. 6(*b*) and Sched. 2, Pt. II of the statutory instruments cited at n. (1) above.
(4) Inserted by art. 6(*c*) and Sched. 2, Pt. II of the statutory instruments cited at n. (1) above.

OBSERVATION

2–10–03 As was noted at 2–07–04 the application fee for registration as a firearms dealer is £118 from January 1, 1995. The fee for renewal will remain £50.

Conditions of registration

2–11–01 36.—(1) The chief officer of police may at any time impose conditions subject to which the registration of a person as a firearms dealer is to have effect and may at any time, of his own motion or on the application of the dealer, vary or revoke any such condition.

(2) The chief officer of police shall specify the conditions for the time being in force under this section in the certificate of registration granted to the firearms dealer and, where any such condition is imposed, varied or revoked during the currency of the certificate of registration, the chief officer of police—

(*a*) shall give to the dealer notice in writing of the condition or variation (giving particulars) or of the revocation, as the case may be; and

(*b*) may by that notice require the dealer to deliver up to him his certificate of registration within twenty-one days from the date of the notice, for the purpose of amending the certificate.

2–11–02 (3) A person aggrieved by the imposition or variation of, or refusal to vary or revoke, any condition of a firearm dealer's registration may in accordance with section 44 of this Act appeal against the imposition, variation or refusal.

OBSERVATION

This section does not deal with removal of dealers from the register. See section 38, *infra*.

Registration of new place of business

37.—(1) A person registered in any area as a firearms dealer 2–12–01 and proposing to carry on business as such at a place of business in that area which is not entered in the register, shall notify the chief officer of police for that area and furnish him with such particulars as may be prescribed; and the officer shall, subject to the provisions of this section, enter that place of business in the register.

(2) The chief officer of police, if he is satisfied that a place of business notified to him by a person under subsection (1) of this section is a place at which that person cannot be permitted to carry on business as a firearms dealer without danger to the public safety or to the peace, may refuse to enter it in the register.

(3) A person aggrieved by the refusal by a chief officer of 2–12–02 police to enter in the register a place of business of his may in accordance with section 44 of this Act appeal against the refusal.

Removal from register of dealer's name or place of business

38.—(1) If the chief officer of police, after giving reasonable 2–13–01 notice to a person whose name is on the register, is satisfied that the person—

(a) is no longer carrying on business as a firearms dealer; or

(b) has ceased to have a place of business in the area; or

(c) cannot be permitted to continue to carry on business as a firearms dealer without danger to the public safety or to the peace,

he shall (subject to this section) cause the name of that person to be removed from the register.

(2) In the case of a person for the time being authorised by 2–13–02 the [1Secretary of State] under section 5 of this Act to manufacture, sell or transfer prohibited weapons or ammunition, the chief officer of police shall not remove his name from the register on the ground that he cannot be permitted to continue to carry on business as a firearms dealer without danger to the public safety or to the peace.

(3) If the chief officer of police is satisfied that a person registered as a firearms dealer has failed to comply with any of the conditions of registration in force under section 36 of this Act, he may remove from the register either that person's name or any place of business of his to which the condition relates.

2–13–03 (4) If the chief officer of police is satisfied that a place entered in the register as a person's place of business is one at which that person cannot be permitted to carry on business as a firearms dealer without danger to the public safety or to the peace, he may remove that place from the register.

(5) The chief officer of police shall cause the name of a person to be removed from the register if the person so desires.

2–13–04 (6) If a person for the time being registered fails to comply with any requirement of section 33(5) of this Act, the chief officer of police shall by notice in writing require him to comply with that requirement and, if the person fails to do so within twenty-one days from the date of the notice or within such further time as the chief officer may in special circumstances allow, shall cause his name to be removed from the register.

(7) A person aggrieved by the removal of his name from the register, or by the removal from the register of a place of business of his, may in accordance with section 44 of this Act appeal against the removal.

2–13–05 (8) Where the chief officer of police causes the name of a firearms dealer to be removed from the register, he shall by notice in writing require the dealer to surrender his certificate of registration [²and the register of transactions kept by him under section 40 of this Act] and it is an offence for the dealer to fail to do so within twenty-one days from the date of the notice:

Provided that, if an appeal is brought against the removal, this subsection shall not apply to that removal unless the appeal is abandoned or dismissed and shall then apply with the substitution, for the reference to the date of the notice, of a reference to the date on which the appeal was abandoned or dismissed.

NOTES

(1) Inserted by S.I. 1968 No. 1200, arts. 2 and 3.
(2) Inserted by the 1988 Act, s.13(3).

OBSERVATION

2–13–06 No definition is given in the Act of the period of notice to be regarded as "reasonable" stipulated in subsection (1).

Offences in connection with registration

39.—(1) A person commits an offence if, for the purpose—   **2–14–01**
(*a*) of procuring the registration of himself or another
     person as a firearms dealer; or
(*b*) of procuring, whether for himself or another person, the
     entry of any place of business in a register of firearms
     dealers,
he makes any statement which he knows to be false.

(2) A person commits an offence if, being a registered **2–14–02**
firearms dealer, he has a place of business which is not entered
in the register for the area in which the place of business is
situated and carries on business as a firearms dealer at that
place.

(3) Without prejudice to section 38(3) above, a person
commits an offence if he fails to comply with any of the
conditions of registration imposed on him by the chief officer of
police under section 36 of this Act.

Supplementary

Compulsory register of transactions in firearms

40.—(1) Subject to section 41 of this Act, every person who by **2–15–01**
way of trade or business manufactures, sells or transfers firearms
or ammunition shall provide and keep a register of transactions
and shall enter or cause to be entered therein the particulars
specified in Schedule 4 to this Act.

(2) In subsection (1) above and in the said Schedule 4, any
reference to firearms is to be construed as not including a
reference to air weapons or component parts of, or accessories
to air weapons; and any reference therein to ammunition is to
be construed as not including—
(*a*) cartridges containing five or more shot, none of which
     exceeds .36 inch in diameter;
(*b*) ammunition for an air gun, air rifle or air pistol; or
(*c*) blank cartridges not more than one inch in diameter
     measured immediately in front of the rim or cannelure of
     the base of the cartridge.

(3) Every entry required by subsection (1) of this section to be **2–15–02**
made in the register shall be made within twenty-four hours
after the transaction to which it relates took place and, in the
case of a sale or transfer, every person to whom that subsection

applies shall at the time of the transaction require the purchaser or transferee, if not known to him, to furnish particulars sufficient for identification and shall immediately enter the said particulars in the register.

[[1](3A) Every person keeping a register in accordance with this section shall (unless required to surrender the register under section 38(3) of this Act) keep it for such a period that each entry made after the coming into force of this subsection will be available for inspection for at least five years from the date on which it was made.]

2–15–03   (4) Every person keeping a register in accordance with this section shall on demand allow [[2]a constable] duly authorised in writing in that behalf by the chief officer of police, to enter and inspect all stock in hand and shall on request by [[2]a constable] so authorised or by an officer of customs and excise produce the register for inspection:

Provided that, where a written authority is required by this subsection, the authority shall be produced on demand.

(5) It is an offence for a person to fail to comply with any provision of this section or knowingly to make any false entry in the register required to be kept thereunder.

2–15–04   (6) Nothing in this section applies to the sale of firearms or ammunition by auction in accordance with the terms of a permit issued under section 9(2) of this Act.

(7) Rules made by the Secretary of State under section 53 of this Act may vary or add to Schedule 4 to this Act, and references in this section to that Schedule shall be construed as references to the Schedule as for the time being so varied or added to.

NOTES

(1) Inserted by the 1988 Act, s.13(4).
(2) Substituted by the 1988 Act, s.23(3).

OBSERVATIONS

2–15–05   (a) Schedule 4 to the Act specifies the information to be completed in each entry in a firearms register.

(b) Subsection (2) specifies the types of ammunition whose sale or transfer need not be recorded in a register of transactions. As section 1(4) indicates, these types of ammunition can be possessed by persons who do not hold a firearms certificate.

Exemption from s.40 in case of trade in shot gun components

41.—If it appears to the chief officer of police that—   **2–16–01**

  (*a*) a person required to be registered as a firearms dealer carries on a trade or business in the course of which he manufactures, tests or repairs component parts or accessories for shot guns, but does not manufacture, test or repair complete shot guns; and

  (*b*) it is impossible to assemble a shot gun from the parts likely to come into that person's possession in the course of that trade or business,

the chief officer of police may, if he thinks fit, by notice in writing given to that person exempt his transactions in those parts and accessories, so long as the notice is in force, from all or any of the requirements of section 40 of this Act and Schedule 4 thereto.

OBSERVATION

This is a discretionary power of the chief constable and as such no appeal is open under the Act against a refusal to exercise it.

Transactions with persons not registered dealers

42.—(1) A person who sells, lets on hire, gives or lends a   **2–17–01** firearm or ammunition to which section 1 of this Act applies to another person in the United Kingdom, not being a registered firearms dealer shall, unless the other person shows that he is by virtue of this Act entitled to purchase or acquire the firearm or ammunition without holding a firearm certificate, comply with any instructions contained in the certificate produced; and in the case of a firearm he shall within [¹seven days] from the transaction, send by registered post or the recorded delivery service notice of the transaction to the chief officer of police by whom the certificate was issued.

[²(1A) The notice under subsection (1) above shall contain a   **2–17–02** description of the firearm (giving the identification number if any) and state the nature of the transaction and the name and address of the other person concerned.]

(2) It is an offence for a person to fail to comply with this section.

NOTES

(1) Words substituted by the 1988 Act, s.23(6).
(2) Subsection (1A) introduced by s.23(6), cited above.

Transactions with persons not registered dealers

2–17–03   [¹42A—(1) A person who sells, lets on hire, gives or lends a shot gun with a magazine to another person who—

    (*a*) shows that he is entitled to purchase or acquire the weapon as the holder of a visitor's shot gun permit under section 17 of the Firearms (Amendment) Act 1988; but

    (*b*) fails to show that the purchase or acquisition falls within subsection (1A)(*c*) or (*d*) of that section (temporary acquisitions or purchases or acquisitions by collectors etc.) or that he resides outside the member States,

shall, within forty-eight hours of the transaction, send by registered post or the recorded delivery service notice of the transaction to the chief officer of police who granted that permit.

    (2) A notice under subsection (1) above shall—

    (*a*) contain a description of the shot gun (giving the identification number if any);

    (*b*) state the nature of the transaction (giving the name of the person to whom the gun has been sold, let on hire, given or lent, his address in the member State where he resides and the number and place of issue of his passport, if any); and

    (*c*) set out the particulars of any licence granted for the purposes of an order made under section 1 of the Import, Export and Customs Powers (Defence) Act 1939 by virtue of which the transaction is authorised under section 17 of that Act of 1988.

    (3) It is an offence for a person to fail to comply with this section.]

NOTE

(1) Inserted by S.I. 1992 No. 2823, reg. 6(2).

OBSERVATIONS

2–17–04   This section introduces controls on the purchase and acquisition of shot guns equipped with a magazine: these are subject to section 1 certification and, as such, fall into Category C of the

European weapons directive. The more common shot guns which require to be certificated in accordance with section 2 of the 1968 Act (single-shot shot guns, side by side, and over-and-under shot guns) are Category D weapons in the directive.

Possession of a visitor's shot gun permit, which is issued in 2–17–05 terms of section 17 of the 1988 Act, does not itself allow the holder to purchase or acquire a shot gun equipped with a magazine where it is intended to remove the gun from Great Britain directly to another E.C. Member State. Such an export would also require the purchaser to obtain a licence from the Department of Trade and Industry; accordingly, section 42A stipulates that all transfers of such weapons shall be promptly notified to the police.

Sales or transfers of these weapons to recognised E.C. collectors are exempt from the section's provisions if obtained solely in connection with such activities.

See 7-18-01, *infra* for a fuller discussion.

Power of Secretary of State to alter fees

43.—(1) Sections 32 and 35 of this Act may be amended by an 2–18–01 order made by the Secretary of State so as to vary any sum specified thereby, or so as to provide that any sum payable thereunder shall cease to be so payable.

(2) An order made under this section may—
  (*a*) be limited to such cases as may be specified by the order and may make different provision for different cases so specified; and
  (*b*) be revoked or varied by a subsequent order so made.

(3) The power to make orders under this section shall be exercisable by statutory instrument and any statutory instrument containing such an order shall be subject to annulment in pursuance of a resolution of either House of Parliament.

OBSERVATION

A power to amend fees for visitors' permits was incorporated by 2–18–02 section 17(9) of the 1988 Act.

Appeals from police decision under Part II

44.—(1) An appeal under section 26, 29, 30, 34, 36, 37 or 38 2–19–01 of this Act lies, in England and Wales, to [¹the Crown Court] and, in Scotland, in accordance with Act of Sederunt to the sheriff.

(2) In relation to an appeal specified in the first column of Part I of Schedule 5 to this Act—

(*a*) [². . .]

(*b*) the third column shows, for Scotland, the sheriff, having jurisdiction to entertain the appeal.

(3) The procedural and other provisions contained in Part II of Schedule 5 to this Act shall have effect (for England and Wales only) on an appeal to [¹the Crown Court] under any provision of this Part of this Act.

NOTES

(1) Words substituted by the Courts Act 1971, s.56(2) and Sched. 9, Pt. I.
(2) Subsection (*a*) repealed by said Act, Sched. 11, Pt. IV.

OBSERVATION

2–19–02 Until the Courts Act 1971 the appellate function in England and Wales was exercised by the court of quarter sessions.

Consequences where registered dealer convicted of offence

2–20–01 **45.**—(1) Where a registered firearms dealer is convicted of an offence relevant for the purposes of this section the court may order—

(*a*) that the name of the dealer be removed from the register; and

(*b*) that neither the dealer nor any person who acquires his business, nor any person who took part in the management of the business and was knowingly a party to the offence, shall be registered as a firearms dealer; and

(*c*) that any person who, after the date of the order, knowingly employs in the management of his business the dealer convicted of the offence or any person who was knowingly a party to the offence, shall not be registered as a firearms dealer or, if so registered, shall be liable to be removed from the register; and

(*d*) that any stock-in-hand of the business shall be disposed of by sale or otherwise in accordance with such directions as may be contained in the order.

2–20–02 (2) The offences relevant for the purposes of this section are:-

(*a*) all offences under this Act, except an offence under section 2, 22(3) or 24(3) or an offence relating specifically to air weapons; and (*b*) offences against the [¹enactments for the time being in force relating to customs or excise] in respect of the import or export of firearms or ammunition to which section 1 of this Act applies, or of shot guns.

(3) A person aggrieved by an order made under this section may appeal against the order in the same manner as against the conviction, and the court may, if it thinks fit, suspend the operation of the order pending the appeal.

NOTE

(1) Words substituted by the Customs and Excise Management Act 1979, s.177(1) and Sched. 4, para. 12.

OBSERVATIONS

(a) There are no reported cases arising from this section's **2–20–03** provisions. The penalties for a firearms dealer convicted under the Act are considerably extended by this section: a sale of the business as a going concern can be proscribed and anyone knowingly employing a convicted dealer, or an associate in the offence giving rise to that conviction, can also be expunged from the register of firearms dealers.

The terms of section 45 suggest that such additional penalties can be imposed only at the time of conviction, and not later, as part of a sentence; it does not appear to be the intention that, for example, the court for the area in which the convicted dealer resides or has a place of business can impose the section's penalties if the court which convicted him did not. Further support for this interpretation may be found if one considers the thorny jurisdictional problems which would otherwise arise: imagine that A, an errant firearms dealer, is convicted of a relevant offence in London arising at his place of business there and is de-registered in terms of section 45 by the court. His former gunsmith, B, elects to start a new life in Scotland working for C, an Edinburgh firearms dealer. Could B (or C) appeal to a Scottish criminal court against an order pronounced under section 45 by a court in London, and would a Scottish sheriff be entitled to review a determination by a superior English court?

Common sense suggests that appeals have to be directed to **2–20–04** the appellate court having jurisdiction over the court which pronounced the original order. Furthermore, the order, as part of a sentence, should be made at the time of sentence during those proceedings and not later.

It is also submitted that it would be necessary to notify an accused of his liability to such additional penalties in a notice of penalty or specifically draw them to the attention of the court when moving for sentence. It should be stressed that the conviction must be a relevant one for the purposes of the Act (as defined in section 45(2)) before this section's provisions can take effect; other criminal convictions would not be relevant, no matter how serious, though they might well be enough to cause the chief constable to exercise his own powers under section 38(1) and (4) to revoke a firearms dealer's registration.

2–20–05 (b) Schedule 6 to the Act (Prosecution and Punishment of Offences) does not refer to section 45 at all, but it is submitted that, for all that, the section is self-evidently penal. No offence is created by section 45, but a person breaching the provisions of the section would arguably also have contravened section 39(1) of the Act by making false statements to procure registration as a firearms dealer, or to have a place of business entered in the register.

2–20–06 (c) Section 44 of the Act (and Schedule 5) provides the framework for other appeals under the Act arising from the refusal or revocation of certificates. As was noted at 2–05–34, it is fruitless to consider whether these are administrative or judicial appeals — they are appeals under the Firearms Act. In contrast, an appeal against a section 45 order made in the course of criminal proceedings has to be taken to an appellate criminal court and is, without doubt, a criminal appeal.

This is the case even where, as in subsection (1)(*c*), the aggrieved party or parties were not convicted in the original criminal proceedings, or, as in the hypothetical instance above where our Edinburgh firearms dealer had no involvement in the proceedings, and lived elsewhere in Great Britain, but could properly regard himself as aggrieved by the court's decision.

A wide range of parties could have a locus to appeal against a section 45 ruling. Quite apart from the convicted dealer, his partners, fellow directors and employees, prospective employers of these persons in the firearms trade and prospective purchasers of the dealer's business could all qualify as having an interest in reviewing the court's decision by way of section 45(3).

2–20–07 (d) It is noted that no timescale is stipulated in the Act to limit the operation of a court order under section 45(1). It is open to question whether in imposing an order the court can limit the period of its currency—an approach which would treat the order as part of the sentencing process and variable depending upon the circumstances of the offence, or as a peremptory order without limit of time.

(e) Subsection (2)(*a*) mentions offences specifically relating to **2–20–08** air weapons; section 57(3) statutorily defines these as sections 22(4), 22(5), 23(1) and 24(4).

PART III

LAW ENFORCEMENT AND PUNISHMENT OF OFFENCES

Power of search with warrant

46.—(1) If a justice of the peace, or in Scotland, the sheriff [1] **3–01–01** . . ., is satisfied by information on oath that there is reasonable ground for suspecting that an offence relevant for the purposes of this section has been, is being, or is about to be committed, he may grant a search warrant authorising a constable [[2] named therein]—

> (*a*) to enter at any time any premises or place named in the warrant, if necessary by force, and to search the premises or place and every person found there;
>
> (*b*) to seize and detain any firearm [[3], imitation firearm] or ammunition which he may find on the premises or place, or on any such person, in respect of which or in connection with which he has reasonable ground for suspecting that an offence relevant for the purposes of this section has been, is being or is about to be committed; and
>
> (*c*) if the premises are those of a registered firearms dealer, to examine any books relating to the business.

(2) The offences relevant for the purposes of this section are **3–01–02** all offences under this Act except an offence under section 22(3) or an offence relating specifically to air weapons.

NOTES

(1) Words deleted by the Local Government (Scotland) Act 1973, Sched. 29.
(2) Repealed (England and Wales only) by the Police and Criminal Evidence Act 1984, s.121, Sched. 7, Pt. I.
(3) Inserted by the Firearms Act 1994, s.2(2).

OBSERVATIONS

(a) The general powers of entry and search are found in this **3–01–03** section. The offences excluded from its provisions are section 22(3), dealing with carriage or possession of exposed shot guns by persons under 15 years, and sections 22(4) and (5), 23(1) and 24(4). Although section 1(3)(*b*) of the Act deals specifically with air guns, and distinguishes between specially dangerous and other air weapons, it does so to exclude low-power air weapons from the certification requirements applicable to all other firearms, and does not create an offence.

3–01–04 Weapons powered by gases other than air are not exempted from these entry and search powers. It is arguable whether the category of de-activated weapons introduced by section 8 of the 1988 Act, which are declared not to be firearms, are to be regarded as imitation firearms and thus subject to the Act's provisions. There is a case for viewing de-activated weapons as an entirely separate species currently beyond the ambit of the Act.

(b) See section 50, *infra*, which empowers the police during a search under warrant to arrest any person found there, reasonably believed to be committing a relevant offence.

Powers of constables to stop and search

3–02–01 47.—(1) A constable may require any person whom he has reasonable cause to suspect—

> (*a*) of having a firearm, with or without ammunition, with him in a public place; or
>
> (*b*) to be committing or about to commit, elsewhere than in a public place, an offence relevant for the purposes of this section,

to hand over the firearm or any ammunition for examination by the constable.

(2) It is an offence for a person having a firearm or ammunition with him to fail to hand it over when required to do so by a constable under subsection (1) of this section.

3–02–02 (3) If a constable has reasonable cause to suspect a person of having a firearm with him in a public place, or to be committing or about to commit, elsewhere than in a public place, an offence relevant for the purposes of this section, the constable may search that person and may detain him for the purpose of doing so.

3–02–03 (4) If a constable has reasonable cause to suspect that there is a firearm in a vehicle in a public place, or that a vehicle is being or is about to be used in connection with the commission of an offence relevant for the purposes of this section elsewhere than in a public place, he may search the vehicle and for that purpose require the person driving or in control of it to stop it.

(5) For the purpose of exercising the powers conferred by this section a constable may enter any place.

(6) The offences relevant for the purposes of this section are those under section 18(1) and (2) and 20 of this Act.

OBSERVATIONS

(a) Section 50(2), *infra*, confers upon the police a power of **3–02–04** arrest without warrant and a power of entry to places without warrant to acquit their duties under section 47.

(b) It is hard to see why subsection (6) refers as it does to section 18(1) and (2) rather than simply to section 18. Contravention of section 18(1) is a relevant offence in England and Wales, but not in Scotland; read in isolation section 47 would only apply to alleged contraventions of section 20 in Scotland. To give full effect to the provisions in Scotland, section 50(2), *infra*, gives a power of arrest without warrant for suspected contraventions of section 18. This is a cumbersome expedient leaving a nagging suspicion that the provisions applying to Scotland were tacked on as an untidy afterthought.

Production of certificates

48.—(1) A constable may demand, from any person whom he **3–03–01** believes to be in possession of a firearm or ammunition to which section 1 of this Act applies, or of a shot gun, the production of his firearm certificate or, as the case may be, his shot gun certificate.

[¹ (1A) Where a person upon whom a demand has been made by a constable under subsection (1) above and whom the constable believes to be in possession of a firearm fails —

(*a*) to produce a firearm certificate or, as the case may be, a shot gun certificate;

(*b*) to show that he is a person who, by reason of his place of residence or any other circumstances, is not entitled to be issued with a document identifying that firearm under any of the provisions which in the other member States correspond to the provisions of this Act for the issue of European firearms passes; or

(*c*) to show that he is in possession of the firearm exclusively in connection with the carrying on of activities in respect of which, he or the person on whose behalf he has possession of the firearm, is recognised, for the purposes of the law of another member State relating to firearms,

as a collector of firearms or a body concerned in the cultural or historical aspects of weapons,
the constable may demand from that person the production of a document which has been issued to that person in another member State under any such corresponding provisions, identifies that firearm as a firearm to which it relates and is for the time being valid.]

3–03–02 (2) If a person upon whom a demand is made under this section fails to produce the certificate [² or document] or to permit the constable to read it, or to show that he is entitled by virtue of this Act to have the firearm, ammunition or shot gun in his possession without holding a certificate, the constable may seize and detain the firearm, ammunition or shot gun and may require the person to declare to him immediately his name and address.

(3) If under this section a person is required to declare to a constable his name and address, it is an offence for him to refuse to declare it or to fail to give his true name and address.

[³ (4) It is an offence for a person who is in possession of a firearm to fail to comply with a demand under subsection (1A) above.]

NOTES

(1) Inserted by S.I. 1992 No. 2328 regulation 7(2).
(2) Inserted by S.I. above, reg. 7(3).
(3) Inserted by S.I. above, reg. 7(4).

Police powers in relation to arms traffic

3–04–01 **49.**—(1) [¹ A constable] may search for and seize any firearms or ammunition which he has reason to believe are being removed, or to have been removed, in contravention of an order made under section 6 of this Act or of a corresponding Northern Irish order within the meaning of subsection (3)(*c*) of that section.

3–04–02 (2) A person having the control or custody of any firearms or ammunition in course of transit shall, on demand by a constable, allow him all reasonable facilities for the examination and inspection thereof and shall produce any documents in his possession relating thereto.

(3) It is an offence for a person to fail to comply with subsection (2) of this section.

NOTE

(1) Words substituted by the 1988 Act, s.23(3).

OBSERVATIONS

The terms of subsection (2) above are extensive and do not **3–04–03**
merely relate to the remover of the weapons or ammunition.
Control or custody can be widely construed and could refer to
both the carrier and sender (or recipient) depending on factual
circumstances. Note too that the obligation upon parties to
produce documents to the police extends to documents in their
possession and is not simply confined to the production of
documents they have with them.

H.M. Customs and Excise are also empowered to stop and
search vehicles or vessels with the assistance of the police,
armed forces or coastguard where there are reasonable grounds
for suspicion that goods being carried are "in the course of
being unlawfully removed from or to any place": see the
Customs and Excise Management Act 1979, section 163(1)(*b*).

Special powers of arrest

50.—(1) A constable making a search of premises under the **3–05–01**
authority of a warrant under section 46 of this Act may arrest
without warrant any person found on the premises whom he has
reason to believe to be guilty of an offence relevant for the
purposes of that section.

(2) A constable may arrest without warrant any person whom
he has reasonable cause to suspect to be committing an offence
under section 19, 20, 21 or 47(2) of this Act and, for the purpose
of exercising the power conferred by this subsection, may enter
any place.

In Scotland, this subsection shall have effect with the inclusion
of a reference to an offence under section 4, 5 or 18 of this Act.

(3) A constable may arrest without warrant a person who
refuses to declare his name and address when required to do so
under section 48(2) of this Act, or whom he in such a case
suspects of giving a false name and address or of intending to
abscond.

Prosecution and punishment of offences

51.—(1) Part I of Schedule 6 to this Act shall have effect with **3–06–01**

respect to the way in which offences under this Act are punishable on conviction.

(2) In relation to an offence under a provision of this Act specified in the first column of the Schedule (the general nature of the offence being described in the second column), —

(*a*) the third column shows whether the offence is punishable on summary conviction or on indictment or either in one way or the other; and

(*b*) the fourth column shows the maximum punishment by way of fine or imprisonment under this Act which may be imposed on a person convicted of the offence in the way specified in relation thereto in the third column (that is to say, summarily or on indictment), any reference in the fourth column to a period of years or months being construed as a reference to a term of imprisonment of that duration.

3–06–02   (3) The provisions contained in Part II of Schedule 6 to this Act (being provisions as to the inclusion in an indictment in Scotland of certain summary offences, the punishments which may be imposed when a person is convicted of more than one offence arising out of the same set of circumstances, alternative verdicts and the orders which, in certain cases, a court may make when a person is convicted by or before it) shall have effect in relation to such of the offences specified in Part I of that Schedule as are indicated by entries against those offences in the fifth column of that Part.

(4) Notwithstanding [¹ section 127(1) of the Magistrates' Courts Act 1980] or [² section 331 of the Criminal Procedure (Scotland) Act 1975] (limitation of time for taking proceedings) summary proceedings for an offence under this Act, other than an offence under section 22(3) or an offence relating specifically to air weapons, may be instituted at any time within four years after the commission of the offence:

Provided that no such proceedings shall be instituted in England after the expiration of six months after the commission of the offence unless they are instituted by, or by the direction of, the Director of Public Prosecutions.

NOTES

(1) Amended (England and Wales) by the Magistrates' Courts Act 1980, s.154 and Sched. 7, para. 72.
(2) Amended (Scotland) by the Criminal Procedure (Scotland) Act 1975, s.460(1)(*b*).

OBSERVATIONS

(a) Section 51(4) is further extended by the 1988 Act, section **3–06–03**
25(5) to include offences created by that Act.

(b) The proviso in subsection (4) plainly does not extend to
Scotland. Presumably the reference to England in this context is
intended to include Wales.

(c) The effect of subsection (3) above was to permit the libelling
of what could be summary charges of possession of a section 1
firearm or ammunition, or a shot gun, without a certificate along
with the (potentially) more serious charges found later in the
Act. Paragraph 1 of Part II to Schedule 6 applied only to
Scotland and was intended to overcome pleas of double
jeopardy, but has since been repealed by the Criminal Justice
(Scotland) Act 1980, section 83(3), Schedule 8.

**Forfeiture and disposal of firearms; cancellation of certificate
by convicting court**

    52.—(1) Where a person —   **3–07–01**
    (*a*) is convicted of an offence under this Act (other than an
        offence under section 22(3) or an offence relating specifi-
        cally to air weapons) or is convicted of a crime for which
        he is sentenced to imprisonment, [¹ . . .] or detention in a
        detention centre or in a young offenders' institution in
        Scotland [² or is subject to a secure training order];
    (*b*) has been ordered to enter into a recognizance to keep
        the peace or to be of good behaviour, a condition of
        which is that he shall not possess, use or carry a firearm;
        or
    (*c*) is subject to a probation order containing a requirement
        that he shall not possess, use or carry a firearm; or
    (*d*) has, in Scotland, been ordained to find caution a condi-
        tion of which is that he shall not possess, use or carry a
        firearm,
the court by or before which he is convicted, or by which the
order is made, may make such order as to the forfeiture or
disposal of any firearm or ammunition found in his possession
as the court thinks fit and may cancel any firearm certificate or
shot gun certificate held by him.

    (2) Where the court cancels a certificate under this section — **3–07–02**
    (*a*) the court shall cause notice to be sent to the chief officer
        of police by whom the certificate was granted; and

(*b*) the chief officer of police shall by notice in writing require the holder of the certificate to surrender it; and

(*c*) it is an offence for the holder to fail to surrender the certificate within twenty-one days from the date of the notice given him by the chief officer of police.

(3) A constable may seize and detain any firearm or ammunition which may be the subject of an order for forfeiture under this section.

(4) A court of summary jurisdiction or, in Scotland, the sheriff may, on the application of the chief officer of police, order any firearm or ammunition seized and detained by a constable under this Act to be destroyed or otherwise disposed of.

NOTES

(1) Words repealed by the Criminal Justice Act 1988, s.123(6) and 170(2) and Sched. 8, para. 6 and Sched. 16.
(2) Inserted by the Criminal Justice and Public Order Act 1994, Sched. 10, para. 24.

OBSERVATION

3–07–03 Use of the word "may" in subsection (3) would excuse the seizure by the police of firearms or ammunition or items mistakenly believed to be the subject of a forfeiture order. Now that sections 27 and 28 of the Act as amended require that certificates, whenever possible, include the identification numbers of weapons included in the certificate (a similar provision also applying to European Firearms Passes) the risk of erroneous seizure ought to be much reduced.

PART IV

MISCELLANEOUS AND GENERAL

Rules for implementing this Act

53.—The Secretary of State may by statutory instrument make **4–01–01** rules—

(*a*) prescribing the form of certificates under this Act, and the register required to be kept under section 40 of this Act and other documents;

(*b*) prescribing any other thing which under this Act is to be prescribed; and

(*c*) generally for carrying this Act into effect;

and rules made under this section may make different provision for different cases.

NOTE

(1) The provisions of s.53 to 56 and s.58 are held also to apply to the provisions of the 1988 Act by s.25(7) thereof.

Application of Parts I and II to Crown servants

54.—(1) Sections 1, 2, 7 to 13 and 26 to 32 of this Act apply, **4–02–01** subject to the modifications specified in subsection (2) of this section, to persons in the service of Her Majesty in their capacity as such so far as those provisions relate to the purchase and acquisition, but not so far as they relate to the possession, of firearms.

(2) The modifications referred to above are the following:—

(*a*) a person in the service of Her Majesty duly authorised in writing in that behalf may purchase or acquire firearms and ammunition for the public service without holding a certificate under this Act;

(*b*) a person in the naval, military or air service of Her Majesty shall, if he satisfies the chief officer of police on an application under section 26 of this Act that he is required to purchase a firearm or ammunition for his own use in his capacity as such, be entitled without payment of any fee to the grant of a firearm certificate authorising the purchase or acquisition or, as the case may be, to the grant of a shot gun certificate.

[¹ (3) For the purposes of this section and of any rule of law whereby any provision of this Act does not bind the Crown, a person shall be deemed to be in the service of Her Majesty if he is —

(*a*) a member of a police force, or

(*b*) a person employed by a police authority who is under the direction and control of a chief officer of police.]

NOTE

(1) Substituted by the Police and Magistrates' Courts Act 1994, s.42.

OBSERVATIONS

4–02–02 (a) These provisions extend to the 1988 Act. See Note (a) to section 53 above.

(b) Subsection (3) was extended by the Atomic Energy Authority (Special Constables) Act 1976 to members of that police force. The changes wrought by the 1994 Act above simply extend this provision to civilian staff employed by police forces. The subsection has also been extended to include officers of the French Republic engaged in policing the control zone formed by the Channel Tunnel and the trains within the tunnel system: see the Channel Tunnel (International Arrangements) Order 1994 (S.I. 1994 No. 1813), art. 7(2), which came into force on August 2, 1994. Reciprocal powers of arrest, including the arrest of police officers, and matters of jurisdiction are dealt with in this Order.

(c) The route available to military personnel to obtain their own firearm or shot gun certificate without fee, as provided by subsection (2)(*b*), was not that followed by Colonel Burditt (see 2-01-04 above), and seems not to have been an option in his circumstances. Note, however, that unusually in the Act, the subsection refers to "the chief officer of police" without the rider "for the area in which the [applicant] resides". Presumably an application should be directed to the police in the area where the applicant is to be found at that time.

The reference to section 26 in section 54(1) suggests that an appeal procedure is available to an unsuccessful applicant; logically it would seem that an application under section 54 could be refused on exactly the same grounds as any other.

There are no reported cases on this question.

Exercise of police functions

4–03–01 **55.**—(1) Rules made under section 53 of this Act may —

(*a*) regulate the manner in which chief officers of police are to carry out their duties under this Act;

(*b*) enable all or any of the functions of a chief officer of police to be discharged by a deputy in the event of his illness or absence, or of a vacancy in the office of chief officer of police.

(2) Without prejudice to subsection (1)(*b*) of this section, the functions of a chief officer of police under this Act shall be exercisable on any occasion by a person, or a person of a particular class, authorised by the chief officer of police to exercise that function on that occasion, or on occasions of that class or on all occasions.

Service of notices

56.—Any notice required or authorised by this Act to be **4–04–01** given to a person may be sent by registered post or by recorded delivery service in a letter addressed to him at his last or usual place of abode or, in the case of a registered firearms dealer, at any place of business in respect of which he is registered.

Interpretation

57.—(1) In this Act, the expression "firearm" means a lethal **4–05–01** barrelled weapon of any description from which any shot, bullet or other missile can be discharged and includes —

(*a*) any prohibited weapon, whether it is such a lethal weapon as aforesaid or not; and

(*b*) any component part of such a lethal or prohibited weapon; and

(*c*) any accessory to any such weapon designed or adapted to diminish the noise or flash caused by firing the weapon;

and so much of section 1 as excludes any description of firearm from the category of firearms to which that section applies shall be construed as also excluding component parts of, and accessories to, firearms of that description.

(2) In this Act, the expression "ammunition" means ammuni- **4–05–02** tion for any firearm and includes grenades, bombs and other like missiles, whether capable of use with a firearm or not, and also includes prohibited ammunition.

[¹ (2A) In this Act "self-loading" and "pump-action" in **4–05–03** relation to any weapon mean respectively that it is designed or adapted (otherwise than as mentioned in section 5(1)(*a*)) so that it is automatically re-loaded or that it is so designed or adapted that it is re-loaded by the manual operation of the fore-end or forestock of the weapon.

4–05–04   (2B) In this Act "revolver", in relation to a smooth-bore gun, means a gun containing a series of chambers which revolve when the gun is fired.]

(3) For purposes of sections 45, 46, 50, 51(4) and 52 of this Act, the offences under this Act relating specifically to air weapons are those under sections 22(4), 22(5), 23(1) and 24(4).

(4) In this Act —

"acquire" means hire, accept as a gift or borrow and "acquisition" shall be construed accordingly;

"air weapon" has the meaning assigned to it by section 1(3)(*b*) of this Act;

[² "another member State" means a member State other than the United Kingdom, and "other member States" shall be construed accordingly;]

"area" means a police area;

[² "Article 7 authority" means a document issued by virtue of section 32A(1)(*b*) or (2) of this Act;]

"certificate" (except in a context relating to the registration of firearms dealers) and "certificate under this Act" mean a firearm certificate or shot gun certificate and —

(*a*) "firearm certificate" means a certificate granted by a chief officer of police under this Act in respect of any firearm or ammunition to which section 1 of this Act applies and includes a certificate granted in Northern Ireland under section 1 of the Firearms Act 1920 or under an enactment of the Parliament of Northern Ireland amending or substituted for that section; and

(*b*) "shot gun certificate" means a certificate granted by a chief officer of police under this Act and authorising a person to possess shot guns;

[² "European firearms pass" means a document to which the holder of a certificate under this Act is entitled by virtue of section 32A(1)(*a*) of this Act;

"European weapons directive" means the directive of the Council of the European Communities No. 91/477EEC (directive on the control of the acquisition and possession of weapons);]

"firearms dealer" means a person who, by way of trade or business, manufactures, sells, transfers, repairs, tests or proves firearms or ammunition to which section 1 of this Act applies, or shot guns;

"imitation firearm" means any thing which has the appearance of being a firearm (other than such a weapon as is mentioned in section 5(1)(b) of this Act) whether or not it is capable of discharging any shot, bullet or other missile;
. . . [3]

"premises" includes any land;

"prescribed" means prescribed by rules made by the Secretary of State under section 53 of this Act;

"prohibited weapon" and "prohibited ammunition" have the meanings assigned to them by section 5(2) of this Act;

"public place" includes any [4]highway and any other premises or place to which at the material time the public have or are permitted to have access, whether on payment or otherwise;

"registered", in relation to a firearms dealer, means registered either —

    (*a*) in Great Britain, under section 33 of this Act, or

    (*b*) in Northern Ireland, under section 8 of the Firearms Act 1920 or any enactment of the Parliament of Northern Ireland amending or substituted for that section,

  and references to "the register", "registration" and a "certificate of registration" shall be construed accordingly, except in section 40,

[[5] "rifle" includes carbine;]

"shot gun" has the meaning assigned to it by section 1(3) (*a*) of this Act and, in sections 3(1) and 45(2) of this Act and in the definition of "firearms dealer", includes any component part of a shot gun and any accessory to a shot gun designed or adapted to diminish the noise or flash caused by firing the gun;

"slaughtering instrument" means a firearm which is specially designed or adapted for the instantaneous slaughter of animals or for the instantaneous stunning of animals with a view to slaughtering them; and

"transfer" includes let on hire, give, lend and part with possession, and "transferee" and "transferor" shall be construed accordingly.

4–05–05   [⁶ (4A) For the purposes of any reference in this Act to the use of any firearm or ammunition for a purpose not authorised by the European weapons directive, the directive shall be taken to authorise the use of a firearm or ammunition as or with a slaughtering instrument and the use of a firearm or ammunition —

    (*a*) for sporting purposes;

    (*b*) for the shooting of vermin, or, in the course of carrying on activities in connection with the management of any estate, of other wildlife; and

    (*c*) for competition purposes and target shooting outside competitions.]

(5) The definitions in subsections (1) to (3) above apply to the provisions of this Act except where the context otherwise requires.

4–05–06   (6) For purposes of this Act —

    (*a*) the length of the barrel of a firearm shall be measured from the muzzle to the point at which the charge is exploded on firing; and

    (*b*) a shot gun or an air weapon shall be deemed to be loaded if there is ammunition in the chamber or barrel or in any magazine or other device which is in such a position that the ammunition can be fed into the chamber or barrel by the manual or automatic operation of some part of the gun or weapon.

4–05–07 NOTES

(1) Inserted by the 1988 Act, s.25(2).
(2) Inserted by S.I. 1992 No. 2823, reg.5(2).
(3) The definition of "indictable offence" was deleted by the Criminal Law Act 1977, Sched. 13.
(4) For Scotland only: the word "highway" in the definition of "public place" is deleted, and inserted in its place is "road (within the meaning of the Roads (Scotland) Act 1984)" as inserted by said Act, s.156(1), Sched. 9, para. 62.
(5) Inserted by the 1988 Act, s.25(3).
(6) Subsection 4A introduced by S.I. 1992 No. 2823, reg.3(5).

OBSERVATIONS

4–05–08   As can be seen the definitions above are lengthy and fundamental to the working of the Act. The principal definitions are discussed individually below for ease of use.

(a) FIREARM.

It is important not to employ the certification provisions of the Act, which apply only to some weapons, ammunition and components, as the determinant of what are, or are not, firearms. The statutory definition is all-encompassing and refers to section 1 firearms, all shot guns, air weapons (whether low or high-powered), all gas propelled weapons and all imitation firearms which are converted or readily capable of conversion to discharge bullets or other projectiles.

In addition as *Flack v. Baldry* and *R. v. Bradish* (cited at 1–05–16 and 1–05–12 above) demonstrate a weapon designed to discharge a noxious thing, in those cases a high-voltage electric current and a CS gas canister respectively, falls within the scope of the Act along with what would conventionally considered to be firearms.

(b) BARREL: definition and length.   **4–05–09**

Given the statutory definition of a firearm at section 57(1) it may be surprising that a rubber-powered speargun which was designed to fire harpoons which were directed via two guide barrels — a weapon much like a crossbow in design — was held to be a section 1 firearm. In the case in question, *Boyd v. McGlennan*, 1994 S.L.T. 1148; 1993 S.C.C.R. 861 it was noted that the barrel was not continuous and the Lord Justice General in his judgment indicated (1994 S.L.T. 1148 at 1149L):

> "It appears to us that it is not a requirement of the definition [lethal barrelled weapon] that the barrel must be continuous. So far as the function is concerned, the two parts of it both appear to have the function of a barrel, in that they are designed to control and guide the harpoon when it is fired. It is clear that the entire projectile is not contained within the barrel before it is fired from the speargun. The harpoon does not pass along either part of the barrel for its entire length when being fired. But here again there is nothing in the definition that appears to us to require that the missile should do so. The sheriff reached the conclusion that this was a firearm with some hesitation. He may well have hesitated because at first sight it might not appear that a speargun of this design was a firearm — although we note that, when charged with a contravention of s1(1)(a) of the 1968 Act, the appellant said that he had just got the weapon and was coming down to see about a certificate."

This appeal was refused. Police tests established that the maximum power generated on firing was comparable to that of a .38 Smith and Wesson bullet.

4–05–10 Note that the statutory definition of barrel length is at section 57(5) of the Act, and this is of some importance since a shot gun whose barrels have been produced, or adapted, to measure under 24 inches in length ceases to be certificated as a shot gun and would require to be licensed (if the police felt able to grant a weapon such as this a certificate) as a section 1 weapon. Section 4 enumerates the offences rising from unauthorised possession of a shortened shot gun (an aggravated offence) or the unauthorised conversion of a gun to produce such a weapon.

The 1988 Act, section 6, has extended the provisions relating to the shortening of barrels to cover those shot guns which had been certificated as section 1 weapons.

The effects of restriction are discussed at 1–04–05, *supra*.

4–05–11 (c) LETHALITY.

Once the object has been identified as a firearm the issue is then to consider its potential lethality. In *Moore v. Gooderham* [1960] 1 W.L.R. 1308; [1960] 3 All E.R. 575, M was charged with selling a Diana-make airgun to a youth under 17 years old. (Although he was charged under section 19(1) of the Firearms Act 1937, the libel was for practical purposes identical to that in section 24(1) of the 1968 Act.) The justices acquitted him on the basis that the gun was not a lethal weapon, and so was not a firearm for the purposes of the Act.

Delivering judgment following a Crown appeal, Lord Parker C.J. ([1960] 1 W.L.R. 1308 at 1310) noted that the only issue was whether the gun was a firearm subject to the Act or not, and added:

> "[The justices] held that it was not, and they came to that conclusion really on the ground that, having regard to the definition in section 32(1) and, in particular, the word lethal, the weapon in question must be one likely to cause injury of the sort which might result in death. They rejected a contention that a lethal weapon was one which was merely capable of causing injury which was unlikely to cause death. In saying that, I understand that they were giving effect to the word lethal in this sense, that the weapon must be of a sort which cause injury of a type from which death would in the ordinary way result. I think that they were fully entitled to give to the word lethal the sense that the injury must be of a kind which may cause death. That is the ordinary meaning of the word,

but it is to be observed that in this connection one is not considering whether a firearm is designed or intended to cause injury from which death results, but rather whether it is a weapon which, however misused, may cause injury from which death may result. . . . Section 19 is designed to prevent, amongst other things, a weapon getting into the hands of a very small child who may misuse it by firing it point blank, and point blank, say, at an eye or ear, or some particularly vulnerable part; and if it is capable of causing more than trifling and trivial injury when misused, then it is a weapon which is capable of causing injury from which death may result."

His Lordship moved to consider the terms of the case stated before finding that the weapon, capable of misuse, fulfilled his test of lethality.

(d) COMPONENT PARTS OF FIREARMS AND PRO- 4–05–12
HIBITED WEAPONS.

The Act is clear that possession of component parts of section 1 and section 5 firearms requires the holding of a firearm certificate or other lawful authority. The effect of the exclusion in section 57(1) is that this does not extend to component parts of shot guns, except those mentioned at 1–01–13 equipped with a magazine, which are treated as section 1 firearms. It is also worth noting that section 41 of the Act allows the police a discretion to exempt from registration procedures a firearms dealer whose business is confined to manufacturing, testing or repairing component parts or accessories for shot guns.

It has been held that possession of a firearm subject to either 4–05–13 section 1 or 5 of the Act without the requisite authority is an absolute offence; by analogy, this might also be said of component parts for such firearms. However, in *R. v. Bradish*, which is discussed at 1–05–12, while repeating that strict liability was a feature of offences against both sections, Auld J. did hint at the possibility that a *mens rea* defence might arise "in relation to some small part of an automatic weapon, perhaps not readily identifiable as such on its own". That apparent concession has not been tested, but it would be difficult for a firearms dealer particularly to rely upon.

The cases of *R. v. Pannell* and *R. v. Clarke (Frederick)*, cited and discussed at 1–05–19 to 1–05–20 above, are pertinent.

4–05–14   It should be appreciated that even where a weapon has been dismantled or disassembled, and might arguably no longer constitute a firearm, the possession of its component parts could still provide an avenue leading to conviction of the possessor. The problem is in defining what would be considered as component parts necessary to the functioning of a firearm (which merit some degree of control) and those parts which are merely incidental and have no role peculiar to the firearm in question. It has been suggested that a more sensible approach would be to focus upon pressure-bearing parts of weapons, since without these a weapon would not fire.

4–05–15   (e) ACCESSORIES

The object of section 57(1)(*c*) is to preclude the circulation of sound moderators (more popularly known as silencers). The Act provides that such accessories have to be separately specified on any firearms certificate and cannot be lawfully possessed without a certificate. Weapons equipped with silencers or flash shields are not generally available in the United Kingdom. However, in *Broome v. Walter* [1989] Crim. L.R. 725, W, a registered firearms dealer, manufactured and sold a firearm equipped with a detachable muzzle intended to diminish the noise of the weapon. The sound moderator enclosed the barrel; the barrel itself was manufactured in two parts, and the muzzle section, incorporating the sound moderator, fitted on by means of a screw fitting. The gun could fire with one or both parts fitted to the weapon. The muzzle fitting was unique to the weapon concerned and could not be purchased separately.

W was prosecuted under section 3 of the Act, the Crown contending that the sound moderator itself constituted a firearm in terms of section 57(1)(*c*). The justices ruled that the fittings were integral parts of the weapon, not accessories requiring separate certification. On appeal this ruling was upheld, though it seems to be very much a matter of degree whether parts of a weapon fall to be considered as component parts of a certificated weapon (and hence exempt from additional certification) or accessories.

4–05–16   (f) AIR WEAPONS

See 1–01–16 to 1–01–18 above.

Peat v. Lees, 1994 S.L.T. 400; 1993 S.C.C.R. 256 illustrates an extreme result of the application of section 5(1)(*ac*) of the Act. The appellant traded in paintball guns which were used in executive wargames. Originally all the weapons seized by the police had been manufactured to operate by means of CO_2 cylinders, but several had been adapted to operate using air cylinders. The guns were all smooth-bore weapons, some operating by pump-action, others by a semi-automatic self-loading action. Despite the fact that the weapons generated no more power than many air weapons, they could in no wise be regarded as such since they were designed to be propelled by a gas other than air; what was worse for the appellant was that the configuration of the paint guns brought them into the realm of prohibited weapons. Defence counsel's efforts to distinguish the explosive chemical charge used as the propellant of a conventional firearm from the compressed force employed in these items (following the line of a similar unsuccessful submission in *R. v. Thorpe*) were rebuffed.

(g) IMITATION FIREARM
4–05–17

An imitation firearm will only require to be licensed if it has either been adapted to discharge a projectile or is capable of being so adapted. In the case of such an item, yet to be adapted, the Act provides a statutory defence in section 1(5) of the 1982 Act that the possessor did not know and had no reason to suspect the true nature of the article.

The Act does not distinguish between the use of a firearm or **4–05–18** an imitation firearm when sections 16(A), 17 or 18 are contravened: the potential penalties are the same. It is of note that the appearance of the imitation firearm at the time of its use, or intended use, in contravention of the Act is the factor that a jury must be directed to consider. In *R. v. Morris; R. v. King* [1984] Crim. L.R. 422, the appellants and a third man used what appeared to be a double-barrelled shot gun to rob a jeweller's shop of stock worth £10,493. The police later found two metal tubes bound with tape in K's car and, at trial, M pleaded guilty to robbery while K was convicted. Both men appealed against conviction, citing alleged misdirection by the trial judge as to the factors determining whether the article was an imitation firearm. The Court of Appeal approved the test outlined above; the jury had to evaluate the evidence of witnesses against whom the article was directed, or who saw it then or at a later time. No doubt evidence would need to be led to substantiate the strength of the resemblance between a real firearm and the item possessed by the accused.

See also the observations following the 1982 Act, *infra* at 6–05–01 onwards.

4–05–19 (h) TRANSFER

This issue is discussed in *Hall v. Cotton,* cited at 1–01–20.

Particular savings

4–06–01 **58.**—(1) Nothing in this Act shall apply to the proof houses of the Master, Wardens and Society of the Mystery of Gunmakers of the City of London and the guardians of the Birmingham proof house or the rifle range at Small Heath in Birmingham where firearms are sighted and tested, so as to interfere in any way with the operations of those two companies in proving firearms under the provisions of the Gun Barrel Proof Act 1868 or any other Acts for the time being in force, or to any person carrying firearms to or from any such proof house when being taken to such proof house for the purposes of proof or being removed therefrom after proof.

4–06–02 (2) Nothing in this Act relating to firearms shall apply to an antique firearm which is sold, transferred, purchased, acquired or possessed as a curiosity or ornament.

(3) The provisions of this Act relating to ammunition shall be in addition to and not in derogation of any enactment relating to the keeping and sale of explosives.

(4) The powers of arrest and entry conferred by Part III of this Act shall be without prejudice to any power of arrest or entry which may exist apart from this Act; and section 52(3) of this Act is not to be taken as prejudicing the power of a constable, when arresting a person for an offence, to seize property found in his possession or any other power of a constable to seize firearms, ammunition or other property, being a power exercisable apart from that subsection.

(5) Nothing in this Act relieves any person using or carrying a firearm from his obligation to take out a licence to kill game under the enactments requiring such a licence.

NOTE

(1) Following the Home Secretary's announcement on July 20, 1994, it seems probable that licences to hunt game will soon be abolished.

OBSERVATIONS

4–06–03 Parliament and the courts alike have declined to provide a definitive meaning for the phrase "antique firearm". An antique weapon is exempted from the certification requirements of the Act only when it is not used, or maintained for use, as a firearm but is kept as a curiosity or ornament.

It is apparent that age alone is not sufficient for categorisation as antique: other factors such as historical or scientific interest, design or workmanship, rarity and value may all have to be scrutinised before a weapon can be regarded as antique.

An imperfect rule of thumb may be that no weapon which could have been available for use in a war this century will be likely to meet the definition, but it will always be a matter of fact and degree. An honest but erroneous belief that a weapon is antique affords no defence.

The case of *R. v. Howells* [1977] Q.B. 614; [1977] 2 W.L.R. **4-06-04** 716; [1977] 3 All E.R. 417 centred upon these issues and the question, already discussed at 1-05-12 above, of whether strict liability attached to possession of a section 1 firearm. H had been convicted of possession of a muzzle-loading percussion revolver without holding a firearm certificate, four other weapons in his possession being ruled, or conceded to be, antiques. Expert evidence established that the revolver was a reproduction probably manufactured within the last 25 years, not in 1860 as the defendant imagined.

In his judgment, Browne L.J. paraphrased defence counsel's submissions thus ([1972] 2 W.L.R. 716 at 719F):

"The first one related to section 58(2), and it was his contention that that subsection should be read as implying that it is subject to a subjective test or element, namely, that of honest and reasonable belief. In other words he submitted that the exclusion from the Act of antique firearms includes those where the seller etc. or the possessor honestly and reasonably believed that the firearm was an antique. One of the arguments put forward in support of this interpretation is based on the words 'possessed as a curiosity or ornament,' which, it was submitted, indicates a subjective element.

A second submission related to section 1 of the 1968 Act, and it was that that provision was not one of strict liability and therefore there was a defence of honest and mistaken belief open to a person charged under that section. It was submitted in the alternative that if the Act was one importing strict liability, then a person does not possess 'a firearm' if he honestly and reasonably believes it to be an antique, as that would amount to possession of something which is of a different nature. . . . What was submitted by [H's counsel in his interpretation of section 58(2)] was that this exclusion from the Act, which was necessary to protect bona fide dealers in and collectors of antique firearms, would be substantially lost if a victim of a fake could not claim that he had an honest and reasonable belief that the firearm was an antique.

We are quite unable to accept this interpretation. This subsection relates to facts and not beliefs; what is excluded is that which is an antique which is sold or possessed as a curiosity or ornament. There is no room, in our opinion, for any other exclusions such as those firearms which are believed by the possessor to be antiques."

4-06-05 Within a month of this judgment the problems of defining "antique" were before the Queen's Bench Division in a prosecution appeal against the dismissal by Greater Manchester magistrates of informations laid by the Chief Constable. In this case, *Richards v. Curwen* [1977] 1 W.L.R. 747; [1977] 3 All E.R. 426, the defendant was prosecuted for the uncertificated possession of two revolvers, which were 83 and 85 years old respectively and which hung on a wall in his livingroom. C was a collector of old firearms and the magistrates held that he had no intention of firing the weapons or keeping them in working use. Subsequent tests showed that each gun could be fired, albeit with some difficulty.

While arguing that antiquity was a matter of fact and degree, counsel for the appellant referred the court to the Pistols Act 1903, which had defined the term "antique pistol", as a guide to construction, and proposed a historical test — say the lapse of a specific passage of time, perhaps 100 years. The court found no assistance in reference to a long-repealed statute; the provisions of the 1903 Act had been adopted in relation to pistols in the Firearms Act 1920 and both statutes were repealed by the 1937 Act, the main statutory predecessor to the 1968 Act.

More importantly, Lord Widgery C.J. ([1977] 1 W.L.R. 747 at 752E) stated:

"It is understandable enough that [the chief constable] would like to have a more precise definition of 'antique firearm' than Parliament has seen fit to give him. Unhappily

we cannot remedy this deficiency. It would be entirely wrong
for us to specify a particular age and say that everything over
that age was antique, and everything below that age was not.
The matter is left to the good sense and judgment of the fact-
finding tribunal".

This reasoning was repeated in *Bennett v. Brown* (1980) 71 **4‑06‑06**
Cr.App.R. 109 which focused upon three firearms found in
Brown's possession when not covered by a section 1 certificate.
The difficulty highlighted by Lord Widgery is shown in sharp
relief in this case: the Mauser rifle seized, which was dated
post-1905, was in working order; a Mauser pistol in poor
condition, dated post-1910 and modified to fire more readily-
available cartridges, subsequently could be made to fire, and an
Enfield .476 revolver dated circa 1886 was in full working order.
A watershed date of the sort proposed in *Howells* might well
have foundered in a situation of this sort.

Upholding the prosecutor's appeal against Brown's acquittal
by magistrates, Eveleigh L.J. noted at 111:

"The sole question . . . is whether the justices were entitled
to hold that the weapons in question qualified for the
description antique firearms. Nothing turns on whether they
were possessed as a curiosity or ornament. That matter was
decided on the evidence in favour of the respondent, and no
criticism is directed in that direction. However, counsel has
submitted in this Court that no reasonable Bench could come
to the conclusion that the weapons in this case were
antiques."

His Lordship noted the difficulty faced by the magistrates who
had been referred to *Richards v. Curwen,* and to Lord Widgery's
remarks, but continued (at 112):

"But turning to the weaponry in the present case, what
does one find? One finds that the rifle was manufactured
post-1905 and the pistol 1910 onwards. Both of those
weapons therefore could rightly be envisaged as weapons
used in the 1914-18 war. That I think is not drawing upon any
particular judicial knowledge, but upon public and general
knowledge. One would not expect an army to be equipped
with weapons that were only manufactured some six or seven

years before the war and would expect modern armies to use
weapons of much greater age than seven, eight or 10 years. It
seems that it would be quite impossible to say that any
weapon that could reasonably be envisaged as available for
use in a war this century could properly be regarded as
antique.

I therefore am of the opinion that the evidence does not
support the conclusion that the 8mm rifle and the Mauser
self-loading pistol were antique within the meaning of section
58(2).

In so far as the .476 revolver is concerned, I am prepared
to approach the matter on the basis that the justices were
entitled to come to that conclusion, although I feel bound to
say that it is not a conclusion I myself would have reached."

It is notable that while restating Lord Justice Eveleigh's view
of the age of weapons which would not qualify as antique,
Watkins J. tended to feel that the justices' conclusion about the
.476 revolver was well-founded.

4–06–07   The only Scottish decision of note in this area is *Walkingshaw
v. Wallace*, 1990 S.C.C.R. 203 which centred upon the accused's
failure to comply with his certificate's conditions as to security of
weapons, as well as the issue of antiquity. The weapon involved
was of historical significance, being the last successful single-shot
breechblock military rifle, produced in 1886, a weapon rendered
obsolete almost immediately by the production of military
repeater rifles.

Wallace believed the weapon to be an antique firearm, and
there was evidence that it had not been fired recently. Nonetheless the weapon was in full working order though no ammunition seems to have been seized from Wallace's home. The very
rarity of the rifle (the only other one in Scotland being in police
hands) made it most difficult, though not impossible, to secure
suitable ammunition. But as the sheriff pointed out (at 206E):

"The terms of the Act, however, do not require the Crown
to show that ammunition was present or available; all that is
required to bring a gun within the terms of the Act is for it to
be 'a lethal barrelled weapon . . . from which any . . . missile
can be discharged".

The police had tested their own, rather than the accused's
weapon, in an exercise which the defence expert, in the sheriff's

words, described as "madness as the gun itself could explode."
The exercise does appear to have impressed the sheriff who
commented at 206F:

> "The test of a firearm, however, is whether a shot *can* be
> discharged and I accept the evidence from the police officers
> that they successfully discharged two bullets from a similar
> gun and accordingly I believed that Mr Wallace was correct
> in the concession which he made when he ultimately gave
> evidence that this gun did count as a firearm as defined by
> section 57(1)".

It is submitted that test firing of a similar weapon was of
limited evidential value and only showed that ammunition could
be obtained for a weapon of this sort; it obviously could not
establish that the weapon in question was capable of discharging
a bullet or other projectile. That surely is the nub of the issue —
the Act refers to a lethal barrelled weapon, not to a type or
model of weapon capable of discharging, etc.

The truly significant factor was that the gun was found to be
in full working order, a fact which could be established without
the need for any firing and which firmly defined it to be a
firearm.

The issue remaining was whether the rifle was indeed an **4-06-08**
antique firearm. Sheriff Dickson put it thus at 207E:

> "The test is not whether the gun is 'an antique'. The word
> 'antique' is used as an adjective governing the noun 'firearm'
> and, accordingly, I consider it is necessary to consider
> whether the gun is 'an antique firearm' and not whether it is a
> firearm which is an antique. The difference, it seems to me, is
> that the wording of the Act is such that the history and
> importance of the gun come into consideration in addition to
> its age and any value it may have."

The sheriff held the gun to be an antique firearm, and as such,
exempt from the certification provisions which would otherwise
have applied to it. He concluded on a cautionary note at 209F:

> "I have reached my decision with some reluctance. I
> consider that the purpose of the Firearms Act is to provide
> protection for the public, and while I accept completely that
> Mr Wallace had no intention whatsoever of using this firearm

for its original purpose, the fact that it is capable of being so used and that ammunition can be obtained for it means that in the wrong hands this gun could be a danger to the public. Why Parliament should choose to exempt an antique firearm when a modern imitation of such an antique is not exempt (*R. v. Howells*) is perhaps difficult to understand when both, in the wrong hands, are equally dangerous. Until such a change in the law is made, however, the words "antique firearm" must have their ordinary meaning".

4–06–09 Wallace was acquitted; but supposing his rifle had not been ruled to be an antique but was found to be a firearm which was incapable of discharging any object, would he then have avoided the Act's provisions? Certainly he would not need a certificate for the gun, but he would still require to have a certificate for the component parts of the weapon in his possession. The mere fact that a gun could not function would not necessarily remove it from the scope of the Act. See *Grace v. D.P.P.* [1989] Crim.L.R. 365; but note that the weapon in that case was an airgun, one firearm whose component parts can be freely possessed.

4–06–10 (b) A guide to enforcement of the Firearms Acts for police use is provided by *Firearms Law: Guidance to the Police* (HMSO). The publication has no legal standing but is intended to assist in achieving uniform standards of enforcement.

Paragraph 2.7 of the guide indicates that all muzzle-loading weapons and some breechloaded guns chambered for obsolete cartridge types may be treated as antiques.

It also has to be recalled that the object of the European weapons directive is to develop a consistent policy for the free movement of legitimate firearms within Member States. The difficulty in achieving a workable definition of "antique firearm" has defied Parliament and the courts throughout this century; only the most extravagant optimist would anticipate more rapid progress by the E.C. States.

4–06–11 Section 5A of the Act, which added firearms disguised as other objects to the list of prohibited weapons, does not extend to antique disguised firearms which are sold, transferred, purchased, acquired or possessed as a curiosity or ornament. Firearms of this sort are particularly popular in Germany and commonly appear in the guise of walking-stick guns, purse-guns and cigarette or cigar cases.

Repeals and general savings

   59.—(1) ...   **4–07–01**

   (2) In so far as any certificate, authority or permit granted, order or rule made, registration effected, or other thing done under an enactment repealed by this Act could have been granted, made, effected or done under a corresponding provision of this Act, it shall not be invalidated by the repeal of that enactment but shall have effect as if granted, made, effected or done under that corresponding provision; and for the purposes of this provision anything which under section 33(1) or (2) of the Firearms Act 1937 had effect as if done under any enactment in that Act shall, so far as may be necessary for the continuity of the law, be treated as done under the corresponding enactment in this Act.

   (3) Any document referring to an enactment repealed by this Act or by the Firearms Act 1937 shall, so far as may be necessary for preserving its effect, be construed as referring, or as including a reference, to the corresponding enactment in this Act.

   (4) The mention of particular matters in this section shall not be taken to affect the general application of section 38 of the Interpretation Act 1889 with regard to the effect of repeals.

NOTE

(1) Subsection (1) serves to repeal the enactments listed in Sched. 7 to the Act.

Short title, commencement and extent

   60.—(1) This Act may be cited as the Firearms Act 1968.   **4–08–01**

   (2) This Act shall come into force on 1st August 1968.

   (3) This Act shall not extend to Northern Ireland.

SCHEDULES

OFFENCES TO WHICH SECTION 17(2) APPLIES

5–01–01

[¹ 1. Offences under section 1 of the Criminal Damage Act 1971.]
2. Offences under any of the following provisions of the Offences Against the Person Act 1861:—

> sections 20 to 22 (inflicting bodily injury; garrotting; criminal use of stupefying drugs);
> section 30 (laying explosive to building etc.);
> section 32 (endangering railway passengers by tampering with track);
> section 38 (assault with intent to commit felony or resist arrest);
> section 47 (criminal assaults);

[² . . .]
[³2A. Offences under Part I of the Child Abduction Act 1984 (abduction of children).]
3. [⁴ . . .]
[⁵ 4. Theft, [⁷ robbery], burglary, blackmail and any offence under section 12(1) (taking of motor vehicle or other conveyance without owner's consent) of the Theft Act 1968.]
5. Offences under section 51(1) of the Police Act 1964 or section 41 of the Police (Scotland) Act 1967 (assaulting constable in execution of his duty).
[⁷ 5A. An offence under section 90(1) of the Criminal Justice Act 1991 (assaulting prisoner custody officer).
5B. An offence under section 13(1) of the Criminal Justice and Public Order Act 1994 (assaulting secure training centre custody officer).]
6. Offences under any of the following provisions of the Sexual Offences Act 1956:-

> section 1 (rape);
> section 17, 18 and 20 (abduction of women).

7. [⁵. . .].
8. Aiding or abetting the commission of any offence specified in [⁵ paragraphs 1 to 6] of this Schedule.
9. Attempting to commit any offence so specified, . . .⁶

NOTES

(1) Paragraph 1 substituted by the Criminal Damage Act 1971, s.11(7).
(2) Paragraph 2 repealed by the Child Abduction Act 1984, s.11(5)(c).
(3) Paragraph 2A inserted by the last-mentioned Act, s.11(2).
(4) Paragraph 3 repealed by the Criminal Attempts Act 1981, s.10, Pt. II of the Schedule.
(5) Substituted by the Theft Act 1968, Sched. 2, Pt. III.
(6) Words deleted by the Criminal Damage Act 1971, Sched., Pt. I.
(7) Inserted by the Criminal Justice and Public Order Act 1994, Sched. 9.

OBSERVATIONS

(a) Paragraph 5 paraphrases in part section 51(1) of the Police   **5–01–02**

Act, which makes assault upon, or resistance or wilful obstruction of, a constable or a person assisting a constable in the execution of his duty, an offence.

Section 41 of the Police (Scotland) Act extends further and refers to an offence where a person assaults, resists, obstructs, molests or hinders a constable in the execution of his duty (or any person assisting a constable therein) or rescues or attempts to rescue, or assists or attempts to assist in the escape of a person in lawful custody.

It is curious that while the Police (Scotland) Act is mentioned in Schedule 1, no reference to the Police Act is made in Schedule 2, which applies only to Scotland.

5–01–03 (b) An aggravation (if it be possible) of an offence stipulated above is also subject to the provisions of the Schedule. See *R. v. Guy* (1991) 93 Cr.App.R. 108, discussed at 1–17–10; the charge in that case was robbery, an offence which is now specifically included in Schedule 1 by dint of the Criminal Justice and Public Order Act 1994.

5–02–01   SCHEDULE 2

OFFENCES TO WHICH SECTIONS 17(2) AND 18 APPLY IN SCOTLAND

Common Law Offences

1. Abduction
2. Administration of drugs with intent to enable or assist the commission of a crime.
3. Assault.
4. Housebreaking with intent to steal.
5. Malicious mischief.
6. Mobbing and rioting.
7. Perverting the course of justice.
8. Prison breaking and breaking into prison to rescue prisoners.
9. Rape.
10. Robbery.
11. Theft.
12. Use of threats with intent to extort money or property.
13. Wilful fireraising and culpable and reckless fireraising.

[*Statutory Offences*]

[¹ 13A. Offences against section 57 of the Civic Government (Scotland) Act 1982.]
14. . . . ¹
15. . . . ¹
16. Offences against sections 2, 3 or 4 of the Explosive Substances Act 1883.
[² 17. Offences against section 175 of the Road Traffic Act 1972.]
18. Offences against section 41 of the Police (Scotland) Act 1967.

[*Attempts*]

19. Attempt to commit any of the offences mentioned in this Schedule.

NOTES

(1) Paragraph 13A was inserted by the Civic Government (Scotland) Act 1982, s.137(2) and Sched. 3, para. 2. The same Act repealed para. 14 and 15 above.
(2) The Road Traffic Act 1988, s.178, superseded section 175 of the 1972 Act of that name. The Road Traffic Act 1988 makes no reference to this Schedule to the Firearms Acts; nor do the Road Traffic Offenders Act and the Road Traffic (Consequential Provisions) Act of that year.

OBSERVATION

For aggravations of offences stipulated above see Observation **5–02–02** (b) to Schedule 1.

SCHEDULE 3   **5–03–01**

JURISDICTION AND PROCEDURE ON APPLICATION UNDER SECTION 21(6)

[PART I]

APPLICATION TO [¹ THE CROWN COURT] (ENGLAND AND WALES)

1. . . . ²
2. Notice of the application, signed by the applicant or by his agent in his behalf and stating the general grounds of the application, shall be given by him to the [³ appropriate officer of the Crown Court] and also to the chief officer of police for the area in which the applicant resides.
3. On receiving notice of the application the [³ appropriate officer of the Crown Court] shall enter the application and give notice to the applicant, and to the chief officer of police to whom the notice of the application is required by

paragraph 2 of this Schedule to be given, of the date, time and place fixed for the hearing; but the date shall not be less than twenty-one clear days after the date when the [³ appropriate officer of the Crown Court] received the notice of the application.

4. The applicant may at any time, not less than two clear days before the date fixed for the hearing, abandon his application by giving notice in writing to the [³ appropriate officer of the Crown Court] and to the chief officer of police; and if he does so the [¹ Crown Court] (hereafter in this Schedule referred to as "the court") may order the applicant to pay the chief officer of police such costs as appear to it to be just and reasonable in respect of expenses properly incurred by him in connection with the application before notice of abandonment was given to him.

5. The chief officer of police may appear and be heard on the hearing of the application.

6. The court may from time to time adjourn the hearing of the application.

7. On the determination of the application, the court may make such order as to payment of costs as it thinks fit, and may fix a sum to be paid by way of costs in lieu of directing a taxation thereof, and any costs ordered to be paid by the court may be recovered summarily as a civil debt and shall not be recoverable in any other manner:

Provided that the chief officer of police shall not under this paragraph be ordered to pay the costs of the applicant.

5–03–02

PART II

APPLICATION TO SHERIFF (SCOTLAND)

8. The application shall be made to the sheriff within whose jurisdiction the applicant resides.

9. Not less than twenty-one days' notice of the application shall be given to the chief officer of police for the area in which the applicant resides.

NOTES

(1) Words substituted by the Courts Act 1971, s.56(2), and Sched. 9, Pt. II.
(2) Paragraph 1 was repealed by the above Act, Sched. 11, Pt. IV.
(3) Words substituted by the said Act, Sched. 8, Pt. I, para. 2.

OBSERVATIONS

5–03–03 This Schedule deals only with the forum, and form, of appeals by persons whose previous convictions have debarred them from lawfully possessing firearms or ammunition in accordance with section 21 of the Act. Appeals against refusal or revocation, etc., of certificates or dealer registration proceed in terms of Schedule 5.

It seems odd (given the thrust of the Firearms Acts) that a disqualified driver who seeks the early restoration of his driving licence has to apply to the court which imposed the disqualification while an individual seeking access to firearms, in the face of his criminal history, applies to the court where he lives, not to the court (or courts) which saw fit to imprison him. It is, of course, open to the police to present information to the court considering the application about the applicant's criminal background; the success of an application for removal of the prohibition does not end the matter — the successful applicant will still have to apply in the normal fashion for the grant of a certificate or for registration as a dealer. Note too that the Act provides no guidance to the court as to the test to be applied to applications arising from section 21(6).

SCHEDULE 4   **5–04–01**

PARTICULARS TO BE ENTERED BY FIREARMS DEALERS IN REGISTER OF TRANSACTIONS

1. The quantities and description of firearms and ammunition manufactured and the dates thereof.
2. The quantities and description of firearms and ammunition purchased or acquired with the names and addresses of the sellers or transferors and the dates of the several transactions.
3. The quantities and description of firearms and ammunition accepted for sale, repair, test, proof, cleaning, storage, destruction or other purpose, with the names and addresses of the transferors and the dates of the several transactions.
[¹ 4. The quantities and description of firearms and ammunition sold or transferred with the names and addresses of the purchasers or transferees and (except in cases where the purchaser or transferee is a registered dealer) the areas in which the firearms certificates were issued, and the dates of the several transactions.]
5. The quantities and description of firearms and ammunition in possession for sale or transfer at the date of the last stocktaking or such other date in each year as may be specified in the register.

NOTE

(1) Substituted (for England and Wales) by S.I. 1989 No. 854, art. 10(5) and (for Scotland) by S.I. 1989 No. 889, art. 10(5).

Firearms

SCHEDULE 5

PROVISIONS AS TO APPEALS UNDER S.44 OF THIS ACT

PART I

COURTS WITH JURISDICTION TO ENTERTAIN APPEAL

Nature of appeal	. . . [1]	Sheriff's jurisdiction
1. Appeal under section 26(4), 29(2) or 30(3) [2 and section 30(4) as amended].		The sheriff within whose jurisdiction the appellant lives.
2. Appeal under section 34(5) by a person aggrieved by police refusal to register him as a firearms dealer.		The sheriff within whose jurisdiction there is situated any place of business in respect of which the appellant has applied to be registered.
3. Appeal under section 34(5) or 37(3) by a person aggrieved by police refusal to enter a place of business of his in the register.		The sheriff within whose jurisdiction there is situated the place of business to which the appeal relates.
4. Appeal under section 36(3).		The sheriff within whose jurisdiction is situated the appellant's place of business in respect of which the condition is in force.
5. Appeal under section 38(7) by a person aggrieved by the removal of his name from the register.		The sheriff within whose jurisdiction there is situated any place of business in respect of which the appellant has been registered.
6. Appeal under section 38(76) by a person aggrieved by the removal from the register of a place of business of his.		The sheriff within whose jurisdiction is situated the place of business to which the appeal relates.

PROCEDURAL PROVISIONS FOR APPEAL TO [³ THE CROWN COURT]

1. Notice of an appeal, signed by the appellant or by his agent on his behalf and stating the general grounds of the appeal, shall be given by him to the [⁴ appropriate officer of the Crown Court] and also to the chief officer of police by whose decision the appellant is aggrieved.

2. A notice of appeal shall be given within twenty-one days after the date on which the appellant has received notice of the decision of the chief officer of police by which he is aggrieved.

3. On receiving notice of an appeal the [⁴ appropriate officer of the Crown Court] shall enter the appeal and give notice to the appellant and to the chief officer of police to whom the notice of the appeal is required by paragraph 1 of this Part of this Schedule to be given, of the date, time and place fixed for the hearing.

4. An appellant may at any time, not less than two clear days before the date fixed for the hearing, abandon his appeal by giving notice in writing to the [⁴ appropriate officer of the Crown Court] and to the chief officer of police; . . .⁵

5. The chief officer of police may appear and be heard on the hearing of an appeal.

6. . . .

7. On the hearing of an appeal the court may either dismiss the appeal or give the chief officer of police such directions as it thinks fit as respects the certificate or register which is the subject of the appeal.

8. . . .

NOTES

(1) Column entry repealed by Courts Act 1971, Sched. 11, Pt. IV. 5-05-03
(2) The phrase in brackets has not been incorporated in the statute's text but the provisions of paragraph 1 have been extended to s.30(4), which was amended by the 1988 Act, s.12(5): this seems the most useful way of dealing with an important appeal provision in the Act. The procedural provisions contained in Pt. II of the Schedule are also extended to appeals under s.30(4) as amended by s.12(5) of the 1988 Act.
(3) Words substituted by Courts Act 1971, s.56(2) and Sched. 9, Pt. I.
(4) Words substituted by Courts Act 1971, Sched. 8, Pt. I, para. 2.
(5) Words repealed by S.I. 1971 No. 1292, Sched. 3.

OBSERVATION

Section 12 of the 1988 Act empowers the police to demand the immediate surrender of firearms, certificated ammunition and certificates. Any appeal procedure in England and Wales is dictated by paragraphs 1 to 5 of Part II of this Schedule. For

Scotland, section 12(5) of the 1988 Act refers back to paragraph 1 of Part I of the Schedule; note, however, that this only identifies the appropriate court for such appeals, not the procedure to be followed. It is submitted that Scottish courts would proceed in accordance with section 44 of the 1968 Act in the absence of any other express provision.

SCHEDULE 6   **5–06–01**

PROSECUTION AND PUNISHMENT OF OFFENCES

PART I

TABLE OF PUNISHMENTS

Section of this Act creating offence	General nature of offence	Mode of Prosecution	Punishment	Additional provisions
Section 1(1) . . .	Possessing etc. firearm or ammunition without firearm certificate.	(a) Summary.	6 months or a level 5 fine on standard scale; or both.	
		(b) On indictment.	(i) Where the offence is committed in an aggravated form within the meaning of Section 4(4) of this act. 7[18] years, or a fine; or both (ii) In any other case, 5[18] years or a fine; or both.	Paragraph 1 of Part II of this Schedule applies.
Section 1(2) . . .	Non-compliance with condition of firearm certificate.	Summary . . .	6 months or a level 5 fine; or both.	Paragraph 1 of Part II of this Schedule applies.
Section 2(1) . . .	Possessing, etc., shot gun without shot gun certificate.	(a) Summary . . .[1]	6 months or the statutory maximum, or both.[1]	Paragraph 1 of Part II of this Schedule applies.
		(b) On indictment.	5[18] years or a fine; or both.	

Section of this Act creating offence	General nature of offence	Mode of Prosecution	Punishment	Additional provisions
Section 2(2) ...	Non-compliance with condition of shot gun certificate.	Summary ...	6 months or a level 5 fine; or both.	Paragraph 1 of Part II of this Schedule applies.
Section 3(1) ...	Trading in firearms without being registered as firearms dealer.	(a) Summary ...	6 months or a level 5 fine; or both.	
		(b) On indictment.	5[18] years or a fine; or both.	
Section 3(2) ...	Selling firearm to person without a certificate.	(a) Summary ...	6 months or a level 5 fine; or both.	
		(b) On indictment.	5[18] years or a fine; or both.	
Section 3(3) ...	Repairing, testing etc, firearm for person without a certificate.	(a) Summary ...	6 months or a level 5 fine; or both.	
		(b) On indictment.	5[18] years or a fine; or both.	
Section 3(5) ...	Falsifying certificate, etc., with view to acquisition of firearm.	(a) Summary ...	6 months or a level 5 fine; or both.	
		(b) On indictment.	5[18] years or a fine; or both.	
Section 3(6) ...	Pawnbroker taking firearm in pawn.	Summary ...	3 months or a level 3 fine.	
Section 4(1) (3)	Shortening a shot gun; conversion of firearms.	(a) Summary ...	6 months or a level 5 fine; or both.	
		(b) On indictment.	7[18] years or a fine; or both.	
Section 5(1) ...	Possessing or distributing prohibited weapons or ammunition.	(a) Summary ...	6 months or a level 5 fine; or both.	

Section of this Act creating offence	General nature of offence	Mode of Prosecution	Punishment	Additional provisions
		(*b*) On indictment.	10[18] years or a fine; or both.	
[²Section 5(1A)]	Possessing or distributing other prohibited weapons or ammunition.	(*a*) Summary ...	6[18] months or a fine of the statutory maximum; or both.	
		(*b*) On indictment	10[18] years or a fine; or both.	
Section 5(5) ...	Non-compliance with condition of [³Secretary of State] authority.	Summary ...	6 months or a fine of level 5 on the standard scale; or both.	
Section 5(6) ...	Non-compliance with requirements to surrender authority to possess, etc., prohibited weapon or ammunition.	Summary ...	A fine of level 3 on the standard scale.	
Section 6(3) ...	Contravention of order under s.6 (or corresponding Northern Irish order) restricting removal of arms.	Summary ...	3 months or for each firearm or parcel of ammunition in respect of which the offence is committed, a fine of level 3; or both.	Paragraph 2 of Part II of this Schedule applies.
Section 7(2) ...	Making false statement in order to obtain police permit.	Summary ...	6 months or a fine of level 5 on the standard scale; or both.	
Section 9(3) ...⁴	Making false statement in order to obtain permit for auction of firearms, etc.	(*a*) Summary ... (*b*) ...	6 months or a fine of level 5 on the standard scale; or both.	

Section of this Act creating offence	General nature of offence	Mode of Prosecution	Punishment	Additional provisions
Section 13(2) ...	Making false statement in order to obtain permit for removal of signalling apparatus.	Summary ...	6 months or a fine of level 5 on the standard scale; or both.	
Section 16 ...	Possession of firearm with intent to endanger life [or injure property].	On indictment ...	14 years or a fine; or, in England and Wales, both.	
[5 Section 16A]	Possession of firearm with intent to cause fear of violence.	On indictment.	10 years or a fine; or both.	
Section 17(1) ...	Use of firearms to resist arrest.	On indictment ...	14 years or a fine; or, in England and Wales, both.	Paragraphs 3 to 5 of Part II of this Schedule apply.
Section 17(2) ...	Possessing firearm while committing an offence specified in Schedule 1 or, in Scotland, an offence specified in Schedule 2.	On indictment ...	[Life imprisonment]6 or a fine; or ... both.	Paragraphs 3 to 6 of Part II of this Schedule apply.
Section 18(1) ...	Carrying firearms or imitation firearm with intent to commit indictable offence (or, in Scotland, an offence specified in Schedule 2) or to resist arrest.	On indictment ...	[Life imprisonment]6 or a fine; or ... both.	

Section of this Act creating offence	General nature of offence	Mode of Prosecution	Punishment	Additional provisions
Section 19 . . .	Carrying loaded firearm in public place.	(a) Summary . . .	6 months or a fine of level 5; or both.	
		(b) On indictment (but not if the firearm is an air weapon).	7[18] years or a fine; or both.	
Section 20(1) . . .	Trespassing with firearm [7 or imitation firearm] in a building.	(a)Summary . . .	6 months or a fine of level 5; or both.	
		(b) On indictment (but not [7 in the case of an imitation firearm or] if the firearm is an air weapon.	7[18] years or a fine; or both.	
Section 20(2) . . .	Trespassing with firearm [7 or imitation firearm] on land.	Summary . . .	3 months or a fine of level 4 on the standard scale.	
Section 21(4) . . .	Contravention of provisions denying firearms to ex-prisoners and the like.	(a) Summary . . .	6 months or a fine of level 5; or both.	
		(b) On indictment	5[18] years or a fine; or both.	
Section 21(5) . . .	Supplying firearms to person denied them under section 21.	(a) Summary . . .	6 months or a level 5 fine; or both.	
		(b) On indictment	5[18] years or a fine; or both.	
Section 22(1) . . .	Person under 17 acquiring firearm.	Summary . . .	6 months or a fine of level 5 on the standard scale; or both.	

Section of this Act creating offence	General nature of offence	Mode of Prosecution	Punishment	Additional provisions
[⁸ Section 22(1A)]	Person under 18 using certificated firearm for unauthorised purpose.	Summary . . .	3 months or a fine of level 5 on the standard scale; or both.	
Section 22(2) . . .	Person under 14 having firearm in his possession without lawful authority.	Summary . . .	3 months or a fine of level 5 on the standard scale; or both.	
Section 22(3) . . .	Person under 15 having with him a shot gun without adult supervision.	Summary . . .	A fine of level 3 on the standard scale.	Paragraph 8 of Part II of this Schedule applies.
Section 22(4) . . .	Person under 14 having with him an air weapon or ammunition therefor.	Summary . . .	A fine of level 3 on the standard scale.	Paragraphs 7 and 8 of Part II of this Schedule apply.
Section 22(5) . . .	Person under 17 having with him an air weapon in a public place.	Summary . . .	A fine of level 3 on the standard scale.	Paragraphs 7 and 8 of Part II of this Schedule apply.
Section 23(1) . . .	Person under 14 making improper use of air weapon when under supervision; person supervising him permitting such use.	Summary . . .	A fine of level 3 on the standard scale.	Paragraphs 7 and 8 of Part II of this Schedule apply.
Section 24(1) . . .	Selling or letting on hire a firearm to person under 17.	Summary . . .	6 months or a fine of level 5 on the standard scale; or both.	

Section of this Act creating offence	General nature of offence	Mode of Prosecution	Punishment	Additional provisions
Section 24(2) . . .	Supplying firearm or ammunition (being of a kind to which section 1 of this Act applies) to person under 14.	Summary . . .	6 months or a fine of level 5 on the standard scale; or both.	
Section 24(3)	Making gift of shot gun to person under 15.	Summary . . .	A fine of level 3 on the standard scale.	Paragraph 9 of Part II of this Schedule applies.
Section 24(4) . . .	Supplying air weapon to person under 14.	Summary . . .	A fine of level 3 on the standard scale.	Paragraphs 7 and 8 of Part II of this Schedule.
Section 25 . . .	Supplying firearm to person drunk or insane.	Summary . . .	3 months or a fine of level 3 on the standard scale; or both.	
Section 26(5)	Making false statement in order to procure grant or renewal of a firearm or shot gun certificate.	Summary . . .	6 months or a fine of level 5 on the standard scale; or both.	
Section 29(3) . . .	Making false statement in order to procure variation of a firearm certificate.	Summary . . .	6 months or a fine of level 5 on the standard scale; or both.	
Section 30(4) . . .	Failing to surrender certificate on revocation.	Summary . . .	A fine of level 3 on the standard scale.	
[⁹Section 32B(5)]	Failure to surrender expired European Firearms pass.	Summary . . .	A fine of level 3 on the standard scale.	

Section of this Act creating offence	General nature of offence	Mode of Prosecution	Punishment	Additional provisions
[⁹Section 32C(6)]	Failure to produce European Firearms pass or Article 7 authority for variation or cancellation etc.; failure to notify loss or theft of firearm identified in pass or to produce pass for endorsement.	Summary . . .	3 months or a fine of level 5 on the standard scale; or both.	
Section 38(8) . . .	Failure to surrender certificate of registration [or register of transactions¹⁰] on removal of firearms dealer's name from register.	Summary . . .	A fine of level 3 on the standard scale.	
Section 39(1) . . .	Making false statement in order to secure registration or entry in register of a place of business.	Summary . . .	6 months or a fine of level 5 on the standard scale; or both.	
Section 39(2) . . .	Registered firearms dealer having place of business not entered in the register.	Summary . . .	6 months or a fine of level 5 on the standard scale; or both.	
Section 39(3) . . .	Non-compliance with condition of registration.	Summary . . .	6 months or a fine of level 5 on the standard scale; or both.	

The Firearms Act 1968   165

Section of this Act creating offence	General nature of offence	Mode of Prosecution	Punishment	Additional provisions
Section 40(5) . . .	Non-compliance by firearms dealer with provisions as to register of transactions; making false entry in register.	Summary . . .	6 months or a fine of level 5 on the standard scale; or both.	
Section 42 . . .	Failure to comply with instructions in firearm certificate when transferring firearm to person other than registered dealer; failure to report transaction to police.	(a) Summary . . . (b) On indictment	6 months or a fine of level 5; or both. 5[18] years or a fine; or both.	
[11Section 42A]	Failure to report transaction authorised by visitor's shot gun permit.	Summary . . .	3 months or a fine of level 5 on the standard scale; or both.	
Section 47(2) . . .	Failure to hand over firearm or ammunition on demand by constable.	Summary . . .	3 months, or a fine of level 4 on the standard scale; or both.	
Section 48(3) . . .	Failure to comply with requirement of a constable that a person shall declare his name and address.	Summary . . .	A fine of level 3 on the standard scale.	

Section of this Act creating offence	General nature of offence	Mode of Prosecution	Punishment	Additional provisions
[¹²Section 48(4)]	Failure to produce firearms pass issued in another member State.	Summary . . .	A fine of level 3 on the standard scale.	
Section 49(3) . . .	Failure to give constable facilities for examination of firearms in transit, or to produce papers.	Summary . . .	3 months or, for each firearm or parcel of ammunition in respect of which the offence is committed, a fine of level 3 on the standard scale; or both.	Paragraph 2 of Part II of this Schedule applies.
Section 52(2)(*c*)	Failure to surrender firearm or shot gun certificate cancelled by court on conviction.	Summary . . .	A fine of level 3 on the standard scale.	

5–06–02

PART II

SUPPLEMENTARY PROVISIONS AS TO TRIAL AND PUNISHMENT OF OFFENCES

1. . . .¹³

2. In the case of an offence against section 6(3) or 49(3) of this Act, the court before which the offender is convicted may, if the offender is the owner of the firearms or ammunition, make such order as to the forfeiture of the firearms or ammunition as the court thinks fit.

[¹⁴ 3.(1) Where in England or Wales a person who has attained the age of seventeen is charged before a magistrates' court with an offence triable either way listed in [¹⁵ Schedule 1 to the Magistrates' Courts Act 1980] ("the listed offence") and is also charged before that court with an offence under section 17(1) or (2) of this Act, the following provisions of this paragraph shall apply.

(2) Subject to the following sub-paragraph the court shall proceed as if the listed offence were triable only on indictment and [¹⁶ sections 18 to 23 of the said Act of 1980] (procedure for determining mode of trial of offences triable either way) shall not apply in relation to that offence.

(3) If [¹⁹ under section 6 of the said Act of 1980,] the court [¹⁹ dismisses the charges against the accused] in respect of the offence under section 17(1) or (2),

or if proceedings before the court for that offence are otherwise discontinued, the preceding sub-paragraph shall cease to apply as from the time when this occurs and—

    (*a*) if at that time the court has not yet begun to [[19] proceed with a view to transferring for trial proceedings for the listed offence], the court shall, in the case of the listed offence, proceed in the ordinary way in accordance with the said [[17] sections 18 to 23]; but

    (*b*) if at that time the court has begun to [[19] proceed in respect of] the listed offence, those sections shall continue not to apply and the court shall proceed with [[19] a view to transferring for trial proceedings for that offence] but shall have power in accordance with [[17] sections 25(3) and (4) of the said Act of 1980] to change to summary trial with the accused's consent.

4. Where a person commits an offence under section 17(1) of this Act in respect of the lawful arrest or detention of himself for any other offence committed by him, he shall be liable to the penalty provided by Part I of this Schedule in addition to any penalty to which he may be sentenced for the other offence.

5. If on the trial of a person for an offence under section 17(1) of this Act the jury are not satisfied that he is guilty of that offence but are satisfied that he is guilty of an offence under section 17(2), the jury may find him guilty of the offence under section 17(2) and he shall then be punishable accordingly.

6. The punishment to which a person is liable for an offence under section 17(2) of this Act shall be in addition to any punishment to which he may be liable for the offence first referred to in section 17(2).

7. The court by which a person is convicted of an offence under section 22(4) or (5), 23(1) or 24(4) of this Act may make such order as it thinks fit as to the forfeiture or disposal of the air weapon or ammunition in respect of which the offence was committed.

8. The court by which a person is convicted of an offence under section 22(3), (4) or (5), 23(1) or 24(4) may make such order as it thinks fit as to the forfeiture or disposal of any firearm or ammunition found in his possession.

9. The court by which a person is convicted of an offence under section 24(3) of this Act may make such order as it thinks fit as to the forfeiture or disposal of the shot gun or ammunition in respect of which the offence was committed.

NOTES

The principal changes to the Table of Punishments were introduced by the **5–06–03** Criminal Justice Act 1972, ss.28 and 66, the Criminal Justice Act 1982 (applicable to England and Wales), ss.38 and 46 and the Criminal Procedure (Scotland) Act 1975, ss.289F and 289G, as amended; the first Act doubled the monetary penalties originally specified in the 1968 Act while the latter two statutes created the standard scale of money fines. While the Table as now published has incorporated these main changes, the value of repeating these derivations constantly must be questionable.

It should also be noted that many of the offences created by the 1988 Act were never inserted in the Table: accordingly it should not be regarded as an exhaustive digest of offences. The notes below detail the less obvious amendments to the Table, and hence have been extended fully.

(1) Entries in Columns 3 and 4 amended and supplemented by the Criminal Justice Act 1988, ss.44 and 123 and Sched. 8, para. 16.

(2) Entry for section 5(1A) inserted by S.I. 1992 No. 2823, reg.3(6).

(3) Words inserted by S.I. 1968 No. 1200, arts. 2 and 3.

(4) Substituted by the 1988 Act, s.23(7).

(5) Inserted by the 1994 Act, s.1(2).

(6) "Life Imprisonment" substituted by the Criminal Justice Act 1988, ss.44(3) and (4), 123(6) and Sched. 8 para. 16.

(7) Entries relating to sections 20(1) and (2) inserted by 1994 Act, s.2(3).

(8) Entry relating to section 22(1A) inserted by S.I. 1992 No. 2823, reg.4(4).

(9) Entries relating to ss.32B(5) and 32C(6) inserted by S.I. 1992 No. 2823, reg.5(3).

(10) Words inserted by 1988 Act, s.13(5).

(11) Entry inserted by S.I. 1992 No. 2823, reg.6(3).

(12) Entry inserted by S.I. 1992 No. 2823, reg.7(4).

(13) Repealed by the Criminal Justice (Scotland) Act 1980, s.83(3) and Sched. 8.

(14) Paragraph 3(1) extended (England and Wales) by the Criminal Attempts Act 1981 s.7(2).

(15) Substituted by the Magistrates' Courts Act 1980, s.154, Sched. 7, para.73(*a*).

(16) Words substituted by the last mentioned Act, para. 73 of said Schedule.

(17) Amendments effected by the above Act, para. 73(*c*) of said Schedule.

(18) Penalties amended by the Criminal Justice and Public Order Act 1994, Sched. 8.

(19) Inserted by the above Act, Sched. 4, para. 17.

OBSERVATIONS

5–06–04 (a) The implications of paragraph 3 of Part II of the Schedule above are discussed in 1–22–07, *supra*.

(b) Paragraphs 4, 5 and 6 of Part II of the Schedule have been discussed at 1-17-12. The primary effect of these provisions is that a person convicted of use of a firearm to resist his own arrest, or in furtherance of a Schedule 1 or 2 offence, can expect to receive a sentence to be served consecutively to any sentence imposed for the original offence: this means that no remission could be earned during the currency of the sentence for the original offence whose full term would have to be served. Remission for good behaviour could only be obtained for the sentence imposed for contravening section 17 itself.

NOTE: This Schedule has been included for information only and does not form part of the Firearms Acts 1968 to 1992.

CATEGORY A

1. Explosive military missiles and their launchers.
2. Automatic firearms.
3. Firearms disguised as other objects.
4. Ammunition with penetrating (armour-piercing), explosive or incendiary projectiles, and the projectiles for such ammunition.
5. Pistol and revolver ammunition with expanding projectiles, and the projectiles for such ammunition, except in the case of weapons for hunting or target shooting, for persons entitled to use them.

CATEGORY B

1. All handguns and short rifles, carbines and smooth-bore guns with a barrel not exceeding 11¾ inches (30 cms) or an overall length not exceeding 23.6 inches (60 cms) except single shot rim-fire pistols with an overall length of 11 inches (28 cm) or more.
2. All semi-automatic rifles and smooth-bore guns:-
    (i) with a magazine and chamber which can together hold more than 3 rounds; or
    (ii) where the magazine and chamber cannot together hold more than three rounds but could be converted to a larger capacity with ordinary tools; or
    (iii) with a detachable magazine; or
    (iv) in the case of smooth-bore guns, which have a barrel less than 24 inches (60.96 cms); or
    (v) which resemble automatic weapons.
3. Repeating (*i.e.* pump-action, bolt-action, lever-action) and other manually loaded, smooth-bore guns, and smooth-bore revolver guns, with a barrel of less than 24 inches (60.96 cms).

CATEGORY C

1. Repeating (*i.e.* pump-action, bolt-action, lever-action) and other manually operated rifles and single-shot rifles.
2. Repeating (*i.e.* pump-action, bolt-action, lever-action) and other manually loaded, smooth-bore guns, and smooth-bore revolver guns, with a barrel of not less than 24 inches (60.96 cms).-
3. Semi-automatic rifles and smooth-bore guns:–
    (i) where the magazine and chamber together cannot hold more than 3 shots and which cannot be converted to a larger capacity using ordinary tools, for example smooth-bore guns which have been adapted in accordance with section 2(3) of the 1988 Act; and
    (ii) which do not have a detachable magazine; and
    (iii) which do not resemble fully automatic weapons; and
    (iv) which, in the case of smooth-bore guns, have a barrel of not less than 24 inches.
4. Single-shot rim-fire pistols with an overall length of more than 11 inches (28 cms).
5. Any shot gun with a magazine.

CATEGORY D

Any shot gun without a magazine.
This includes single-barrel single-shot shot guns, over and under, and side by side, shot guns, or any multi-barrelled shot guns which can only fire one shot from each barrel without reloading.

FIREARMS ACT 1982

An Act to apply the provisions of the Firearms Act 1968 (with certain exceptions) to imitation firearms which are readily convertible into firearms to which section 1 of that Act applies.

[13th July 1982]

Control of imitation firearms readily convertible into firearms to which Section 1 of the 1968 Act applies

1.—(1) This Act applies to an imitation firearm if— **6–01–01**
  (*a*) it has the appearance of being a firearm to which section 1 of the 1968 Act (firearms requiring a firearm certificate) applies; and
  (*b*) it is so constructed or adapted as to be readily convertible into a firearm to which that section applies.

(2) Subject to section 2(2) of this Act and the following provisions of this section, the 1968 Act shall apply in relation to an imitation firearm to which this Act applies as it applies in relation to a firearm to which section 1 of that Act applies.

(3) Subject to the modifications in subsection (4) below, any expression given a meaning for the purposes of the 1968 Act has the same meaning in this Act.

(4) For the purposes of this section and the 1968 Act, as it applies by virtue of this section—
  (*a*) the definition of air weapon in section 1(3)(*b*) of that Act (air weapons excepted from requirement of firearm certificate) shall have effect without the exclusion of any type declared by rules made by the Secretary of State under section 53 of that Act to be specially dangerous; and
  (*b*) the definition of firearm in section 57(1) of that Act shall have effect without paragraphs (*b*) and (*c*) of that subsection (component parts and accessories).

(5) In any proceedings brought by virtue of this section for an offence under the 1968 Act involving an imitation firearm to which this Act applies, it shall be a defence for the accused to show that he did not know and had no reason to suspect that the

imitation firearm was so constructed or adapted as to be readily convertible into a firearm to which section 1 of that Act applies.

(6) For the purposes of this section an imitation firearm shall be regarded as readily convertible into a firearm to which section 1 of the 1968 Act applies if—

> (*a*) it can be so converted without any special skill on the part of the person converting it in the construction or adaptation of firearms of any description; and

> (*b*) the work involved in converting it does not require equipment or tools other than such as are in common use by persons carrying out works of construction and maintenance in their own homes.

Provisions supplementary to section 1

6–02–01   **2.**—(1) Subject to subsection (2) below, references in the 1968 Act, and in any order made under section 6 of that Act (orders prohibiting movement of firearms or ammunition) before this Act comes into force—

> (*a*) to firearms (without qualification); or

> (*b*) to firearms to which section 1 of that Act applies;

shall be read as including imitation firearms to which this Act applies.

(2) The following provisions of the 1968 Act do not apply by virtue of this Act to an imitation firearm to which this Act applies, that is to say—

> (*a*) section 4(3) and (4) (offence to convert anything having appearance of firearm into a firearm and aggravated offence under section 1 involving a converted firearm); and

> (*b*) the provisions of that Act which relate to, or to the enforcement of control over, the manner in which a firearm is used or the circumstances in which it is carried;

but without prejudice, in the case of the provisions mentioned in paragraph (*b*) above, to the application to such an imitation firearm of such of those provisions as apply to imitation firearms apart from this Act.

(6) The provisions referred to in subsection (2)(*b*) above are sections 16 to 20 and section 47.

Corresponding provision for Northern Ireland

6–03–01   **3.**—An Order in Council under paragraph 1(1)(*b*) of Schedule

1 to the Northern Ireland Act 1974 (legislation for Northern
Ireland in the interim period) which contains a statement that is
made only for purposes corresponding to the purposes of this
Act—

- (*a*) shall not be subject to paragraph 1(4) and (5) of that
    Schedule (affirmative resolution of both Houses of Par-
    liament); but
- (*b*) shall be subject to annulment in pursuance of a resolu-
    tion of either House of Parliament.

Citation, interpretation, commencement and extent

4.—(1) This Act may be cited as the Firearms Act 1982, and **6–04–01**
this Act and the 1968 Act may be cited together as the Firearms
Act 1968 and 1982.

(2) In this Act "the 1968 Act" means the Firearms Acts 1968.

(3) This Act shall come into force on such day as the
Secretary of State may by order made by statutory instrument
appoint.

(4) This Act, except section 3, does not extend to Northern
Ireland.

OBSERVATIONS

Imitation firearms are statutorily defined by section 57(4) of **6–05–01**
the 1968 Act, and ordinarily can be freely possessed without the
need for a firearms certificate — see 4–05–17 and 4–05–18
above. These items should not be confused with firearms
disguised as other objects which are prohibited weapons: imitation firearms have the appearance of working firearms but are
meant to be incapable of discharging ammunition.

The use of such an imitation firearm in the pursuance of
crime, or to resist arrest, or (following section 20 of the
Firearms Act 1994) in the course of trespass, is as much an
offence as would be the use of a firearm; only section 20 of the
1968 Act, as amended, makes any concession in terms of penalty
where an imitation firearm, rather than a firearm, is carried,
restricting the mode of prosecution in that event to summary
proceedings.

It is essential to grasp that even in situations where sections
16 to 20 of the 1968 Act (as amended by the 1994 Act) are
breached by a person carrying an imitation firearm, there will be

no offence against sections 1 or 2 of that Act, which demand possession of a firearm or shot gun certificate, unless the imitation used has been converted or adapted, or is capable of being so converted or adapted, to discharge bullets or other objects.

The 1982 Act provides that imitation firearms which are capable of easy conversion into working firearms can only be lawfully possessed by the holder of a firearms certificate. The 1968 Act was sufficiently widely drafted to ensure that imitation firearms converted or adapted to fire ammunition were already subject to the same licensing regime as other working firearms. The problem has been, and remains, in the policing provisions of the Firearms Acts, since, unlike conventional firearms, imitation firearms are outwith the licensing provisions of the Acts and can be sold or possessed by anyone. This problem is accentuated when it is recalled that an individual whose past criminal conduct renders him liable to the provisions of section 21 of the 1968 Act (discussed at 1–21–07) can freely possess an imitation firearm provided it has not been converted, or is not adaptable, to fire ammunition. Since section 21 enacts against such a person possessing so much as an air weapon pellet, it takes no great sagacity to appreciate the attractions which imitation firearms hold for the criminally-inclined.

Obscure as it is, section 1(4)(a) of the 1982 Act does no more than provide that imitation firearms which have been converted into low-power air weapons are exempted from the Act's certification requirements.

6–05–02   It has been observed (at 1–01–09) that possession of a section 1 weapon without holding a certificate, or other lawful authority, is an absolute offence. However, section 1(5) of the 1982 Act creates a statutory defence for possessors of convertible imitation firearms, this being the only clear exception to the rule of strict liability which the Act applies to possession of firearms, ammunition and shot guns.

In any proceedings under the 1982 Act, it is unlikely that much evidence will be necessary to satisfy section 1(1)(a); the close resemblance between the replica firearm and its antecedent firearm was, after all, the manufacturer's aim in the first place. It is much more likely that the issue before the court will be the ease, or otherwise, of conversion of the imitation into a working firearm. To that end it is likely that the prosecution will place some emphasis upon the results of tests conducted by the Home Office Forensic Science Service Laboratory at Huntingdon.

The laboratory, with the co-operation of the manufacturers **6–05–03** and importers of replica firearms, undertakes examinations of imitation firearms to determine the relative ease of methods of conversion, having regard to the strictures of section 1(6) of the 1982 Act. Each examination results in the preparation of a Model Firearm Report (M.F.E.), which presents a finding as to whether or not conversion, or adaptation, of the replica into a working firearm can readily be achieved, and if so, how. Where a conversion can be effected the method is described and the findings are circulated to the importer or manufacturer, and to police forces, interested government departments and the Gun Trade Association. The intention is to ensure that sales of convertible replicas remain restricted to the gun trade. Obviously, given the potential for misuse of the information contained in M.F.E.s, these reports enjoy only restricted circulation; but the Home Office issues a leaflet, *Guidelines on the Design, Construction or Adaptation of Imitation Firearms*, which provides some general guidance to the public.

It is essential to ensure that the M.F.E. referred to in any ballistic report does in fact relate to the particular replica variant which is the subject of proceedings; it is not unknown for a manufacturer to produce as many as 10 variants of the same replica firearm, each with different internal features, and some models may be more easy to convert into functioning firearms than others. Furthermore, it must be emphasised that the results of an examination of a replica weapon conducted by Huntingdon, or any other forensic laboratory, enjoy no particular legal status and cannot be regarded as exhaustive of the methods which may be employed to overcome barrel blockages thereby enabling an imitation firearm to discharge shot. The Home Office leaflet mentioned above may equally be persuasive evidence before a court, but again it has no special evidential standing.

Thus in *Campbell v. Normand,* 1993 G.W.D. 37–2426, the **6–05–04** appellant was found in possession, amongst other things, of an 8mm replica pistol (one of ten variants produced by the Italian manufacturer). He held no firearms certificate but reference to the Huntingdon M.F.E. reports indicated that the model seized was one of five of these variants which could be converted, though not easily. A defence expert in his report noted indeed that "In most instances the difference between versions was so indistinguishable as to be recognised only by those with access to the detailed results of the Huntingdon reports and, in at least two of the versions, could only be differentiated by the use of X-ray equipment."

The method of conversion considered at Huntingdon required the removal of hardened steel inserts and then boring out the barrel to produce a smooth-bore weapon, a task which would require expertise and access to industrial engineering equipment and would be eased by use of commercial X-ray equipment. By no stretch of the imagination could it be asserted that this method fell within the definition of "readily convertible" found in the 1982 Act. However, the prosecution produced evidence from police ballistics experts that, while they had previously shared Huntingdon's opinion as to the difficulty of conversion of these replicas, the regular appearance of converted imitation firearms of this model in criminative circumstances had forced them to reconsider their view. Indeed they achieved conversion by a method not attempted at Huntingdon within 15 minutes, causing the sheriff to conclude: "In view of the nature of the task which became obvious to me after hearing evidence and elementary skills and tools required to effect conversion combined with the firing capability of the pistol (which was agreed) I concluded that [the pistol] was so constructed as to be readily convertible into a firearm without any special skill or equipment and convicted the appellant."

It is worth noting that, on appeal, the High Court of Justiciary ruled that the test to be met in section 1(6) of the Act was not a subjective one; the court should not consider whether the accused himself possessed the skills necessary to effect conversion but simply whether the application of such skills by any person would produce a converted imitation firearm.

FIREARMS (AMENDMENT) ACT 1988

An Act to amend the Firearms Act 1968 and to make further provision for regulating the possession of, and transactions relating to, firearms and ammunition. [15th November 1988]

[Specially dangerous weapons]

Prohibited weapons and ammunition

1.—(1) Section 5 of the Firearms Act 1968 (in this Act **7–01–01** referred to as "the principal Act") shall have effect with the following amendments the purpose of which is to extend the class of prohibited weapons and ammunition, that is to say weapons and ammunition the possession, purchase, acquisition, manufacture, sale or transfer of which requires the authority of the Secretary of State.

(2) [Text inserted as section 5(1)(*a*) to (*ae*) of the 1968 Act]

(3) [Text inserted as section 5(1)(*c*) of the 1968 Act]

(4) If it appears to the Secretary of State that the provisions of the principal Act relating to prohibited weapons or ammunition should apply to—

(*a*) any firearm (not being an air weapon) which is not for the time being specified in subsection (1) of section 5, was not lawfully on sale in Great Britain in substantial numbers at any time before 1988 and appears to him to be—

(i) specially dangerous; or

(ii) wholly or partly composed of material making it not readily detectable by apparatus used for detecting metal objects; or

(*b*) any ammunition which is not for the time being specified in that subsection but appears to him to be specially dangerous, he may by order add it to the weapons or ammunition specified in that subsection whether by altering the description of any weapon or ammunition for the time being there specified or otherwise.

(5) The power to make an order under subsection (4) above shall be exercisable by statutory instrument and no such order shall be made unless a draft of it has been laid before and approved by a resolution of each House of Parliament.

[*Weapons requiring firearm certificate*]

Re-definition of exempted shot guns

7–02–01   **2.**—(1) Section 1 of the principal Act shall have effect with the following amendments the purpose of which is to require a firearm certificate for certain types of shot gun.

(2) [Text inserted as section 1(3)(*a*) of the 1968 Act]

(3) [Text inserted as section 1(3A) of that Act]

OBSERVATIONS

The intention of this section is to restrict the range of weapons which may be possessed by the holder of a shot gun certificate to shot guns whose barrel or barrels exceed 24 inches in length and are capable of discharging no more than two shots without reloading.

Repeating shot guns, *i.e.* those weapons designed with magazines capable of holding more than two cartridges, require the possessor to hold a firearm certificate; to qualify for certification as a shot gun, such a gun must now have its magazine made non-detachable and restricted in such a way as to render the weapon incapable of firing more than two rounds.

Section 1(3)(*a*)(ii) of the 1968 Act, as amended by section 2(2) of the 1982 Act, stipulates that once so modified, the gun must be approved by one of the two proof houses as restricted in a manner meeting the Secretary of State's approval. The magazine of the weapon will be stamped with the appropriate proof stamp to denote compliance; this is an essential step for a repeating shot gun to qualify as a shot gun for certification purposes in view of the terms of the above section.

Substitution of a non-approved magazine in order to permit the discharge of more than two shots would offend against section 1 of the 1968 Act. It follows that the replacement of a proofed magazine by an unproofed one, even if it complied with the technical specifications to limit its cartridge capacity, would be an offence against the same section.

See also 1–01–13, above.

[*Shot guns*]

Grant and renewal of shot gun certificates

3.—(1) For section 28(1) of the principal Act (criteria for grant of shot gun certificates) there shall be substituted—   **7–03–01**

[Text inserted as section 28(1) to (1B) of the 1968 Act]

(2) After section 28(2) of the principal Act (form and contents of shot gun certificates) there shall be inserted—

[Text inserted as section 28(2A) of the 1968 Act]

Transfers of shot guns

4.—(1) This section applies where a person—   **7–04–01**

    (*a*) sells, lets on hire or gives a shot gun; or

    (*b*) lends a shot gun for a period of more than seventy-two hours,

to another person in the United Kingdom who is neither a registered firearms dealer nor a person who shows he is by virtue of the principal Act or this Act entitled to purchase or acquire the shot gun without holding a shot gun certificate.

(2) The transferor shall—

    (*a*) comply with any instructions contained in the certificate produced by the transferee; and

    (*b*) within seven days of the transaction send a notice of the transaction to the chief officer of police who issued the transferor's certificate or, if he is by virtue of the principal Act or this Act entitled to be in possession of the shot gun without holding a certificate, to the chief officer of police who issued the transferee's certificate.

(3) The transferee shall, within seven days of the transaction, send a notice of the transaction to the chief officer of police who issued his certificate.

(4) The notice of transaction under subsection (2) or (3) shall contain a description of the shot gun in question (giving the identification number if any) and state the nature of the

transaction and the name and address of the other person concerned; and any such notice shall be sent by registered post or the recorded delivery service.

(5) It is an offence to fail to comply with this section and that offence shall be punishable on summary conviction with imprisonment for a term not exceeding six months or a fine not exceeding level 5 on the standard scale or both.

OBSERVATIONS

(a) Note that the penalty for contravening section 4's provisions has not been included in the Table of Punishments in the 1968 Act.

(b) It will be appreciated that the object of this section is to restrict the traffic in shot guns so far as practicable.

Restriction on sale of ammunition for smooth-bore guns

7–05–01   **5.**—(1) This section applies to ammunition to which section 1 of the principal Act does not apply and which is capable of being used in a shot gun or in a smooth-bore gun to which that section applies.

(2) It is an offence for a person to sell any such ammunition to another person in the United Kingdom who is neither a registered firearms dealer nor a person who sells such ammunition by way of trade or business unless that other person—

(*a*) produces a certificate authorising him to possess a gun of a kind mentioned in subsection (1) above; or

(*b*) shows that he is by virtue of that Act or this Act entitled to have possession of such a gun without holding a certificate; or

(*c*) produces a certificate authorising another person to possess such a gun, together with that person's written authority to purchase the ammunition on his behalf.

(3) An offence under this section shall be punishable on summary conviction with imprisonment for a term not exceeding six months or a fine not exceeding level 5 on the standard scale or both.

OBSERVATION

Ordinarily shot gun ammunition can be freely possessed. This section provides, however, that ammunition for shot guns or smooth-bore guns which fall to be certificated as firearms may only be sold to a person fulfilling the requirements laid down in subsection (2) above. Oddly, the section does not prevent the certificated purchaser of such ammunition then transferring it on to other persons.

[*Converted and de-activated weapons*]

Shortening of barrels

6.—(1) Subject to subsection (2) below, it is an offence to **7–06–01** shorten to a length less than 24 inches the barrel of any smooth-bore gun to which section 1 of the principal Act applies other than one which has a barrel with a bore exceeding 2 inches in diameter; and that offence shall be punishable—
  (*a*) on summary conviction, with imprisonment for a term not exceeding six months or a fine not exceeding the statutory maximum or both;
  (*b*) on indictment, with imprisonment for a term not exceeding five years or a fine or both.
(2) It is not an offence under this section for a registered firearms dealer to shorten the barrel of a gun for the sole purpose of replacing a defective part of the barrel so as to produce a barrel not less than 24 inches in length.

OBSERVATION

The effect of section 6(1) above is, in effect, to extend the prohibition upon shortening the barrel (or barrels) of shot guns certificated under section 2 of the 1968 Act to those shot guns currently requiring section 1 certificates.

Conversion not to affect classification

7.—(1) Any weapon which— **7–07–01**
  (*a*) has at any time (whether before or after the passing of this Act) been a weapon of a kind described in section 5(1) of the principal Act as amended by or under section 1 above; and
  (*b*) is not a self-loading or pump-action smooth-bore gun which has at any such time been such a weapon by reason only of having had a barrel less than 24 inches in length,

shall be treated as a prohibited weapon notwithstanding anything done for the purpose of converting it into a weapon of a
different kind.

(2) Any weapon which—

(*a*) has at any time since the coming into force of section 2
above been a weapon to which section 1 of the principal
Act applies; or

(*b*) would at any previous time have been such a weapon if
those sections had then been in force,

shall, if it has, or at any time has had, a rifled barrel less than 24
inches in length, be treated as a weapon to which section 1 of
the principal Act applies notwithstanding anything done for the
purpose of converting it into a shot gun or an air weapon.

(3) For the purposes of subsection (2) above there shall be
disregarded the shortening of a barrel by a registered firearms
dealer for the sole purpose of replacing part of it so as to
produce a barrel not less than 24 inches in length.

OBSERVATIONS

7–07–02   (a) Section 2 above came into force on June 1, 1989.

(b) Subsection (1) can be paraphrased thus: once a prohibited
weapon, always a prohibited weapon, but subject to the provisions of section 8 below, which has created a class of de-
activated weapons.

Subsection (1) stipulates that any weapon which has at any
time been a prohibited weapon (as defined in section 5(1) of the
1968 Act) shall remain such even if it has subsequently been
converted into a firearm or shot gun to obtain certification.
Presumably what is envisaged is the sort of conversion undertaken (unsuccessfully) in *R. v. Clarke (Frederick)* or in *R. v.
Pannell*, cases discussed at 1–05–19.

At one time modifications to restrict the automatic firing
capabilities of a prohibited weapon might well have produced a
firearm qualifying for a section 1 certificate if it could be
established that it could only fire single shots and was incapable
of continuous firing. The 1968 Act focused upon the physical
character of weapons (whether rifled or smooth-bore, barrel
lengths or dynamic capabilities) to determine how each should
be classified in Part I of the Act. So in *Creaser v. Tunnicliffe*
[1977] 1 W.L.R. 1493; [1978] 1 All E.R. 569 in his dissenting
judgment (approved subsequently in *R. v. Hucklebridge*, which is

cited and discussed at 1–02–03) Lord Widgery considered the actual capabilities of a bored-out rifle, rather than its original design and purpose, and concluded that the weapon in that case fulfilled the statutory definition of a shot gun. That approach is still valid in respect of section 1 and section 2 firearms but, as a result of subsection (1) above, it has no application to any weapon which has at any time been a prohibited weapon. However, a gun no longer capable of discharging a bullet, etc., logically can no longer be viewed as a weapon and, it is submitted, ceases to be subject to the provisions of the Firearms Acts.

Subsection (2) provides that efforts to convert a shorter rifled firearm (usually a pistol) into either a shot gun or an air weapon will not alter its classification as a section 1 firearm.

De-activated weapons

8.—For the purposes of the principal Act and this Act it shall **7-08-01** be presumed, unless the contrary is shown, that a firearm has been rendered incapable of discharging any shot, bullet or other missile, and has consequently ceased to be a firearm within the meaning of those Acts, if—

(*a*) it bears a mark which has been approved by the Secretary of State for denoting that fact and which has been made either by one of the two companies mentioned in section 58(1) of the principal Act or by such other person as may be approved by the Secretary of State for the purposes of this section; and

(*b*) that company or person has certified in writing that work has been carried out on the firearm in a manner approved by the Secretary of State for rendering it incapable of discharging any shot, bullet or other missile.

OBSERVATIONS

(a) The marginal note refers to "De-activated weapons" and it is **7–08–02** apparent that this section has created an additional class of weapon distinct from the firearms or imitation firearms defined in section 57 of the 1968 Act. Quite how radical this addition has been remains a matter of conjecture since there are, as yet, no reported cases on the topic.

Certainly it is intended that any firearm or shot gun which has been de-activated in the approved manner will cease to be subject to the 1968 Act's certification requirements and can then be freely possessed. It will be noted that de-activated weapons can, but need not, be scrutinised by either of the proof houses to receive that classification, provided that the person who neutralises the weapon is someone approved in that regard by the Secretary of State. Two issues are much less clear: what is the standing of a de-activated prohibited weapon and its component parts; and how do the Firearms Acts treat the use of a de-activated weapon in the furtherance of a crime specified in Schedules 1 or 2 to the 1968 Act?

Section 8 stipulates that a firearm rendered (by means of an approved method) incapable of firing ceases to be a firearm for the purposes of the Act. However, section 7, which relates to prohibited weapons, admonishes that any such weapon remains a prohibited weapon irrespective of anything done to convert it "into a weapon of a different kind". Common sense suggests that a de-activated prohibited weapon should be regarded as having ceased to be a firearm and cannot then be regarded as "a weapon" at all; that seems to accord with the legislature's intentions.

7–08–03 Reference to the statutory definition of "firearm" in section 57(1) indicates that this expression extends to any component part. Component parts of either section 1 or section 5 firearms cannot ordinarily be freely possessed, but it seems to be the case that provided they are integral to a de-activated weapon, and the gun or weapon has been rendered ineffective in an approved fashion, then such components can be possessed without any form of lawful authority. It is stressed that there is no settled authority on the issue which, it may be argued, is one of technical, rather than practical, significance.

The second issue mentioned earlier, namely how the Acts deal with the carrying of a de-activated firearm by a person then contravening sections 16A, 17, 18 or 20 of the 1968 Act, is much more fundamental. It would appear that Parliament's intention is to regard a de-activated weapon as an imitation firearm as defined in section 57(4) of the 1968 Act. If that interpretation is echoed by the courts, then there is little difficulty in applying the Acts as they stand, but the question remains as to whether such an interpretation is well-founded. To date there is no reported authority on the subject.

7–08–04 Section 8, above, stipulates that a de-activated weapon ceases to be a firearm; that being so, sections 16 and 19 of the principal

Act, which refer to offences committed by use of a firearm, can for the present purpose be ignored. Sections 16A, 17, 18 or 20 are pertinent since they can be contravened by use of either a firearm or an imitation firearm. It will be recalled that section 57(4) of the 1968 Act defines an imitation firearm as "any thing which has the appearance of being a firearm ... whether or not it is capable of discharging any shot, bullet or other missile". (The 1982 Act relates to convertible imitation firearms and, by definition, should not apply to any de-activated firearm.)

It could surely be asserted that a de-activated firearm is not an artificial likeness, copy or replica as the word "imitation" suggests, but rather (to coin a phrase) the real thing, which has subsequently been neutralised. The courts may well repeat the statutory definition of an imitation firearm and apply that to de-activated firearms both on public policy grounds and in an effort to make sense of the Acts, but it may not only be lexicographers who will feel uneasy at such an approach. Of course the issue need not have arisen at all if the 1988 Act had been more judiciously drafted.

(b) It is anticipated that de-activated weapons will usually be **7–08–05** certified as such by the one or other of the two proof houses by the impress or engraving of their coat of arms on the barrel, breech and action of the weapon. As was mentioned earlier, there is no requirement that such weapons must be so certified and, in any event, to preserve the outward appearance (and collectability) of these weapons, any inspection marks will not be readily apparent. We can fairly conclude that the fact that a weapon has been de-activated and poses no offensive threat is more likely to be appreciated after the event.

Falsification or alteration of proof house markings and the use of barrels so marked is struck at by the Gun Barrel Proof Act 1868, as amended by the 1978 statute of the same name.

[Firearm and shot gun certificates]

9. [Amends section 26(2)(a) of the 1968 Act] **7–09–01**
10. [Amends section 26(2)(b) of the 1968 Act] **7–10–01**

Grant of co-terminous certificates

11.—(1) Where a person who holds a firearm certificate **7–11–01**

applies for the grant or renewal of a shot gun certificate that certificate may, if he so requests, be granted or renewed for such period less than that specified in [¹subsection (3), or in an order made under subsection (3A), of section 26] of the principal Act as will secure that it ceases to be in force at the same time as the firearm certificate.

(2) Where a person who holds a shot gun certificate, or both such a certificate and a firearm certificate, applies for the grant of a firearm certificate, or for the renewal of the firearm certificate held by him, he may, on surrendering his shot gun certificate, apply for a new shot gun certificate to take effect on the same day as that on which the firearm certificate is granted or renewed.

(3) Where a shot gun certificate is granted to a person or such a certificate held by him is renewed and on the same occassion he is granted a firearm certificate or such a certificate held by him is renewed the fee payable on the grant or renewal of the shot gun certificate shall be £5 instead of that specified in section 32 of the principal Act.

(4) Subsection (3) above shall be included in the provisions that may be amended by an order under section 43 of the principal Act.

NOTE

(1) Inserted by the Firearms (Amendment) Act 1992, s.1(2).

OBSERVATION

For fees effective from January 1, 1995, see 2–07–04 above.

Revocation of certificates

7–12–01 **12.**—(1) Where a certificate is revoked by the chief officer of police under section 30(1)(*a*) or (2) of the principal Act he may by notice in writing require the holder of the certificate to surrender forthwith the certificate and any firearms and ammunition which are in the holder's possession by virtue of the certificate.

(2) It is an offence to fail to comply with a notice under subsection (1) above; and that offence shall be punishable on summary conviction with imprisonment for a term not exceeding three months or a fine not exceeding level 4 on the standard scale or both.

(3) Where a firearm or ammunition is surrendered in pursuance of a notice under subsection (1) above, then—

(*a*) if an appeal against the revocation of the certificate succeeds, the firearm or ammunition shall be returned;

(*b*) if such an appeal is dismissed, the court may make such order for the disposal of the firearm or ammunition as it thinks fit;

(*c*) if no such appeal is brought or such an appeal is abandoned, the firearm or ammunition shall be disposed of—

   (i) in such manner as the chief officer of police and the owner may agree; or

   (ii) in default of agreement, in such manner as the chief officer may decide;

but subject, in a case within sub-paragraph (ii), to the provisions of subsection (4) below.

(4) The chief officer of police shall give the owner notice in writing of any decision under subsection (3)(*c*)(ii) above, the owner may appeal against that decision in accordance with section 44 of the principal Act and on such appeal the court may either dismiss the appeal or make such order as to the disposal of the firearm or ammunition as it thinks fit.

(5) Subsection (4) of section 30 of the principal Act (surrender of revoked certificate within twenty-one days with extension in cases of appeal) shall not apply where the revocation is under subsection (1)(*a*) or (2) of that section and a notice is served under subsection (1) above; and paragraph 1 of Part I and paragraphs 1 to 5 of Part II of Schedule 5 to that Act (appeal jurisdiction and procedure) shall apply to an appeal against the revocation of a certificate.

OBSERVATION

It is intended that the peremptory power to revoke a certificate under this section should be used only where continued retention of the firearm or section 1 ammunition, or shot gun, would pose a direct and immediate threat to public safety or the peace.

[Firearms dealers and other businesses]

Firearms dealers

7–13–01   **13.**—(1) [Text inserted in section 33(5) of the 1968 Act]
(2) [Text inserted as subsection (1A) of section 34 of the 1968 Act]
(3) [Text added to section 38(8) of the 1968 Act]
(4) [Text inserted as section 40(3A) of the 1968 Act]
(5) [Words added to column 1 of the entry relating to section 38(8) in the Table of Punishments; see 5–06–01 above]

OBSERVATIONS

7–13–02   Subsection (2) allows the police to refuse an application for registration as a firearms dealer unless they are satisfied that a substantial volume of business will be developed. This suggests that factors such as the suitability of the premises for the level of anticipated business, and the nature of any other business conducted in tandem, may have to be considered.

Dealing with new-start business, it may be no easy task to assess such factors. See also 2–09–05, above.

Auctioneers, carriers and warehousemen

7–14–01   **14.**—(1) It is an offence for an auctioneer, carrier or warehouseman—

(*a*) to fail to take reasonable precautions for the safe custody of any firearm or ammunition which, by virtue of section 9(1) of the principal Act, he or any servant of his has in his possession without holding a certificate; or

(*b*) to fail to report forthwith to the police the loss or theft of any such firearm or ammunition.

(2) An offence under this section shall be punishable on summary conviction with imprisonment for a term not exceeding six months or a fine not exceeding level 5 on the standard scale or both.

OBSERVATION

The main provision in the Acts concerning auctioneers is found at section 9 of the 1968 Act. (See 1–09–01.) Strictly this section does not include shot gun ammunition (except that subject to section 1 certification) since the purpose of section 9 was to exempt carriers, auctioneers, etc., from the certification requirements otherwise imposed by virtue of the Act.

[*Exemptions*]

Rifle and pistol clubs

15.—(1) A member of a rifle club, miniature rifle club or **7–15–01** pistol club approved by the Secretary of State may, without holding a firearm certificate, have in his possession a firearm and ammunition when engaged as a member of the club in, or in connection with, target practice.

(2) Any approval under this section may be limited so as to apply to target practice with only such types of rifles or pistols as are specified in the approval.

(3) An approval under this section shall, unless withdrawn, continue in force for six years from the date on which it is granted but may be renewed for further periods of six years at a time.

(4) There shall be payable on the grant or renewal of an approval under this section a fee of [1£84] but this subsection shall be included in the provisions that may be amended by an order under section 43 of the principal Act.

(5) A constable duly authorised in writing in that behalf by a chief officer of police may, on producing if required his authority, enter any premises occupied or used by a club approved under this section and inspect those premises, and anything on them, for the purpose of ascertaining whether the provisions of this section and any limitations in the approval are being complied with.

(6) It is an offence for a person intentionally to obstruct a constable in the exercise of his powers under subsection (5) above; and that offence shall be punishable on summary conviction with a fine not exceeding level 3 on the standard scale.

(7) [Words "rifle club or miniature rifle club" and "club or" deleted from the 1968 Act section 11(3).]

(8) [Words inserted in section 32(2) of the 1968 Act.]

(9) Any approval of a rifle or miniature rifle club under section 11(3) of the principal Act shall have effect as if it were

an approval under this section except that (without prejudice to renewal) it shall expire at the end of the period of three years beginning with the day on which this section comes into force.

NOTE

(1) Fee amended by S.I. 1994 No. 2615 (England & Wales) and S.I. 1994 No. 2652 (Scotland). See also 2–07–04, above.

Borrowed rifles on private premises

7–16–01   16.—(1) A person of or over the age of seventeen may, without holding a firearm certificate, borrow a rifle from the occupier of private premises and use it on those premises in the presence either of the occupier or of a servant of the occupier if—

(*a*) the occupier or servant in whose presence it is used holds a firearm certificate in respect of that rifle; and

(*b*) the borrower's possession and use of it complies with any conditions as to those matters specified in the certificate.

(2) A person who by virtue of subsection (1) above is entitled without holding a firearm certificate to borrow and use a rifle in another person's presence may also, without holding such a certificate, purchase or acquire ammunition for use in the rifle and have it in his possession during the period for which the rifle is borrowed if—

(*a*) the firearm certificate held by that other person authorises the holder to have in his possession at that time ammunition for the rifle of a quantity not less than that purchased or acquired by, and in the possession of, the borrower; and

(*b*) the borrower's possession and use of the ammunition complies with any conditions as to those matters specified in the certificate.

OBSERVATIONS

7–16–02 This section allows non-certificate holders visiting shooting estates to borrow a rifle from the occupier there and use it under supervision. However, the section could have been more comprehensively expressed to avoid doubt: it would seem that the "occupier" can refer either to the owner or to the lessee of the subjects, and, following section 57(4), the expression "premises" includes land.

It will be appreciated that the main beneficiaries of this **7–16–03** provision are those who operate, and the guests (paying or otherwise) of those who operate, shooting estates although strictly the section could equally apply to supervised use of a rifle for other lawful purposes, clay or target shooting on private land.

To a degree this section's provisions and those in section 17, *infra*, relating to visitors' firearm permits, might appear to cover similar ground and serve to confuse. The latter section provides for the issue of certificates for those visiting from abroad who bring their firearms with them for sporting or recreational purposes. Since this necessarily demands the carriage of firearms into and about Great Britain it may be preferable that section 16 be accorded a liberal, not a restrictive, interpretation. Section 16 applies equally to British residents who could likewise borrow rifles on an estate rather than having to obtain and convey such weapons of their own.

While the section requires the presence of the certificate holder as an added safeguard, the Act does nothing to define the extent of supervision to be exercised nor to provide penalties for those who fail in such a task. Saving provisions in subsection (2)(*a*) and (*b*) stipulate that a borrowed rifle may only be used for the purposes detailed in the weapon owner's certificate and that quantities of ammunition obtained for the borrower cannot exceed those permitted to be held by the certificate holder. Again the intention appears to be that some portion of the ammunition cache allowed the certificate holder can be allocated temporarily to the guest; an alternative reading would be that both the certificate holder and the guest can possess up to the quantities of ammunition for the rifle as approved in the relevant certificate.

Finally, while subsection (2) refers to the purchase or acquisi- **7–16–04** tion of ammunition, subsection (1) uses only the word "borrow" in regard to a rifle. The expression "acquire", statutorily defined in section 57(4), means "hire, accept as a gift or borrow": it may be a cavil but in this definition the words "hire" and "borrow" are hardly synonymous—indeed "hire" does not appear in subsection (1), although its use might be thought singularly apposite.

Visitors' permits

17.—(1) The holder of a visitor's firearm permit may, without **7–17–01** holding a firearm certificate, have in his possession any firearm, and have in his possession, purchase or acquire any ammunition, to which section 1 of the principal Act applies; and [¹subject to subsection (1A) below] the holder of a visitor's shot gun permit may, without holding a shot gun certificate, have shot guns in his possession and purchase or acquire shot guns.

[²(1A) A visitor's shot gun permit shall not authorise the purchase or acquisition by any person of any shot gun with a magazine except where—

    (a) that person is for the time being the holder of a licence granted, for the purposes of any order made under section 1 of the Import, Export and Customs Powers (Defence) Act 1939, in respect of the exportation of that shot gun;

    (b) the shot gun is to be exported from Great Britain to a place outside the member States without first being taken to another member State;

    (c) the shot gun is acquired on terms which restrict that person's possession of the gun to the whole or part of the period of his visit to Great Britain and preclude the removal of the gun from Great Britain;
    or

    (d) the shot gun is purchased or acquired by that person exclusively in connection with the carrying on of activities in respect of which—

      (i) that person; or

      (ii) the person on whose behalf he makes the purchase or acquisition, is recognised, for the purposes of the law of another member State relating to firearms, as a collector of firearms or a body concerned in the cultural or historical aspects of weapons.]

(2) The chief officer of police for an area may, on an application in the prescribed form made by a person resident in that area on behalf of a person specified in the application, grant a permit under this section to the specified person if satisfied that he is visiting or intending to visit Great Britain and—

    (a) in the case of a visitor's firearm permit, that he has a good reason for having each firearm and the ammunition to which the permit relates in his possession, or, as respects ammunition, for purchasing or acquiring it, while he is a visitor to Great Britain;

(*b*) in the case of a visitor's shot gun permit, that he has a good reason for having each shot gun to which the permit relates in his possession, or for purchasing or acquiring it, while he is such a visitor.

(3) No permit shall be granted under this section to a person if the chief officer of police has reason to believe—

(*a*) that his possession of the weapons or ammunition in question would represent a danger to the public safety or to the peace; or

(*b*) that he is prohibited by the principal Act from possessing them.

[³(3A) No permit shall be granted under this section as respects any firearm unless—

(*a*) there is produced to the chief officer of police a document which—

    (i) has been issued in another member State under provisions corresponding to the provisions of the principal Act for the issue of European firearms passes;

    (ii) identifies that firearm as a firearm to which it relates; and

    (iii) is for the time being valid;

(*b*) the applicant shows that the person specified in the application is a person who, by reason of his place of residence or any other circumstances, is not entitled to be issued with such a document in any of the other member States; or

(*c*) the applicant shows that the person specified in the application requires the permit exclusively in connection with the carrying on of activities in respect of which—

    (i) that person; or

    (ii) the person on whose behalf he is proposing to make use of the authorisation conferred by the permit,

is recognised, for the purposes of the law of another member State relating to firearms, as a collector of firearms or a body concerned in the cultural or historical aspects of weapons;

and a chief officer of police who grants a permit under this section in a case where a document has been produced to him in pursuance of paragraph (a) above shall endorse on the document a statement which identifies the permit and the firearm to which it relates and briefly describes the effect of the permit.]

(4) A permit under this section shall be in the prescribed form, shall specify the conditions subject to which it is held and—

    (*a*) in the case of a visitor's firearm permit, shall specify the number and description of the firearms to which it relates, including their identification numbers, and, as respects ammunition, the quantities authorised to be purchased or acquired and to be held at any one time;

    (*b*) in the case of a visitor's shot gun permit, shall specify the number and description of the shot guns to which it relates, including, if known, their identification numbers.

(5) The chief officer of police by whom a permit under this section is granted may by notice in writing to the holder vary the conditions subject to which the permit is held but, in the case of a visitor's shot gun permit, no condition shall be imposed or varied so as to restrict the premises where the shot gun or guns to which the permit relates may be used.

(6) A permit under this section shall come into force on such date as is specified in it and continue in force for such period, not exceeding twelve months, as is so specified.

(7) A single application (a "group application") may be made under this section for the grant of not more than twenty permits to persons specified in the application if it is shown to the satisfaction of the chief officer of police that their purpose in having the weapons in question in their possession while visiting Great Britain is—

    (*a*) using them for sporting purposes on the same private premises during the same period; or

    (*b*) participating in the same competition or other event or the same series of competitions or other events.

(8) There shall be payable on the grant of a permit under this section a fee of £12 except that where six or more permits are granted on a group application the fee shall be £60 in respect of those permits taken together.

(9) Subsection (8) above shall be included in the provisions that may be amended by an order under section 43 of the principal Act.

(10) It is an offence for a person—

    (*a*) to make any statement which he knows to be false for the purpose of procuring the grant of a permit under this section; or (*b*) to fail to comply with a condition subject to which such a permit is held by him;

and each of those offences shall be punishable on summary conviction with imprisonment for a term not exceeding six months or a fine not exceeding level 5 on the standard scale or both.

NOTES

(1) Inserted by S.I. 1992 No. 2823, reg. 6(1).
(2) Derivation as above.
(3) Subsection inserted by reg. 7(1) of S.I. 1992 No. 2823.

OBSERVATIONS

(a) These provisions supersede section 14 of the 1968 Act, which 7–17–02 was repealed by section 23(8) of the present Act. The repealed provision applied only to shot guns and ammunition, unlike the provisions of section 18 above, which can also apply to section 1 firearms and ammunition.

While the rationale of the European weapons directive was to abolish controls on the movement of firearms within Member States and replace such controls with a harmonised system of firearms policing, this can only function when Member States share similar views as to the classification of firearms. Annex I (reproduced at 5–07–01) is an obvious step in that direction but does not entirely ensure harmonisation; as was noted at 1–01–13, certain smooth-bore weapons require section 1, not section 2, certificates in order to be lawfully possessed in Great Britain, and while on any technical definition such weapons are shot guns (and licensed as such elsewhere in the E.C.) they could not be brought into Great Britain on the authority of another Member State's shot gun certificate. Similar difficulties may well exist in relation to de-activated weapons and to antique firearms; it remains to be seen to what extent parameters for assessing the suitability of individual applicants for firearm certificates will be harmonised in the E.C., and that is likely to be an even more important and difficult task.

(b) It will be noted that there is no provision for an appeal procedure against refusal by the police to issue a visitor's permit. Nor does the Act provide a mechanism for revocation of permits once they are issued.

Firearms acquired for export

 18.—(1) A person may, without holding a firearm or shot gun 7–18–01

certificate, purchase a firearm from a registered firearms dealer
if—

    (*a*) that person has not been in Great Britain for more than
        thirty days in the preceding twelve months; and

    (*b*) the firearm is purchased for the purpose only of being
        exported from Great Britain without first coming into
        that person's possession.

[[1](1A) A person shall not be entitled under subsection (1)
above to purchase any firearm which falls within category B for
the purposes of Annex I to the European weapons directive
unless he—

    (*a*) produces to the dealer from whom he purchases it a
        document which—

        (i) has been issued under provisions which, in the
            member State where he resides, correspond to the
            provisions of the principal Act for the issue of
            Article 7 authorities; and

        (ii) contains the prior agreement to the purchase of that
            firearm which is required by Article 7 of the Euro-
            pean weapons directive;

    (*b*) shows that he is purchasing the firearm exclusively in
        connection with the carrying on of activities in respect of
        which he, or the person on whose behalf he is purchasing
        the firearm, is recognised, for the purposes of the law of
        another member State relating to firearms, as a collector
        of firearms or a body concerned in the cultural or
        historical aspects of weapons; or

    (*c*) shows that he resides in the United Kingdom or outside
        the member States.]

7–18–02   (2) A registered firearms dealer who sells a firearm to a
person who shows that he is entitled by virtue of subsection (1)
above to purchase it without holding a certificate shall within
forty-eight hours from the transaction send a notice of the
transaction to the chief officer of police in whose register the
premises where the transaction took place are entered.

    (3) The notice of a transaction under subsection (2) above
shall contain the particulars of the transaction which the dealer
is required to enter in the register kept by him under section 40
of the principal Act and every such notice shall be sent by
registered post or the recorded delivery service.

    (4) In the case of a transaction to which subsection (2) above
applies the particulars to be entered in the register kept under

section 40 of the principal Act (and accordingly contained in a notice under subsection (3) above) shall include the number and place of issue of the purchaser's passport, if any [²and, in a case where the transaction is one for the purposes of which a document such as is mentioned in subsection (1A)(*a*) above is required to be produced, particulars of the agreement contained in that document].

(5) It is an offence for a registered firearms dealer to fail to comply with subsection (2) above; and that offence shall be punishable on summary conviction with imprisonment for a term not exceeding six months or a fine not exceeding level 5 on the standard scale or both.

[³(6) In the case of any failure to comply with subsection (2) above which is confined to the omission from a notice of particulars of an agreement contained in a document such as is mentioned in subsection (1A)(a) above, subsection (5) above shall have effect as if for "six months" there were substituted "three months".]

[⁴**18A.**—(1) Subject to subsections (2) and (3) below, where—   **7–18–03**
  (*a*) a person who resides in Great Britain purchases or acquires a firearm in another member State; and
  (*b*) that firearm is a firearm which falls within category C for the purposes of Annex I to the European weapons directive,

he shall, within 14 days of the transaction, send notice of the transaction to the chief officer of police for the area where he resides.

(2) A person shall not be required to give notice under subsection (1) above of a transaction under which he acquires a firearm on terms which—
  (*a*) restrict his possession of the firearm to the whole or a part of the period of a visit to the member State where the transaction takes place; and
  (*b*) preclude the removal of the firearm from that member State.

(3) A person shall not be required to give notice under subsection (1) above of a transaction under which he purchases or acquires a firearm if—
  (*a*) he is for the time being the holder of a certificate under the principal Act relating to that firearm and containing, in relation to that firearm, a condition that he may have

the firearm in his possession only for the purpose of its being kept or exhibited as part of a collection; or

(*b*) he would, if in Great Britain, be authorised by virtue of a licence under the Schedule to this Act to have that firearm in his possession.

(4) A notice under subsection (1) above shall contain a description of the firearm (giving the identification number if any) and state the nature of the transaction and the name and address in Great Britain of the person giving the notice.

(5) A notice under subsection (1) above which is sent from a place in Great Britain shall be sent by registered post or by the recorded delivery service and, in any other case, shall be sent in such manner as most closely corresponds to the use of registered post or recorded delivery service.

(6) It is an offence for a person to fail to comply with this section; and that offence shall be punishable on summary conviction with imprisonment for a term not exceeding three months or a fine not exceeding level 5 on the standard scale or both.]

NOTES

(1) Inserted by S.I. 1992 No. 2823, reg. 8(1).
(2) Words added by S.I. 1992 No. 2823 reg. 8(2).
(3) Subsection added by reg. 8(3), as above.
(4) Section added by said regulations, reg. 9.

Firearms and ammunition in museums

7–19–01   **19.** The Schedule to this Act shall have effect for exempting firearms and ammunition in museums from certain provisions of the principal Act.

Removal of arms and ammunition to Northern Ireland

7–20–01   **20.**—(1) Section 6 of the principal Act (power to control movement of arms and ammunition) shall be amended as follows.

(2) [Text inserted as section 6(1A) of the 1968 Act]

(3) [Deletes section 6(1)(*b*) of the 1968 Act which is superseded by the last-mentioned provision]

Payments in respect of prohibited weapons

7–21–01   **21.** The Secretary of State shall, in accordance with a scheme

made by him, make payments to persons who surrender or
otherwise dispose of firearms—

(*a*) which they had, and were entitled to have, in their
possession immediately before 23rd September 1987 by
virtue of firearm or shot gun certificates held by them; or

(*b*) which before that date they had contracted to acquire
and were entitled to have in their possession on or after
that date by virtue of such certificates held by them,

and the possession of which will become, or has become,
unlawful by virtue of section 1(2) or 7(1) above.

Firearms consultative committee

22.—(1) There shall be established in accordance with the **7–22–01**
provisions of this section a firearms consultative committee
consisting of a chairman and not less than twelve other members
appointed by the Secretary of State, being persons appearing to
him to have knowledge and experience of one or more of the
following matters—

(*a*) the possession, use or keeping of, or transactions in,
firearms;

(*b*) weapon technology; and

(*c*) the administration or enforcement of the provisions of
the principal Act, the Firearms Act 1982 and this Act.

(2) The reference in subsection (1)(*a*) above to the use of
firearms includes in particular a reference to their use for sport
or competition.

(3) Subject to subsection (4) below, a member of the committee shall hold and vacate office in accordance with the terms
of his appointment.

(4) Any member of the committee may resign by notice in
writing to the Secretary of State; and the chairman may by such
a notice resign his office as such.

(5) It shall be the function of the committee—

(*a*) to keep under review the working of the provisions
mentioned in subsection (1)(*c*) above and to make to the
Secretary of State such recommendations as the committee may from time to time think necessary for the
improvement of the working of those provisions;

(*b*) to make proposals for amending those provisions if it
thinks fit; and

(*c*) to advise the Secretary of State on any other matter relating to those provisions which he may refer to the committee.

(6) The committee shall in each year make a report on its activities to the Secretary of State who shall lay copies of the report before Parliament.

(7) The Secretary of State may make members of the committee such payments as he may determine in respect of expenses incurred by them in the performance of their duties.

(8) The committee shall cease to exist at the end of the period of five years beginning with the day on which this section comes into force unless the Secretary of State provides by an order made by statutory instrument for it to continue thereafter, but no such order shall continue the committee for more than three years at a time.

Minor and consequential amendments and repeals

7–23–01   23.—(1) [Inserts words in section 4(4) of the 1968 Act]

(2) [Amends section 12(2) of said Act]

(3) [Substitutes in sections 13(1)(c), 40(4) and 49(1) of said Act the words "a constable"]

(4) [Adds to sections 22(2), 24(2)(b) and 23(2)(a) of the 1968 Act]

(5) [Adds to section 27(2) of said Act]

(6) [Inserts section 42(1A) in said Act]

(7) [Alters columns 3 and 4 in Part I of Schedule 6 (Table of Punishments) in relation to section 9(3)]

(8) [Repeals section 14 of the 1968 Act]

Expenses and receipts

7–24–01   24.—(1) Any administrative expenses incurred by the Secretary of State under section 15 or 22 above or the Schedule to this Act and any sums required by him for making payments under section 21 or 22 above shall be paid out of money provided by Parliament.

(2) Any fees received by the Secretary of State under section 15 above or the Schedule to this Act shall be paid into the Consolidated Fund.

Interpretation and supplementary provisions

7–25–01   25.—(1) In this Act "the principal Act" means the Firearms

Act 1968 and any expression which is also used in that Act has the same meaning as in that Act.

(2) [Adds subsections (2A) and (2B) to section 57 of the 1968 Act]

(3) [Amends the definition "rifle" in section 57(4) of that Act]

(4) Any reference in the principal Act to a person who is by virtue of that Act entitled to possess, purchase or acquire any weapon or ammunition without holding a certificate shall include a reference to a person who is so entitled by virtue of any provisions of this Act.

(5) Sections 46, 51(4) and 52 of the principal Act (powers of search, time-limit for prosecutions and forfeiture and cancellation orders on conviction) shall apply also to offences under this Act except that on the conviction of a person for an offence under the Schedule to this Act no order shall be made for the forfeiture of anything in his possession for the purposes of the museum in question.

(6) Sections 53 to 56 and section 58 of the principal Act (rules, Crown application, service of notices and savings) shall have effect as if this Act were contained in that Act.

(7) The provisions of this Act other than sections 15 and 17 shall be treated as contained in the principal Act for the purposes of the Firearms Act 1982 (imitation firearms readily convertible into firearms to which section 1 of the principal Act applies).

Corresponding provisions for Northern Ireland

26.—(1) An Order in Council under paragraph 1(1)(*b*) of **7–26–01** Schedule 1 to the Northern Ireland Act 1974 (legislation for Northern Ireland in the interim period) which states that it is made only for purposes corresponding to those of the provisions of this Act to which this section applies—

(*a*) shall not be subject to paragraph 1(4) and (5) of that Schedule (affirmative resolution of both Houses of Parliament); but

(*b*) shall be subject to annulment in pursuance of a resolution of either House.

(2) This section applies to—

(a) section 1(1), (2) and (3);

(b) section 9;

(c) section 13(1), (3) and (5);

(d) section 14;

(e) section 15(5) and (6);

(f) section 23(2);

(g) section 25(1), (2), (5), (6) and (7).

Short title, citation, commencement and extent

7–27–01   **27.**—(1) This Act may be cited as the Firearms (Amendment) Act 1988.

(2) This Act and the Firearms Act 1968 and 1982 may be cited together as the Firearms Acts 1968 to 1988.

(3) Except for section 26 and this section the provisions of this Act shall not come into force until such day as the Secretary of State may appoint by an order made by statutory instrument; and any such order may appoint different days for different provisions or different purposes and contain such transitional provisions as appear to the Secretary of State to be necessary or expedient in connection with any provision brought into force.

(4) Except for section 26 and this section this Act does not extend to Northern Ireland.

SCHEDULE

Firearms and Ammunition in Museums

Museum firearms licences

7–28–01   **1.**—(1) The Secretary of State may, on an application in writing made on behalf of a museum to which this Schedule applies, grant a museum firearms licence in respect of that museum.

(2) While a museum firearms licence (in this Schedule referred to as a "licence") is in force in respect of a museum the persons responsible for its management and their servants—

    (*a*) may, without holding a firearm certificate or shot gun certificate, have in their possession, and purchase or acquire, for the purposes of the museum firearms and ammunition which are or are to be normally exhibited or kept on its premises or on such of them as are specified in the licence; and

    (*b*) if the licence so provides, may, without the authority of the Secretary of State under section 5 of the principal Act, have in their possession, purchase or acquire for those purposes any prohibited weapons and ammunition which are or are to be normally exhibited or kept as aforesaid.

(3) The Secretary of State shall not grant a licence in respect of a museum unless, after consulting the chief officer of police for the area in which the premises to which the licence is to apply are situated, he is satisfied that the arrangements for exhibiting and keeping the firearms and ammunition in question are or will be such as not to endanger the public safety or the peace.

(4) A licence shall be in writing and be subject to such conditions specified in it as the Secretary of State thinks necessary for securing the safe custody of the firearms and ammunition in question.

(5) A licence shall, unless previously revoked or cancelled, continue in force for five years from the date on which it is granted but shall be renewable for further periods of five years at a time and sub-paragraph (3) above shall apply to the renewal of a licence as it applies to a grant.

(6) The Secretary of State may by order substitute for the periods mentioned in sub-paragraph (5) above such longer or shorter periods as are specified in the order.

(7) The power to make an order under sub-paragraph (6) above shall be exercisable by statutory instrument subject to annulment in pursuance of a resolution of either House of Parliament.

Variation and Revocation

2.—(1) The Secretary of State may by notice in writing to the persons **7–28–02** responsible for the management of a museum—

(*a*) vary the conditions specified in a licence held in respect of the museum; or

(*b*) vary the licence so as to extend or restrict the premises to which it applies.

(2) A notice under sub-paragraph (1) above may require the persons in question to deliver up the licence to the Secretary of State within twenty-one days of the date of the notice for the purpose of having it amended in accordance with the variation.

(3) The Secretary of State may by notice in writing to the persons responsible for the management of a museum revoke a licence held in respect of the museum if—

(a) at any time, after consulting the chief officer of police for the area in which the premises to which it applies are situated, he is satisfied that the continuation of the exemption conferred by the licence would result in danger to the public safety or to the peace; or

(b) those persons or any of them or any servant of theirs has been convicted of an offence under this Schedule; or

(c) those persons have failed to comply with a notice under this paragraph requiring them to deliver up the licence.

(4) Where a licence is revoked the Secretary of State shall by notice in writing require the persons responsible for the management of the museum in question to surrender the licence to him.

Fees

3.—(1) There shall be payable— **7–28–03**

(a) on the grant or renewal of a licence a fee of £200 or of such lesser amount as the Secretary of State may in any particular case determine;

(b) on the extension of a licence to additional premises, a fee of £75.

(2) This paragraph shall be included in the provisions that may be amended by an order under section 43 of the principal Act.

Offences and Enforcement

7–28–04 **4.**—(1) It is an offence—

(a) for a person to make any statement which he knows to be false for the purpose of procuring the grant, renewal or variation of a licence;

(b) for the persons or any of the persons responsible for the management of a museum to fail to comply or to cause or permit another person to fail to comply with any condition specified in the licence held in respect of that museum.

(2) An offence under sub-paragraph (1) above shall be punishable on summary conviction with imprisonment for a term not exceeding six months or a fine not exceeding level 5 on the standard scale or both.

(3) It is an offence for a person to fail to comply with a notice under paragraph 2(4) above; and that offence shall be punishable on summary conviction with a fine not exceeding level 3 on the standard scale.

(4) In proceedings against any person for an offence under sub-paragraph (1)(b) above it is a defence for him to prove that he took all reasonable precautions and exercised all due diligence to avoid the commission of the offence.

(5) Where an offence under this paragraph committed by a body corporate is proved to have been committed with the consent or connivance of, or to be attributable to any neglect on the part of, any director, manager, secretary or other similar officer of the body corporate, or any person who was purporting to act in any such capacity, he, as well as the body corporate, shall be guilty of that offence and be liable to be proceeded against and punished accordingly.

(6) Where the affairs of a body corporate are managed by its members sub-paragraph (5) above shall apply in relation to the acts and defaults of a member in connection with his functions of management as if he were a director of the body corporate.

Museums to which this Schedule applies

7–28–05 **5.** This Schedule applies to the following museums—
The Armouries, H.M. Tower of London
The National Army Museum
The National Museum of Wales
The Royal Air Force Museum
The Science Museum
The Victoria and Albert Museum
The Royal Marines Museum
The Fleet Air Arm Museum
The Royal Navy Museum
The Royal Navy Submarine Museum
The British Museum
The Imperial War Museum
The National Maritime Museum

The National Museums of Scotland
The National Museums and Galleries on Merseyside
The Wallace Collection
Any other museum or similar institution in Great Britain which has as its
    purpose, or one of its purposes, the preservation for the public benefit of
    a collection of historical, artistic or scientific interest which includes or is
    to include firearms and which is maintained wholly or mainly out of
    money provided by Parliament or by a local authority.

Interpretation

6. In this Schedule references to the persons responsible for the management
of a museum are to the board of trustees, governing body or other person or
persons (whether or not incorporated) exercising corresponding functions.

FIREARMS (AMENDMENT) ACT 1992

An Act to empower the Secretary of State to extend the period
for which firearm and shot gun certificates are granted or
renewed. [16th March 1992]

Duration of firearm and shot gun certificates
1.—(1) (a) [Amends section 26(3) of the 1968 Act] **8–01–01**
   (b) [Inserts subsections (3A), (3B) and (3C) in section 26(3)
     of the 1968 Act]
  (2) [Amends section 11(1) of the 1988 Act]

Northern Ireland
2.—(1) Section 1 above does not extend to Northern Ireland. **8–02–01**
  (2) An Order in Council under paragraph 1(1)(b) of Schedule
1 to the Northern Ireland Act 1974 (legislation for Northern
Ireland in the interim period) which states that it is made only
for purposes corresponding to those of section 1 above—
- (a) shall not be subject to paragraph 1(4) and (5) of that
Schedule (affirmative resolution of both Houses of Parliament); but
- (b) shall be subject to annulment in pursuance of a resolution of either House.

Citation
3.—(1) This Act may be cited as the Firearms (Amendment) **8–03–01**
Act 1992.
  (2) This Act and the Firearms Acts 1968 to 1988 may be cited
together as the Firearms Acts 1968 to 1992.

THE FIREARMS ACTS (AMENDMENT) REGULATIONS 1992

(S.I. 1992 No.2823)

1.—(1) These Regulations may be cited as the Firearms **9–01–01** (Amendment) Regulations 1992.

(2) These Regulations shall come into force on 1st January 1993.

(3) These Regulations do not extend to Northern Ireland.

2.—In these Regulations **9–02–01**
    "the 1968 Act" means the Firearms Act 1968; and
    "the 1988 Act" means the Firearms (Amendment) Act 1988.

3.—(1) [Inserts section 5(1A) into the 1968 Act] **9–03–01**

(2) [Amends section 5(2) of that Act]

(3) [Adds subsection (7) to section 5 of that Act]

(4) [Inserts section 5A in the 1968 Act]

(5) [Adds section 57(4A) to the 1968 Act]

(6) [Adds entry relating to section 5(1A) to the Table of Punishments in part I to Schedule 6 of the 1968 Act]

4.—(1) [Adds subsection (1A) to section 22 of the 1968 Act] **9–04–01**

(2) [Adds subsection (1A) to section 27 of said Act]

(3) [Adds subsection (1C) to section 28 of said Act]

(4) [Adds entry relating to section 22(1A) to the Table of Punishments in Part I to Schedule 6 of the 1968 Act]

5.—(1) [Inserts sections 32A, 32B and 32C in the 1968 Act] **9–05–01**

(2) [Adds to section 57(4) of 1968 Act definitions of "another member State", "Article 7 authority", "European firearms pass" and "European weapons directive"]

(3) [Adds entries relating to sections 32B(5) and 32C(6) to the Table of Punishments in Part I to Schedule 6 of the 1968 Act]

6.—(1) [Inserts section 17(1A) in the 1988 Act and amends **9–06–01** section 17(1) accordingly]

(2) [Adds section 42A to the 1968 Act]

(3) [Adds entry relating to section 42A to the Table of Punishments in Part I to Schedule 6 of the 1968 Act]

7.—(1) [Inserts section 17(3A) in the 1988 Act] **9–07–01**

Firearms

(2) [Inserts section 48(1A) in the 1968 Act]

(3) [Amends section 48(2) above]

(4) [Adds subsection (4) to section 48 above]

(5) [Adds entry relating to section 48(4) to the Table of Punishments in Part I to Schedule 6 of the 1968 Act]

9–08–01 **8.**—(1) [Inserts subsection (1A) in section 18 of the 1988 Act]

(2) [Adds to section 18(4) of the 1988 Act]

(3) [Inserts subsection (6) to section 18 above]

9–09–01 **9.** [Inserts section 18A in the 1988 Act]

9–10–01 **10.**—(1) No obligation as to secrecy or other restriction upon the disclosure of information imposed by statute or otherwise shall preclude—

(a) the disclosure by the Secretary of State or an officer of his to the competent authorities of a member State other than the United Kingdom of any information which is required to be disclosed in pursuance of the directive of the Council of the European Communities No. 91/477/ EEC (directive on the control of the acquisition and possession of weapons); or

(b) the disclosure to the Secretary of State or any officer of his by a chief officer of police, or by any government department or officer of a government department, of any information required by the Secretary of State for the purpose of facilitating the communication or exchange of information in pursuance of that directive.

(2) The reference in paragraph (1) above to the competent authorities of a member State is a reference to the persons appointed by that member State to deal with the communication or exchange of information in pursuance of the directive mentioned in that paragraph.

FIREARMS (AMENDMENT) ACT 1994

An Act to create a new offence of possessing a firearm or imitation firearm with intent to cause fear of violence; to apply certain provisions of the Firearms Act 1968 to imitation firearms; and for connected purposes. [21st July 1994]

Possession of firearm or imitation firearm with intent to cause fear of violence

1.—(1) [Inserts section 16A in the 1968 Act]   10–01–01

(2) [Adds entry relating to section 16A in the Table of Punishments in Part I to Schedule 6 of the 1968 Act]

Application of sections 20 and 46 of 1968 Act to imitation firearms

2.—(1) [Inserts the words "or imitation firearm" in section 20 **10–02–01** of the 1968 Act]

(2) [Inserts the words "imitation firearm" in section 46(1)(b) of the 1968 Act]

(3) [Amends the entries relating to sections 20(1) and (2) in the Table of Punishments in Part I to Schedule 6 of the 1968 Act to take account of section 2(1) above]

Northern Ireland

3.—(1) Sections 1 and 2 do not extend to Northern Ireland.   **10–03–01**

(2) An Order in Council under paragraph 1(1)*(b)* of Schedule 1 to the Northern Ireland Act 1974 (legislation for Northern Ireland in the interim period) which contains a statement that it is made only for purposes corresponding to those of section 1 and 2 above—

(*a*) shall not be subject to paragraph 1(4) and (5) of that Schedule (affirmative resolution of both Houses of Parliament); but

(*b*) shall be subject to annulment in pursuance of a resolution of either House of Parliament.

Short title and commencement

4.—(1) This Act may be cited as the Firearms (Amendment) **10–04–01** Act 1994.

(2) This Act shall come into force at the end of the period of two months beginning with the day on which it is passed.

(3) This Act shall not have effect in relation to anything done before it comes into force.

INDEX

FORFEITURE—(cont'd)
assembled shot gun carried by
person under 15, 5–06–02
contravening sections 6 or 49 of
Act, 5–06–02
conviction generally, 3–07–01
imposition of probation, 3–07–01
offences involving air weapons
and ammunition, 5–06–02
shot gun or its ammunition
gifted to person under 15,
5–06–02

HAVE WITH HIM,
and possession contrasted,
1–18–05,
1–18–07
HIGHWAY,
(England and Wales) as public
place,
4–05–05

IMITATION FIREARM,
appearance at time of offence
relevant, 4–05–18
conversion into:
firearm, 1–04–03, 1–04–07
low power air weapon, 6–05–01
converted/convertible weapons
need certification, 6–05–01
convicted persons and, 6–05–01
de-activated firearms and, 7–08–04
defence (to charge of possession of
convertible firearm), 6–01–01,
6–05–01
definition of readily convertible,
6–01–01
discussed, 1–04–07
extent of exemption from Act's
certification provisions, 6–05–01
Home Office guidelines upon,
6–05–03
Model Firearm Report (MFE):
discussed, 6–05–03
evidential status of, 6–05–03

IMITATION FIREARM—(cont'd)
offences:
possession during arrest for
Schedule offence, 1–17–02,
1–17–07
possession during commission of
Schedule offence, 1–17–02,
1–17–06
use of to induce fear of violence,
1–16–10
use to assault prison officer,
1–17–05
with intent to resist arrest,
1–17–01
readily convertible into
firearm—test,
6–01–01
skills necessary to effect
conversion—test, 6–05–04
trespass with, 1–20–1, 6–05–01
use in pursuance of crime, 6–05–01

LETHALITY,
discussed, 4–05–11
LICENSING PROVISIONS,
appeal procedures:
against refusal of grant or
renewal of certificate, 2–01–02
revocation of certificate, 2–05–03
applications, format of, 2–01–01
cancellation of certificate on
conviction, 3–07–02
court conduct of appeals: see
APPEALS
co-terminous firearm/shot gun
certificates, 7–11–01
duration of certificates, 2–01–01,
2–01–03
fees for certificates, 2–01–03
format of:
firearm certificate, 2–02–01
shot gun certificate, 2–03–03
grant of:
group applications (Visitor's
permit), 7–17–01
s.1 certificate, criteria, 2–02–01